Afro-American Writing Today

Afro-American Writing Today

AN ANNIVERSARY ISSUE
OF THE
SOUTHERN REVIEW

Edited by James Olney

Louisiana State University Press
Baton Rouge and London

Copyright © 1985 by Louisiana State University, 1989 by Louisiana State University Press
All rights reserved
Manufactured in the United States of America
First printing

98 97 96 95 94 93 92 91 90 89   5 4 3 2 1

Printer: Thomson-Shore, Inc.
Binder: John H. Dekker & Sons, Inc.

This volume is a reprint of the *Southern Review,* n.s., XXI (Summer, 1985), except for the omission of "A Conversation," by Gloria Naylor and Toni Morrison. The cover photograph and the photographs displayed herein are copyrighted by Roland L. Freeman, photographer, and are reproduced with his permission.

Library of Congress Cataloging-in-Publication Data

Afro-American writing today: an anniversary issue of the Southern
  Review/edited by James Olney.
       p.   cm.
    ISBN 0-8071-1482-0
    1. American literature—Afro-American authors.   2. American
  literature—20th century.   3. American literature—Afro-American
  authors—History and criticism.   4. American literature—20th
  century—History and criticism.   5. Afro-American authors—
  Interviews.   6. Afro-Americans—Intellectual life.   7. Afro-
  Americans—Literary collections.   I. Olney, James.   II. Southern
  review (Baton Rouge, La.)
  PS508.N3A38   1989
  810'.8'0896073—dc19   88-39021
                                                                    CIP

The paper in this book meets the guidelines for permanence and durability of the Committee on Production Guidelines for Book Longevity of the Council on Library Resources. ∞

Contents

CONTENTS

DRAMA

Acknowledgments

WHAT WAS SAID by way of acknowledgments in the "Editorial Note" to the Afro-American number of the *Southern Review* I would like to repeat here: I doubt that I will ever again receive, for a single issue, so much help from so many people as for this one. I hesitate to list the names, for I fear that I will forget some, but I cannot fail to thank at least the following for assistance, advice, encouragement, and good words in general: Houston A. Baker, Jr., Thadious Davis, Henry Louis Gates, Jr., Robert Hemenway, Joyce A. Joyce, Toni Morrison, Gloria Naylor, Robert O'Meally, Charlotte Pierce-Baker, Arnold Rampersad, Charles H. Rowell, John Sekora, Robert B. Stepto, Claudia Tate, John Edgar Tidwell, and Mary Helen Washington. Anthony Barthelemy served as associate editor of the Afro-American special number, and his presence is discernible throughout this volume. Donna Perreault's assistance in transforming the special number into a manuscript for Louisiana State University Press has been invaluable. Likewise, Beverly Jarrett and Catherine Landry of LSU Press have demonstrated editorial wisdom at every stage of the transfiguration from journal issue to published book. I am deeply grateful to all these people who have assisted in bringing this volume into being twice over.

Afro-American Writing Today

Introduction

THIS VOLUME IS intended to put into more lasting form a special number of the *Southern Review* (Summer, 1985) devoted to Afro-American writing. That issue of the *Review* enjoyed a very considerable success and an eager demand. Indeed, it was sold out, through new subscriptions and requests for individual copies, before the number ever arrived from the printer in the *Southern Review* offices, which says something about the timeliness of devoting a special number of the journal to the subject of Afro-American writing and also about the lively interest that exists in many quarters, both within and without the South, in this liveliest of literatures. Putting aside for a moment the liveliness of the literature, I might say something first about how and why it seemed particularly appropriate in 1985 to devote a number of the *Southern Review* to Afro-American writing. I should emphasize in this regard four points: the very title of the *Southern Review;* the history and present situation of the *Southern Review;* the historical and current circumstances of Afro-American writing; and the state of Afro-American criticism, both literary criticism and cultural criticism more broadly, in recent years and today.

As to the title of the *Southern Review:* I assume that it would be generally agreed, and I take it pretty much as a given, that the South is uniquely what it is in large part because of the black presence in that section of the country. This is doubtless true of the entire nation (C. G. Jung used to claim that Americans of all races differ from Europeans because of the subtly pervasive influence of black rhythms and black styles), but for historical, economic, and social reasons it is true to a much greater degree of the South than of America in general. Ralph Ellison has said that the peculiar blend of possibility and denial faced by the Negro provides a kind of heightened metaphor for the American experiment and indeed for the human condition, and one might well

1

suggest that this emblematic significance that can be read in the situation of the Negro generally is not diminished but only intensified in the South, which itself, in the pages of writers both black and white, has often enough been seen as a compressed image of the problems and possibilities of the entire country. If this is so, then a "southern" review that is going to do justice to the literary, historical, and cultural realities of the region and its relationship to the nation must necessarily accord a fair portion of its time, attention, and space to the black presence in the life and the literature of the South and throughout the United States. Although much of the writing collected in this volume comes from outside the South, the roots of Afro-American literature and culture unquestionably go deep into southern soil, and thus it seemed as natural and fitting to devote a special number of the *Southern Review* to Afro-American writing as it was to devote special numbers to the southern writer and to T. S. Eliot.

That there should have been these three special numbers in a single year was determined by the history of the *Southern Review:* the journal was founded in 1935 under the editorship of Charles W. Pipkin, Cleanth Brooks, and Robert Penn Warren and refounded, in a new series, in 1965 under the editorship of Lewis P. Simpson and Donald E. Stanford. Thus 1985 was a dual anniversary year, marking fifty years since the founding of the original *Southern Review* and twenty years since its refounding in a new series (coincidentally, it was also the fiftieth anniversary of Louisiana State University Press and the 125th anniversary of the founding of Louisiana State University)—hence a year for celebration and for commemorative issues of the *Southern Review.* The spring number bore on its cover the legend "An Anniversary Issue: The Southern Writer," the summer number was designated "An Anniversary Issue: Afro-American Writing," and the autumn number declared itself "An Anniversary Issue: T. S. Eliot." As to the history that led up to these anniversary issues, the original series of the *Southern Review,* although it lasted only seven years, was astonishingly, brilliantly successful, and when the editors designate were planning the editorial direction for the new series, they believed, and no doubt rightly, that they should follow to a considerable extent the lead that had proved so successful in the journal's brief first incarnation. That is to say, the new series, like the original series, has had a dual focus on the literature of the southern United States and on modernist literature, which the editors, however, perceived not as two polarized interests, all too likely to yield a divided, schizophrenic publication, but as complementary and fruitful ways to a better understanding of both southern and modernist writing. Southern writing, in their view, was not a provincial literature (unless Yeats, for example, and the Irish literary renaissance could also be labeled "provincial") but was, on the contrary, very near the center of whatever could profitably be called "modernism"; and whatever was alive and well in the literature of the South was hand in glove with the shaping of the modernist canon that was going on not only in the South but simultaneously in the northern states, in Great Britain and Ireland, and on the European continent as well. One might say, then, that special issues devoted to the southern writer and to T. S. Eliot constituted recognition of this historically determined dual focus of the *Southern Review*—as it were, the journal's two-eyed, single-visioned understanding of modern literature published as two discrete numbers. But this is not yet a full explanation of the Afro-American issue, which appeared, appropriately, in the middle of the *Southern Review*'s anniversary year.

In the planning stages of the new series of the *Southern Review*, according to the account given in Thomas Cutrer's *Parnassus on the Mississippi: The "Southern Review" and the Baton Rouge Literary Community, 1935–1942*, the new editors consulted Cleanth Brooks on the direction that he felt the journal should take after more than twenty years of nonpublication. "It should take [a direction] as different from that of the magazine of 1935–1942 as the literary situation demanded," was Mr. Brooks's advice. The literary situation of the late 1930s was, in many ways, not especially conducive to the publication of significant amounts of Afro-American writing, but in recent years, and certainly by 1983, when I was appointed to succeed Donald E. Stanford upon his retirement as editor of the *Southern Review*, that situation had changed dramatically. And so it seemed to me and to my colleague, Lewis P. Simpson, who gave his enthusiastic support to the Afro-American special number from start to finish, that personal and historic circumstances had conspired to offer us a unique opportunity to do something that would be altogether in keeping with the editorial purview and vision of the *Southern Review* and that would yet, at the same time, extend it in the different direction that, as Mr. Brooks said, "the literary situation demanded." Afro-American writing has not been prominent in the pages of the *Southern Review*, and, as suggested above, there have no doubt been good historical reasons for this relative neglect; all historical explanations aside, however, there seemed to both Lewis Simpson and me to be compelling reasons for changing this situation and thus realizing the added dimension that was potentially available and altogether appropriate to the journal's editorial vision. And this brings me to the third of my four points, namely, the historical and current circumstances of Afro-American writing.

One reason for bringing Afro-American writing into greater prominence in the pages of the *Southern Review* is that in this literature the modernist mode and the southern literary and cultural heritage are more fully joined and more completely engaged with each other than in probably any other writing. Moreover, one can perceive from the perspective of the mid-eighties that this merger of modernism with a southern heritage characterizes Afro-American writing not only today but historically from the Harlem Renaissance to the present—from Jean Toomer, Zora Neale Hurston, and Langston Hughes through Richard Wright, Ralph Ellison, and James Baldwin to Amiri Baraka and Ishmael Reed. Toomer, Hurston, and Hughes were, in their various ways, modernists, and so have been those who came after them—to the degree, indeed, that Afro-American writing may well come to be seen as the primary locus of modernist literature in the eighties. Moreover, while the South may or may not have been always at the center of the black writer's consciousness, Afro-American writing, for whatever reasons personal, social, and historical, has rehearsed again and again the drama of departure from the South and return to it—a return not always in fact (though often enough it has been) but at least in imagination, a return that would uncover obscured traces, that would discover and recover the cultural and ancestral past. Afro-American writing might thus be said to be both quintessentially modern (or modernist) and quintessentially southern, and as such a more than appropriate literature, indeed a central literature, for the pages of the *Southern Review.*

Another compelling reason for giving prominence to Afro-American writing now has nothing to do with the fact that the *Southern Review* is a specifically southern journal or that it has traditionally had an eager interest in modernist literature but lies instead, very simply, in the quality of contemporary Afro-American writing and the vitality of the tradition it embodies. Any literature that can boast of the poets, dramatist, critics, and fiction writers included in this volume can claim something much more than mere good fortune or a state of being blessed. There is here a long tradition, a tradition both of living and of literature, very much alive in writing now, and one would be hard pressed to name another body of writing with quite the same vitality and variety and drive as this one shows. What editor would not be grateful for the opportunity to publish any or all of the writers (not to mention the photographer) represented here? From an editor's point of view, *opportunity* is the exact and right word: it was an opportunity not to be missed and one that I am happy to say was embraced with enthusiasm and gratitude.

Perhaps the most appropriate way to say something about the current state of Afro-American literary and cultural criticism is to look at a pair of motifs that appear in a number of the pieces in this collection, namely, jazz music (specifically, the blues) and quilts or quilting. These two subtexts, as it were, developed quite spontaneously and independently—they were not planned, and pieces were not chosen because one or the other motif was present—and, taken together, they say something of great importance about Afro-American literature and culture. Also—and this again is important—the motifs occur both in pieces that might be described as "creative" and in pieces that might be described as "critical." (One reason for using quotation marks here is that the line between the two modes in this collection is a flexible, indistinct, and shifting one.) That the motifs appear in critical essays as well as in fiction and poetry (and in the photographs as well) suggests that they have in common a deep-running significance in and for the black community, a significance that goes far beyond the genres of literature or the different means of expression in language, in musical sounds, and in images. Even in those pieces in which quilting or the blues do not explicitly appear, it might well be argued that they are present in spirit and that together they represent a principle of thinking, of relating, of tradition, and of living that is essential to the black community both literary and extraliterary.

"Weaving, shaping, sculpting, or quilting in order to create a kaleidoscopic and momentary array," Houston A. Baker, Jr., and Charlotte Pierce-Baker remark in their essay on quilting and community in a story of Alice Walker, "is tantamount to providing an improvisational response to chaos." That this formulation is in essence rather like Robert Frost's famous description of poetry ("a momentary stay against confusion") does not make it the less exact or fitting as a description of specifically black artistic and cultural forms. On the contrary, I would suggest, on the one hand, that in spirit this formulation has to do with a world and an activity that are Frostean by nature but, on the other hand, that in introducing the word *improvisational*, it serves to draw quilting together with jazz music and points to a highly significant aspect of all sorts of cultural forms of the Afro-American community. It is improvisation and recurrence with variation or revision that characterize not only blues and quilting but also Afro-American poetry, fiction, drama, and criticism—and indeed the phrase "improvisation and recurrence with variation or revision" might be taken as a fair description of Afro-American literary tradition and literary history. And beyond strictly literary concerns, this all has to do with community—community of spirit in the present and community of creative expression across generations. (One thing that struck me forcefully about the pieces that came in for the Afro-American number—in contrast to the flood of regular submissions, presumably largely from white writers, dealing with erotic situations, marital conflicts, and generational antagonisms—was the constant emphasis on family, on ancestry, on, in a word, community.) Quilts might be seen as a visible symbol of ancestry and heritage and communal piecing together just as the literary tradition that started even before the writing of the slave narratives in the nineteenth century and that flows through writers of the Harlem Renaissance and Zora Neale Hurston and Richard Wright to writers of the present moment can be conceived of as an analogue to the blues tradition of repetition and variation, recurrence and increase.

To express it as Henry Louis Gates, Jr., and Houston Baker have notably done, the artistic and cultural forms of the black community are intimately bound up with the activity known as signifying. Signifying is playing on and against a previous expression, a previous form, and in Afro-American writing, as in the Afro-American community, it is both substance and style; in other words, where signifying is the mode, style *is* substance. Because oral/aural signifying obtains in linguistic, verbal exchanges as it does in the recurrences and variations of jazz music, it is a metaphor not only for the local ways of individual jazz performances but for those of individual Afro-American texts, and a metaphor as well for the extended tradition and history established in many performances and over many texts. Signifying constitutes an interpretation, a variation, a revision, and an extension of what has gone before. In his poem "Sr/Sd: for an African Chronicle," Houston Baker refers to "an endless play of signifiers," and this is at once a nice indication of the way in which style-as-meaning is everywhere in Afro-American expression and a clear demonstration of how Afro-American writers allow modernist and postmodernist critical terminology (*signifier* and *signified*, for example) a place in their discursive practice while making it, at the same time, all their own. The discourse recently produced by linguistic critics of French and other persuasions has been a fact of the Afro-American community, literary and otherwise, for about as far back as one can see. Signifying is the network of expression, interpretation, and meaning that binds together a community in the present by drawing that community into interpretive league, into interpretive exchange and interchange, with its own past.

This sense of community is perhaps even more overwhelmingly present in Roland Freeman's eloquent photographs. A great many of them depict someone in the act of weaving or braiding or patching or improvising or piecing together—in the act, in short, of signifying. There is the picture of the girl with her hair in cornrows learning the means and the meaning of quilting from a woman one might guess to be her grandmother. That photograph is in spirit precisely the same as the one of an elderly woman showing a youngster (grandmother and grandson in this case) something in a tattered and worn book that would appear to be the family Bible—showing something, it might be supposed, about births and deaths, about family history, about heritage and ancestry. It might seem a great leap, an unjustifiable leap, from these photographs to the poetry of Amiri Baraka and Michael Harper and Marilyn Nelson Waniek, or to the fiction of Richard Perry and John E. Wideman, or to the essays of Anthony Barthelemy and Clyde Taylor, but the truth is, I believe, that these and all the other pieces gathered together in this volume, like the photographs themselves, enact an improvisational drama of generational recurrence and revitalization and variation, a revision that means new life for the predecessor as for the reviser and, indeed, means new life for the community as a whole and for the tradition that is embodied and extended in the photographs, drama, stories, interviews, poems, and essays of this volume. Those readers familiar with the original issue of the *Southern Review* will notice that one of the strongest pieces contained therein, the conversation between Gloria Naylor and Toni Morrison, is omitted from the present volume. I very much regret that Toni Morrison would not give her permission to reproduce that piece.

HENRY LOUIS GATES, JR.

An Interview with
Josephine Baker and James Baldwin

I N 1973, HENRY LOUIS GATES, JR., was in Paris interviewing black American expatriates. He sought to know why, after the "gains" of the sixties, so many black Americans still found it necessary to live abroad. In addition to interviewing Leroy Haynes, proprietor of a Parisian Soul Food restaurant, Beauford Delaney, painter, and Bob Reid, musician, Gates interviewed Josephine Baker and James Baldwin. Although some twelve years have passed since these interviews, the observations and comments of Baker and Baldwin offer us insights into the expatriate experience then, and America now.

The interview with Josephine Baker began in her home, "Villa Maryvonne," in Monte Carlo. Later, while she and Gates were dinner guests at James Baldwin's home in St. Paul-de-Vence in the south of France, Gates concluded his interview with Baker and interviewed Baldwin. Although all of the conversation over dinner that night was not preserved, Baker's and Baldwin's responses to Gates's questions were. The individual interviews I have edited to read as a single conversation so that the genial ambience of that evening in St. Paul could be captured. Gates speaks of that evening and the events that led up to it in his own introduction to this piece.—Anthony Barthelemy

So many questions that I should have asked that night, but did not! I was so captivated by the moment: under the widest star-filled evening sky that I can remember, in the backyard of Baldwin's villa at St. Paul, drunk on conversation, burgundy, and a peasant stew, drunk on the fact that James Baldwin and Josephine Baker were seated on my right and left. It was my twenty-second summer; a sublime awe, later that evening, led me to tears.

Those few days in the south of France probably had more to do with my subsequent career as a literary critic than any other single event. At the time, I was a correspondent at the London bureau of *Time* magazine, a training that is, probably, largely responsible for the quantity of my later critical writing, and for its anecdotal opening paragraphs. I had just graduated from Yale College in June, as a Scholar of the House in History. *Time*, to even my great surprise, had hired me to work as a correspondent during the six month collective vacations at the University of Cambridge. I figured that I would "read" philosophy or literature at Cambridge, take the M.A. degree, then join permanently the staff at *Time*.

So, I sailed to Southampton from New York on the *France* in June, 1973. After a week of pure fright and anxiety—after all, what *does* a *Time* correspondent *do?*, and *how?*—I decided to go for my fantasy. I proposed doing a story on "Black Expatriates," perhaps every young Afro-American would-be-intellectual's dream. To my astonishment, the story suggestion was approved. So, off we (Sharon Adams, to whom I am married, and I) went by boat, train, and automobile to Europe, in search of blackness and black people.

In the Paris bureau of *Time*—Paris was the only logical point of departure, after all—I dialed Jo Baker's phone number. (*Time* can get to virtually *anyone*.) She answered her own phone! Stumbling around, interrupting my tortured speech with loads of "uh's" and "um's," I asked her if she would allow me to interview her. On one condition, she responded: "Bring Jimmy Baldwin with you to Monte Carlo." Not missing a beat, I promised that I would bring him with me.

Baldwin agreed to see me, after I had begged one of his companions and told him that I was heading south anyway to see Jo Baker. Cecil Brown, the companion told me, was living there as well, so maybe I could interview him as well? Cecil Brown, I thought. Def-i-nite-ly! (*Jive-ass Nigger* had been a cult classic among us younger nationalists in the early seventies.) So, off we went.

Imagine sitting on a train, from Paris to Nice, on the hottest night of August, 1973, wondering how I could drag Baldwin from St. Paul to Monte Carlo, and scared to death of Baldwin in the first place. It was a thoroughly Maalox evening; to top everything else, our train broke down in a tunnel. We must have lost twenty pounds in that tunnel. Finally, just after dawn, we arrived at Nice, rented a car, then drove the short distance to St. Paul.

After the best midday meal that I had ever eaten, before or since, I trekked with great trepidation over to Baldwin's "house." "When I grow up . . . ," I remember thinking as I walked through the gate. I won't bore you with details; suffice it to say that if you ever get the chance to have dinner with Jimmy Baldwin at his house at St. Paul, then *do* it. "Maybe *I* could write *Notes of a Native Son* if I lived here," I thought.

I am about to confess something that literary critics should not confess: James Baldwin *was* literature for me, especially the essay. No doubt like everyone who is reading these pages, I started reading "black books" avidly, voraciously, at the age of thirteen or fourteen. I read *everything* written by black authors that could be ordered from Red Bowl's paper store in Piedmont, West Virginia. LeRoi Jones's *Home* and *Blues People*, Malcolm's *Autobiography*, and *Invisible Man* moved me beyond words—beyond my own experience, which is even a further piece, I would suppose. But nothing could surpass my love for the Complete Works of James Baldwin. In fact, I have never before written about Baldwin just because I cannot read his words outside of an extremely personal nexus of adolescent sensations and emotions. "Poignancy" only begins to describe those feelings. I learned to love written literature, of any sort, through the language of James Baldwin.

When Baldwin came into the garden to be interviewed, I was so excited that I could not blink back the tears. That probably explains why he suggested that we begin with wine. Well into that first (of several) bottles, I confessed to him my promise to Jo Baker. Not missing a beat, he told me to bring Jo *here*. Did he think that she would drive back from Monte Carlo with me? Just tell her that dinner is served at nine.

And she did, after a warm and loving lunch with her family (we met *eleven* of the legendary twelve children), at her favorite restaurant overlooking Cape Martin. She had recently returned from a pilgrimage to Israel, and was looking forward to her return to the stage, her marvelous comeback. She was tall, as gracious and as warm as she was elegant, sensuous at sixty-five. Pablo this; Robeson that; Salvador so and so: she had been friends with the Western tradition, and its modernists. Everywhere we drove, people waved from the sidewalks or ran over to the car. She was so very *thoughtful*, so intellectual, and so learned of the sort of experience that, perhaps, takes six decades or so to ferment. I cannot drink a glass of Cantenac Brown without recreating her in its bouquet.

How did all of this lead to my present career? *Time* would not print the story, because, they said, "Baldwin is passé, and Baker a memory of the thirties and forties." My narrative remains unpublished, but shall appear in a new essay collection called *With the Flow*. When I went "up" to Cambridge from *Time* and London in October, 1973, I was so angered by the idiocy of that decision that I threw myself into the B.A. curriculum for English Language and Literature. A year later, I was admitted into the Ph.D. program, and four years later, I was awarded my degree.

That evening was the very last time that my two heroes saw each other, and the last time that Jo Baker would be interviewed at her home. She would die, on the stage, too soon thereafter. One day I hope to be forced to write about my other hero, James Baldwin.—HLG

GATES: Mrs. Baker, why did you leave the United States?

BAKER: I left in 1924, but the roots extend long before that. One of the first things I remember was the East St. Louis Race Riots (1906). I was hanging on to my mother's skirts, I was so little. All the sky was red with people's houses burning. On the bridge, there were running people with their tongues cut out. There was a woman who'd been pregnant with her insides cut out. That was the beginning of my feeling.

One day I realized I was living in a country where I was afraid to be black. It was only a country for white people, not black, so I left. I had been suffocating in the United States. I can't live anywhere that I can't breathe freedom. I must be free. Haven't I that right? I was created free. No chains did I wear when I came here. A lot of us left, not because we wanted to leave, but because we couldn't stand it anymore. Branded, banded, cut off. Canada Lee, Dr. Dubois, Paul Robeson, Marcus Garvey —all of us, forced to leave.

GATES: Did the French people offer you a respite from race prejudice?

BAKER: The French adopted me immediately. They all went to the beaches to get dark like Josephine Baker. They had a contest to see who could be the darkest, like Josephine Baker, they said. The French got sick, trying to get black—café au lait—you weren't anything unless you were café au lait.

I felt liberated in Paris. People didn't stare at me. But when I heard an American accent in the streets of Paris, I became afraid. I would tremble in my stomach. I was afraid they'd humiliate me.

I was afraid to go into prominent restaurants in Paris. Once, I dined in a certain restaurant with friends. An American lady looked at our table and called the waiter. "Tell her to get out," the lady said. "In my country, she is belonging only in the kitchen." The French management asked the American lady to leave. To tell the truth, I was afraid of not being wanted.

GATES: Mr. Baldwin, when did you leave the United States and for what reasons?

BALDWIN: It was November, 1948, Armistice Day as a matter of fact. I left because I was a writer. I had discovered writing and I had a family to save. I had only one weapon to save them, my writing. And I couldn't write in the United States.

GATES: But why did you flee to France?

BALDWIN: I had to go somewhere where I could learn that it was possible for me to thrive as a writer. The French, you see, didn't see me; on the other hand, they watched me. Some people took care of me. Else I would have died. But the French left me alone.

GATES: Was it important for you to be left alone?

BALDWIN: The only thing standing between my writing had to be me: it was I, it was me—I had to see that. Because the French left me alone, I was freed of crutches, the crutches of race. That's a scary thing.

GATES: Did you find any basic differences between Americans and Europeans, since you said that you could at least be left alone in Paris?

BALDWIN: There was a difference, but now the difference is a superficial one. When I first came to Paris, it was poor—everybody was broke. Now, Europe thinks it has something again, that it has regained the material things it lost. So Europeans are becoming Americans. The irony, of course, is that Europe began the trend even before America was formed. The price of becoming "American" is beating the hell out of everybody else.

GATES: Mrs. Baker, you said you felt "liberated" in France. Did the freedom you found here in France sour you towards the United States?

BAKER: I love the country within which I was born. These people are my people. I don't care what color they are—we are all Americans. We must have the application to stand up again.

Once I fought against the discriminatory laws in America but America was strong then. Now, she is weak. I only want to extend my fingers to pull it out of the quicksand, because that's where it is. I have all the hope in the world, though. The storm will come; we can't stop it. But that's all right. America will still be—but it will be the America it was intended to be. We were a small train on the track. We fell off. We'll get on again.

GATES: Where do you think the United States is heading, with distrust in government so apparent, with Watergate attracting worldwide attention?

BAKER: America was the promised land. I just want to give them my spirit; they've lost the path. That makes me suffer. I was so unhappy in the United States; I saw my brothers and sisters so afraid. The problem is deep—it has long roots. It is basic. The soil must be purified, not only must the root be pruned. It makes me unhappy to think that—I wouldn't be human if I weren't made unhappy by that. Needlessly, people will suffer. They need someone who can give them more than money. Someone to offer his hand, not just his money.

GATES: Mr. Baldwin, do you think that Watergate is a new, a significant departure in American history, or do you think it is the logical extension of policies begun long before Nixon, before this century even?

BALDWIN: Simply stated, Watergate was a bunch of incompetent hoods who got caught in the White House in the name of law and order.

GATES: Do you think the public hearings, indictments, and possible convictions could purge America, could allow it to change those things which you do not like about it?

BALDWIN: America is my country. Not only am I fond of it, I love it. America would change itself if it could, if that change didn't hurt, but people rarely change. Take the German people, for example. The German experiment during the war was catastrophic. It was a horror not to be believed. But they haven't changed: the German nation is basically the same today as it was before the war.

In a different sense, it is easy to be a rebel at age eighteen; it is harder to be one at age twenty-five. A nation may change when it realizes it has to. But people don't give up things. They have things taken away from them. One does not give up a lover; you lose her.

GATES: What do you see as the significance of Vietnam to America?

BAKER: I won't criticize America today. She is weak. I said all this years ago. It all came true. But it is never too late. It can be saved, but we Americans are so proud—false dignity, though. It's nothing to be ashamed about to acknowledge our mistakes; Vietnam was a mistake. All that money for no progress, that turned the whole world against America.

But actually, My Lai happened first with the Indians. We brought on our own enemies—nobody, no matter how powerful, needs enemies.

GATES: Did you ever regret that you had left the United States, or did you ever feel guilty, particularly during the Civil Rights Era, for not being there to participate?

BAKER: Some of my own people called me an Uncle Tom; they said I was more French than the French. I've thought often about your question, about running away from the problem. At first, I wondered if it was cowardice, wondered whether I should have stayed to fight. But I couldn't have done anything. I would have been thwarted in ways in which I was free in France. I probably would have been killed.

But really, I belong to the world now. You know, America represented that: people coming from all over to make a nation. But America has forgotten that. I love all people at the same time. Our country is people of all countries. How else could there have been an America? And they made a beautiful nation. Each one depositing a little of his own beauty.

It's a sad thing to leave your country. How very often I've felt like the Wandering Jew with my twelve children on my arms. I've been able to bear it, though. It might be a mistake to love my country where brothers are humiliated, where they kill each other, but I do love it. We are a wealthy people, a cultivated people. I wish people there would love. They can't go on like that. There's going to be a horrible storm. It's going to be a disaster. They'll torture each other through hate. It's ironic: people ran from slavery in Europe to find freedom in America, and now. . . .

GATES: Why don't you return to live in America now; aren't things a lot better for blacks?

BAKER: I don't think I could help America. I want to be useful, where I can help. America is desperate. In New York last year, I regretted for the first time not being young again. Young Americans need understanding and love. Children don't want to hear words; they want to see examples, not words—not blah, blah, blah—profound love, without malice, without hate.

GATES: When did you eventually return to the United States and why?

BAKER: It was in 1963. I kept reading about the "March on Washington," about preparation for the march. I so much wanted to attend. But I was afraid they wouldn't let me.

You see, for years I was not allowed to enter the United States. They said I was a Communist, during President Eisenhower's administration. They would make a black soldier—to humiliate me—they would make a black soldier lead me from a plane to a private room. It was so terrible, so painful. But I survived.

Then, in 1963, we applied to President Kennedy for permission to go to the March on Washington. He issued me a permanent visa. I wore the uniform I went through the war with, with all its medals. Thank God for John Kennedy for helping me get into America.

They had humiliated me so much; but still, I love them as if nothing happened. They didn't know what they were doing—digging their own grave through their hate. Then came Vietnam.

GATES: So you were actually forbidden to return to the United States between 1924 and 1963?

BAKER: Yes. They said I was a Communist because I dared love— thrown out for preferring freedom to riches, feelings to gold. I am not to be sold; no one can buy me. I lost America; I had nothing in my pockets, but I had my soul. I was so rich. For all this, they called me a Communist. America drives some of its most sensitive people away. Take Jimmy Baldwin: he had to leave the States to say what he felt.

GATES: And what were your first impressions of life in "exile"?

BALDWIN: I was no longer a captive nigger. I was the exotic attraction of the beast no longer in the cage. People paid attention. Of course you must realize that I am remembering the impression years later.

GATES: Did life abroad give you any particular insight into American society?

BALDWIN: I realized that the truth of American history was not and had never been in the White House. The truth is what had happened to black people, since slavery.

GATES: What do you think characterized Europeans to make them more ready to accept you at a time when you felt uncomfortable living in America?

BAKER: America has only been around for less than four hundred years; that's not a long time, really. Apparently it takes more than that to realize that a human being is a human being. Europeans are more basic. They see colors of the skin as colors of nature, like the flowers, for example.

GATES: Did you find any difference between the manner in which French men and women viewed you as a black man?

BALDWIN: That's a very important question. Before the Algerian war, and that's crucial in this, the black man did not exist in the French imagination; neither did the Algerian. After Dien Bien Phu, and after the "Civil War" as the French persist in calling it, there began to be a discernible difference between the way women and police had treated you before and after the war.

GATES: But were black Americans treated like Algerians were during their quest for independence?

BALDWIN: Of course I was removed, but you became a personal threat as a black American. You were a threat because you were visible. The French became conscious of your visibility because of the Algerians. You see, the French did not and don't know what a black man is. They'd like to put the blacks against the Algerians, to divide and rule, but the Arabs and black Americans were both slaves, one group was the slaves in Europe, the other back in America.

GATES: But surely you must believe that social change can come, that great men can effect change?

BALDWIN: Change does come, but not when or in the ways we want it to come. George Jackson, Malcolm X—now people all over the world were changed by them. Because they told the secret; now, the secret was out.

GATES: And the secret?

BALDWIN: Put it this way. In 1968, along with Lord Caradon (British Delegate to the United Nations then), I addressed an assembly of the World Council of Churches in Switzerland on "white racism or world community?" When Lord Caradon was asked why the West couldn't break relations with South Africa, he brought out charts and figures that showed that the West would be bankrupt if they did that: the prosperity of the West is standing on the back of the South African miner. When he stands up, the whole thing will be over.

GATES: How do you assess the results of the war in Vietnam on the American people?

BALDWIN: Americans are terrified. For the first time they know that they are capable of genocide. History is built on genocide. But they can't face it. And it doesn't make any difference what Americans think that they think—they are terrified.

GATES: From your vantage point, where do you think not only America but Western Civilization is heading?

BALDWIN: The old survivals of my generation will be wiped out. Western Civilization is heading for an apocalypse.

MEL WATKINS

An Interview with Ishmael Reed

ON A RECENT TRIP to *New York City from his home in Oakland, California, the essayist, poet and novelist Ishmael Reed took the time to sit for an interview concerning his own writing and his thoughts about the state of Afro-American literature specifically and American literature in general. In addition to his writing, Reed teaches literature at the University of California at Berkeley, operates his own publishing company, I. Reed Books, and frequently travels throughout the country as a lecturer. On the day of this interview, he was preparing to participate in a panel discussion with Toni Morrison and other writers. Even though the time for our conversation was limited, we managed to touch on many of the problems and concerns of those who, like ourselves, are extremely interested in the development of American literature. The following transcript reflects some of the more important and, I hope, more interesting issues discussed.—MW*

MW: There are obviously many places to start a talk about Afro-American literature, but, if only to give things a sense of context, let's begin by talking about the so-called second renaissance of black literature, which really got underway in the 1960s, and go on from there. At that point, there were more outlets for black writers, and a few publications such as *Black World* edited by Hoyt Fuller seemed to have more influence than many publications do today. What is your opinion of that magazine?

IR: *Black World* gave a more or less Afro-American point of view about the literature that was coming out. A lot of the stuff that was being pushed as Afro-American into the mainstream did not meet the approval of *Black World* magazine. I was at odds with them on some questions, but most of the time I could still get my writing published there, get my point of view across. In a way they had the most varied representation of different viewpoints of any black, intellectual magazine.

MW: I agree. Even though I think their viewpoint was kind of provincial, they did occasionally run something that was totally at odds with the literary line they pushed.

IR: It was like a bulletin board. If you wanted to know what was happening among Afro-American writers, or what was going on with the small presses, you could read *Black World*. But now that it has failed, all the people in the New York intellectual crowd—

MW: Do you mean black intellectuals?

IR: No, no! I mean those East Coast intellectuals who began to make the choices and determine what was significant black writing—what Norman Podhoretz calls the avant-garde. Populism is a dirty word to them. Anyway, in his book *Making It* he wrote about these "avant-garde" critics. But in reality he's an assimilationist and elitist; most of that crowd are assimilationists. They became disillusioned with Communism —some of them, the *Partisan Review* crowd, went into something they called "aesthetic traditionalism." Others went into what they called "neoconservatism," which from my point of view would be more accurately described as neo-Nazism. I see it as neo-Nazism. It was those New York intellectuals who promoted James Baldwin—notwithstanding his immense talents—the *Commentary* crowd and the *New Yorker* magazine crowd. Saul Bellow and Alfred Kazin were instrumental in Ralph Ellison's getting the National Book Award for *Invisible Man*. They were the judges, and his book epitomizes the modernist values they supported. In the book, Ellison jokes about Rastafarianism, although that movement has outlived the Modernist movement that championed Freudianism, Marxism, and Existentialism (which, according to William Barrett, author of *The Truants*, Sartre repudiated shortly before his death). Rastafarianism is still a worldwide movement, and I think it's growing. I used some of the Rastafarian aesthetic and morality in *The Terrible Twos*. So I think Ellison's satire was misdirected. I also think that *Invisible Man* is a fine book, but the motives of the Modernist 1950s critics who promoted it are not pure. They like the anti-Stalinism, the impotent first person, the incest and the satire of Rastafarianism.

MW: I don't think there's any doubt that the control was not coming from the black community.

I think that in the 1960s *Black World* competed with the eastern clique for influence on black literary trends. Hoyt Fuller and his people were more avant-garde than anything going on in New York at the time, and some of the other ethnic scholars and writers followed their example in the 1970s.

The thing that put me at odds with *Black World* magazine and the nationalist movement as far as the arts go was the insistence on a Black Aesthetic.

IR: Yes, they were fooling around with that idea, but again the idea came from the New York City environment. The people who were pushing the Black Aesthetic were from the East Coast and steeped in the white aesthetic. They were here and they were influenced by their intellectual friends in this town, right?

MW: True, but Hoyt Fuller, the editor of *Black World* at the time, identified very much with the black scene, and he was one of the major advocates of the Black Aesthetic.

IR: Well, I saw Hoyt in Atlanta about a year or so before he died, and he said something that made me think that he realized—despite his position—who was in control. He said we're all tokens, and he was right. He said for every Ishmael Reed there are hundreds of other talented black writers. I'm aware that I'm one of them, the tokens—a few of us have been picked out. There are many black writers who are very good but just don't get the publicity that prominent tokens get. The point is that the East Coast intellectuals permitted the idea of a Black Aesthetic to be talked about in mainstream magazines and newspapers. They made the choice—it was almost a kind of nonaggression pact in which they said, "All right, even though we don't agree with it, we'll let you guys have the Black Aesthetic." It is possible to contrast European and Afro-American styles, but the proponents of the Black Aesthetic kept pushing Stalinism upon black writers instead of defining the Black Aesthetic. But, even with that concession and all the talk about blueprints for black writing and such, the whole thing failed. The people who were in control in the 1950s are back in control now. And now Susan Brownmiller and Gloria Steinem, members of the third generation of New York intellectuals, have more control than we do. They have more power to create trends in Afro-American literature than I have. Yet, in a recent issue of *Contact* magazine, an insulated black feminist said that I headed some kind of black literary mafia. I'm small potatoes compared to Brownmiller and Steinem.

MW: It's that impotence, then, the lack of any real power despite one's position, that makes the term *tokenism* applicable?

IR: Correct. It's the assumption by whites that Afro-American talent is rare. And if you do have talent, if you're a genius and have a lot of talent, it's because you have white blood. That notion hasn't changed much since the nineteenth century. I was down in Lexington, Kentucky, recently and, seeing the stables and the horses being bred, something occurred to me about the condition of our literature. Every liberal and every conservative has a pet horse that he's trying to enter into the American literary sweepstakes where authors' personalities are packaged like soaps. Do you know what Ronald Reagan said when he met the people at the advertising firm that does publicity for him? "Thought you'd want to meet the soap," revealing the extent to which anything in America can be nickeled and dimed.

I had an exchange of letters with a reviewer for the *New York Review of Books* that illustrates what I mean. At the time he was trying to push a black feminist writer who said that black males are all evil. He reviewed my novel *The Terrible Twos* along with hers—a book that critics praised for its "dialect," which many black readers say they cannot understand—and wrote that the books didn't have much in common. So I asked him why he reviewed them together and said that he wouldn't do that with two Irish writers or two Jewish writers who had "nothing in common." He said that her book represented the most successful use of black English by any writer, when the exchange of letters revealed that he was not informed enough to make such a comparison. In a follow-up letter, while discussing writers who have done a lot with Afro-American speech styles in their works, I brought up Margaret Walker and Ernest Gaines. He said these people were just obscure writers.

MW: Ernest Gaines an obscure writer?

IR: Yeah, Ernest Gaines, and I think that was the week "Miss Jane Pittman" was being aired on national television. I see it all the time. They really don't know anything about Afro-American literature or literature written by white male writers for that matter, so when they review a book by a black writer they feel they have to be king-makers or queen-makers. Everyone's work is compared to a few token black novels that have been set up as the standard; there's no room for diversity. And every reviewer feels he or she has discovered THE black writer. They write things like, "This writer has done what no black writer, etc." I just don't see those kinds of comments made about other American or European writers. They don't write, "This is the greatest white writer."

MW: Or Jewish writer or writer of any other nationality. The only time you find it—and I say this from the point of view of an editor involved with what is normally taken out of reviews—is if it's said about blacks or other minorities such as American Indians, Chicanos. If it's said about any other American writer, it's taken out. You can make those kinds of remarks about foreign writers, whether they are Russian or Greek or what have you, just as long as they are from Russia or Greece. You're right and, in that sense, we're the only American citizens who are treated as if we were in permanent exile.

IR: We're treated as guests or visitors. (*laughs*) That reminds me of an incident involving William Phillips, a former member of the Coordinating Council of Literary Magazines. I was in the organization at the same time he was and, although I liked the guy, we had some run-ins about philosophy. Later he wrote a book entitled *A Partisan View*, in which he wrote that I had used Populist tactics to get my way.

They accused me of using Populist tactics so often that I went out and did some research on Populism. It's a very interesting tradition. The old agrarian alliances of the nineteenth century led to the creation of the modern labor movement. Although the Knights of Labor became racist towards the end, at the peak of its power it brought thousands of black and white workers together. But, anyway, he said that I was trying to get people on the board who didn't really have qualifications. The two people in question—the two that I nominated—were Leslie Silko, the great Native American writer and—

MW: She's part Mexican also, isn't she?

IR: That's right, she's a Mexican-American Indian and she won a MacArthur Foundation grant. She's a great writer. And the other person I nominated was Toni Cade Bambara. The women on the board and the staff had never heard of her and questioned her qualifications. The week after I nominated her, there was a full-page story about her in *Newsweek* magazine. The point is, again, that it's common for us to know their literature, but, unlike African, Asian and European readers and critics, they don't know anything about ours.

MW: Well, we have to know theirs.

IR: Still, we are finally the multicultural writers. And even though they attribute it to us, I think they are much more provincial. And if an ethnic view of literature means having limited concerns, then they are the ones who are limited. For instance there is a writer on the *Times*; she's Japanese I believe.

MW: Yes, Michiko Kakutani.

IR: Anyway, she did an essay on detective novels and didn't even mention Chester Himes. Then she did a piece on war novels and didn't mention John A. Williams. She also wrote an article on faction, books in which fiction and fact are merged, and didn't mention Alex Haley, who invented the term. I said, "Wow, what happened to poor Alex?" I always look at the New York *Times* as a wonderful thing to have on Sunday. It's an essential part of my equipment. Like no other magazine or newspaper, it provides a chronicle of American civilization. But at other times it reminds me of that county in Arkansas where they have been having Ku Klux Klan meetings even though there are no blacks in the county. I remember a piece in the *Times* by Cynthia Ozick in which she talked about a black American author who had never been published—it was one of the most patronizing things I'd ever read. This was her entry in the Kentucky Derby for black writers. The guy had never been published and there was more space devoted to him than to John E. Wideman or Paule Marshall or John McCluskey. She was congratulating this unknown writer for not "mythologizing negritude," as she put it. Now if I'd said that she was mythologizing her culture, you know what the reaction would have been.

MW: You can't turn it around, though. They wouldn't know what you were talking about. For instance, when you talk about writers inventing certain literary forms you have to consider that James Baldwin invented the personalized essay or personalized journalism, whatever name you wish to give it. Still, Norman Mailer and Tom Wolfe are usually given credit for it. A few years back, I talked about this with an editor at the *Times* and he argued that, yes, Baldwin was the first, but that was a different thing. In other words, it was different, distinct, because he was black or his essays were unique. They didn't have anything to do with this mainstream thing we call personalized journalism. There is a blind spot with regard to black accomplishment for many white intellectuals.

IR: It happens in music, dance, and other fields just as often. It's as if the only reason we're around is to provide white males with artistic inspiration. In other words, the importance of Chuck Berry is that he influenced Mick Jagger. The importance of Native American writers is that they influenced "white shamans" and other Anglo-Americans who write about American Indians. I see it everywhere. It's what I call "Settler Paranoia," a term I picked up from Native Americans. I used to think it was racism, but it isn't. The original literary and cultural creations of Afro-Americans are popular all over the world, Europe included. And certainly in Europe some of the people who admire it and accept it are white. I don't think that describing the dynamics of this situation in terms of black and white is accurate. *Black* and *white* are polarizing terms anyway. To describe it as a conflict between black and white is polarizing and not very precise. It's more subtle than that. For instance, I came out of the closet a couple of years ago about my Irish ancestry and there was an interesting reaction. I said, "Well you know, I'm forty-six years old now and I feel I should start finding out what I am—start defining myself instead of leaving that up to others." Still, the media rarely gives credit to Afro-Americans for contributing to trends in American culture. Take Michael Jackson, for instance. According to one article, the reason he got across is because of the influence of Al Jolson and Fred Astaire upon his music and dance, when actually both Jolson and Astaire were professional black imitators. That, to me, is an instance of the settlers becoming paranoid. The result is a kind of brain dysfunction that occurs when settlers feel themselves surrounded by too many nonwhites.

MW: That idea won't sell as many books, but it certainly makes sense.

IR: The point is, finally, that it's not racism. The kind of literature that I'm interested in—a kind that is produced in this country but is not reviewed by the major book review outlets—is known all over Asia and South America, while here its creators are subjected to Settler Paranoia. Atrocities that happen to us don't mean anything to them because to them we only exist in a state of near-humanity anyway. Benjamin De-Mott once reviewed a Leon Forrest novel and criticized it for what he called "the all too familiar details of slavery." Suppose I wrote about the all too familiar details of the Holocaust—all hell would break loose. He also criticized black leaders for not imparting intellectual ideas to the masses. I hit the ceiling when I read that. Doesn't he know that W.E.B. DuBois had a Ph.D., that Huey P. Newton—who can hold his own in a discussion of phenomenology—has a Ph.D., that Martin Luther King had a Ph.D., etc.? And even many of those who don't have degrees were self-taught geniuses like Malcolm X and Frederick Douglass.

MW: Maybe even more important—how does he explain Ronald Reagan?

IR: I don't know, but DeMott suggested that anyone who thought that the statement "black leaders have not promoted intellectual values" was a racist statement, was stupid. Well, he may not be stupid, but he is certainly inaccurate. Proportionately, Afro-American leaders probably have more Ph.D.'s among them than white leaders.

MW: The dynamics and nature of this culture would demand that overall they'd have to be more educated.

IR: Sure, but he was wrong. Anyway, I'm writing a book about the black-Jewish situation. It seems to me that the last time Jews cooperated with blacks was in the Middle Ages when the Jews showed Africans how to get into Spain—how to take over the country. They provided the Moors with an invasion route because the Jews were catching hell in Spain. There were Spanish Christian fundamentalists who were trying to force the Jews into conversion; together the Jews and the blacks created a renaissance. It happened about 900 A.D.

MW: The book sounds fascinating and I'd like to talk more about it, but before we get to that, I'd like to discuss the rather unique style of your writing. Is the new novel stylistically similar to your previous work?

IR: I don't think my novels have all been alike. They all had different subjects. I think *Terrible Twos* was a different kind of book from *Flight to Canada*, which was different from *Mumbo Jumbo*.

MW: Yes, the subjects were very different, but the narrative style seemed similar in each novel.

IR: Well, yes, I think there is a distinct approach that carries through in my fiction. It's a combination of different influences, you know; I try to combine elements from different arts, cultures, and disciplines. I think that the tone is probably different.

MW: True, but I remember your saying a few years ago, while I was in Berkeley, that you were thinking of writing a "straight" novel.

IR: Sure, if straight means traditional, my approach owes more to the Afro-American oral tradition and to folk art than to any literary tradition. The oral tradition includes techniques like satire, hyperbole, invective, and bawdiness. It's a comic tradition in the same way that the Native American tradition is comic. Gerald Vizenor, a Native American scholar, for instance, says that tragedy is Western. I use a lot of techniques that are Western and many that are Afro-American. I read a book recently by [Henry] Louis Gates at Yale, about signifying—

MW: The one about the signifying monkey?

IR: Right, and when I read the manuscript it led me to think about some of the influences that shape my writing. It's a terrific book! He is a very good writer—I think he comes as close to defining the Afro-American literary style as anyone I've read.

MW: This is his new book?

IR: Yes. I think of it as a kind of Rosetta stone—I mean, that may be a bit of hyperbole, but the book does develop a theory of Afro-American literature that people only had hunches about in the 1960s. But Gates lays it all out for you in this new book.

Satire is a prominent part of it. If you look at our traditions all the way back to the plantations you see that satire and signifying are widely used. It's a way of subverting the wishes of the people in power. And that is one of the techniques I've used a lot in my work. One could call it "magic populism."

MW: Could you define magic populism a little more specifically?

IR: Well, it's a variation of the usual social realism approach. Only I don't employ a naturalistic style of writing; many approaches and techniques are incorporated into it. At the same time it takes the side of the poor against the rich, and it takes aim at some of the same targets as the early populist movement—the church, for instance, the concentration of wealth in the hands of a few, and racism. The narrative, however, is strange and fantastic. I discovered through viewing murals in Mexico and other places that social realism in art does not have to be confined to the purely naturalistic. Look at José Orozco. And I started to use this approach in my work. *The Terrible Twos* was the first time. And I hope to write two more novels along that same line: *The Terrible Threes* and *The Terrible Fours*.

But my new book, which I call *Reckless Eyeballing*, is basically about the parallelism between the Jewish and Afro-American experiences. The similarities are quite vivid. I'm studying the Nazi movement and I'm looking at Nazi films and literature. I found some surprises that will be a major part of the book. I also found some interesting parallels between the period leading up to the national denunciation of Jews—their acceptance as scapegoats by Germans—and some things that are going on in America today. That's what makes Susan Brownmiller and people like that frightening to me. Using the collective pronoun, she wrote that the black man encouraged rape and supported rape, which suggests that one person stands for the whole group and implicates all black men. This is the kind of generalization that you used to hear about Jewish males in Germany.

When her book was published everybody rushed out to congratulate her; *Time* magazine called her work the book of the year. It's that kind of feminist attitude that I have trouble with. As a matter of fact, the Before Columbus Foundation had a panel in Berkeley to discuss the question; it was called "Are Third World Men the Scapegoats of Feminist Writers?" It's about time this question was addressed. In his book *The Crisis of the Negro Intellectual*, Harold Cruse wrote that one problem with the black intellectual was the lack of response to spurious criticism and attacks in print by critics. I also think that the inability of minorities to rebut some of these neo-Nazi charges and presumptions in an organized fashion is a serious matter. Jesse Jackson used an unfortunate slur during his campaign and the whole white press came down on him, but he did not say that white people or Jewish people were biologically inferior, which is the kind of remark I hear from some of these neoconservatives. They actually use some of the same rhetoric that the Nazis used. The "Crisis" that Cruse wrote about actually became real when Afro-American intellectuals didn't challenge all these slurs. They showed how otherworldly and abstract they were—they were about as involved as monks, something like Afro-American Buddhists.

MW: I'm looking forward to seeing the book; obviously, it's going to be controversial as hell.

IR: Well, in a way, I'm doing a real tightrope act with this thing. As one character in the book, a writer, says, his treatment of other ethnic groups will be fairer than the treatment afforded black characters by their white male creators. The characters he writes about, he says, will have more class and culture than, say, the black characters of William Styron or Saul Bellow.

MW: Is this character black or white?

IR: He's a black character. He feels that Jewish writers have stolen all the material about blacks. He hasn't written a book in twenty years because he feels that there is nothing left to write about blacks, since their culture has been exploited by others. There's nothing left; they've taken it all.

MW: What about his anti-Semitism?

IR: Well, as you know, people reform in my novels. We'll see. The point is, how can these writers get away with the disparaging remarks about black men? And, more, what makes them feel that they know more about Afro-American culture than blacks do? Like the *Times* drama critic who wrote that the author of *Dreamgirls* knows more about black people than Charles Fuller, the author of *A Soldier's Story*. If that's so, why do they call the experience ethnic? If it's available to William Styron and Mick Jagger, then it has become a part of the American cultural heritage, which means that the majority of American-Europeans have a dual heritage. There is no other ethnic culture with this kind of prominence in American society. I mean, there is the influence in dance, music, style and language. If it's out there for everybody, why do they continue insisting that it's ethnic?

But in universities and among intellectuals you still get these people who say it's ethnic and limited. The same people, the same groups, will go to Hollywood and make millions of dollars from it. Actually from us—it's crazy! But the point is if they can write about Afro-Americans then we can write about other ethnic groups. We can show that we are above cheap-shot bigotry. And I think we can write about those other groups with more class and knowledge than they can write about us.

MW: About Afro-Americans?

IR: Yes. And the reason is that, as I've said, we are the ones who are actually multicultural. They are more limited and ethnic. I became truly aware of that advantage when I got to the West Coast. I began to realize that being black or Chicano or Native American, you are forced to see and be aware of disparate cultures. We had to become multicultural, and I think this will be a major factor in determining who finally survives in this country. It's like evolution—if you have a limited viewpoint you are at a disadvantage. Those who have incorporated other perspectives and allowed their vision to embrace other ways of looking at the world have a better chance of surviving.

MW: I think any black in this country who has gotten to the point that you have must have incorporated and understood his culture. You had to deal with it in order to be successful. Even though you have maintained much of that black cultural perspective, you've had to learn their traditions. In a sense, it's like absorbing a second culture.

IR: Oh, absolutely.

MW: It's not only the culture but the language. When I first went to college my most difficult adjustment was the language. Much of that time I didn't know what the hell they were talking about. I really sat there trying to figure out, translate, parts of the lectures. My parents were southern blacks and, at home, we simply didn't talk that way. And the vocabulary I'd learned in high school didn't prepare me for the experience. If my parents were listening to this conversation right now, they wouldn't understand half of what we are saying.

IR: Sure, some of the people who are against black English and Spanish remind me of the Russian campaign against Yiddish. Or the Catholic campaign against Arabic when the Moors were in Spain. That kind of suppression happens often. It's why I call many members of the European ethnic groups assimilationists—they have forgotten their own traditions, or given them up because they don't want to deal with the hassles that come with maintaining them. It's the assimilationists that we have problems with.

MW: *Assimilationist* is a good term for that faction, since it puts into perspective the idea that they are not standing up for any particular ethnic heritage.

IR: There are American-European intellectuals, of course, like Russell Banks, Lawrence Levine and the late Truman Capote, who have gone beyond these limits, who are willing to accept the contributions of blacks and other minorities and give credit to the original sources of much of what has become part of American culture.

MW: Gone beyond Settler Paranoia, you mean.

IR: Yes.

MW: I agree, and I hope we see more of that. But, to get back to you— what are your plans beyond the new book?

IR: I think the most important thing is to take Afro-American and other minority literature across our borders, into those countries where there is a real demand for it. I've been buying remainders, and I plan to take them to the book fairs and make them available to European, Asian, African, Central and South American readers. I think I can show that the neglect of minority culture in this country doesn't reflect the attitudes of other countries.

MW: Well, I hope you're as successful at that as you have been with your writing. Just as important, I think, is the new book. I am looking forward to reading *Reckless Eyeballing*, and I'm sure others are also.

ROLAND L. FREEMAN

Black Folk

THE PHOTOGRAPHS PRESENTED HERE are from a much larger cultural research project which employs photodocumentation for historical preservation and interpretation of Black life throughout the African diaspora.

At this point in American history, it is probably not necessary to define the need for documenting the past, especially that which might otherwise be lost to us, or for documenting the creative contributions of African-Americans, especially where they are known only to a few, or for documenting the rural genius of the Black South, especially when it is rapidly slipping away from us and deserves recognition and preservation.

Photography transcends boundaries of literacy and language and has immediate impact on, perhaps, the very people who need most to believe in the value of their cultural heritage, African-Americans. I think these images, in spite of outwardly depressing conditions, have the special value of showing the inner strengths of the people.

But there is perhaps another reason why a project of this kind is more than a preservation of the past, however important. In America, the world of forever expanding affluence, which has just begun to open to African-Americans, seems to be coming to an end. In the rest of the world, most especially among the poorer nations, it is becoming clear that the ability to just hold on to what they now have is very much endangered, and any hope of real prosperity is rapidly fading. Peoples of the world are beginning to re-examine themselves in the light of their inner, rather than material, needs. In rural Black America, it is my conviction that there is a lesson to be learned for now, and for the future. It is impossible to look at the photographs which have formed the bulk of my work without seeing, in the very poorest of conditions, just those qualities of wisdom, compassion, creativity, and just plain fun that we all so badly need. The American South, and Mississippi in particular, provide fertile soil for the growth of this idea, through photodocumentation.

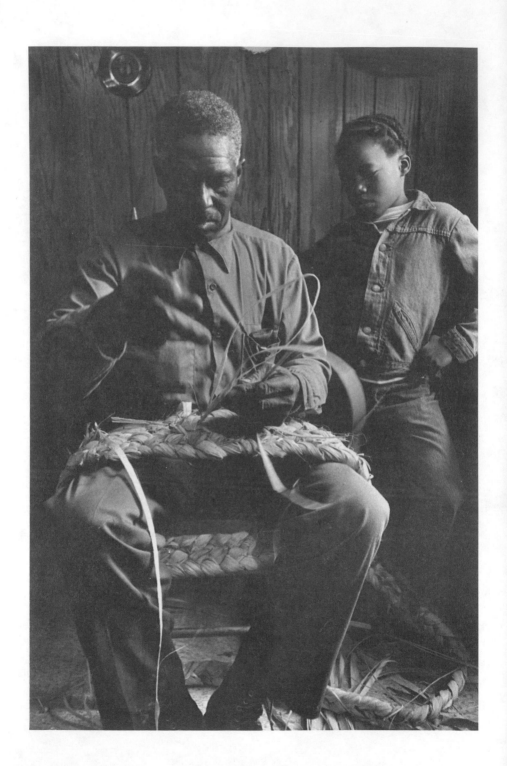

JOHN E. WIDEMAN

Surfiction

Among my notes on the first chapter of Charles Chesnutt's "Deep Sleeper" there are these remarks:

> Not reality but a culturally learned code—that is out of the infinite number of ways one might apprehend, be conscious, be aware, a certain arbitrary pattern, or finite set of indicators is sanctioned and over time becomes identical with reality. The signifier becomes the signified. For Chesnutt's contemporaries reality was "I" (eye) centered, the relationship between man and nature disjunctive rather than organic, time was chronological, linear, measured by man-made units—minutes, hours, days, months, etc. To capture this reality was then a rather mechanical procedure—a voice at the center of the story would begin to unravel reality: a catalog of sensuous detail, with the visual dominant, to indicate nature, "out-there" in the form of clouds, birdsong, etc. A classical painting rendered according to the laws of perspective, the convention of the window frame through which the passive spectator observes. The voice gains its authority because it is literate, educated, perceptive, because it has aligned itself correctly with the frame, because it drops the cues, or elements of the code methodically. The voice is reductive, as any code ultimately is; an implicit reinforcement occurs as the text elaborates itself through the voice: the voice gains authority because things are in order, the order gains authority because it is established by a voice we trust. For example the opening lines of "Deep Sleeper" . . .
>
> It was four o'clock on Sunday afternoon, in the month of July. The air had been hot and sultry, but a light, cool breeze had sprung up; and occasional cirrus clouds overspread the sun, and for a while subdued his fierceness. We were all out on the piazza—as the coolest place we could find—my wife, my sister-

46

in-law and I. The only sounds that broke the Sabbath stillness were the hum of an occasional vagrant bumblebee, or the fragmentary song of a mockingbird in a neighboring elm . . .

Rereading, I realize "my remarks" are a pastiche of received opinions from Barthes, certain cultural anthropologists and linguistically oriented critics and Russian formalists, and if I am beginning a story rather than an essay the whole stew suggests the preoccupations of Borges or perhaps a footnote in Barthelme. Already I have managed to embed several texts within other texts, already a rather unstable mix of genres and disciplines and literary allusion. Perhaps for all of this, already a grim exhaustion of energy and possibility, readers fall away as if each word is a well-aimed bullet.

More Chesnutt. This time from the text of the story, a passage unremarked upon except that in the margin of the xeroxed copy of the story I am copying this passage from, several penciled comments appear. I'll reproduce the entire discussion.

Latin: secundus-tertius quartus-quintus.

"Tom's gran'daddy wuz name' Skundus," he began. "He had a brudder name' Tushus en' ernudder name' Cottus en ernudder name' Squinchus." The old man paused a moment and gave his leg another hitch.

"drawing out Negroes"—custom in old south, new north, a constant in America. Ignorance of one kind delighting ignorance of another. Mask to mask. The real joke.

My sister-in-law was shaking with laughter. "What remarkable names!" she exclaimed. "Where in the world did they get them?"

Naming: plantation owner usurps privilege of family. Logos. Word made flesh. Power. Slaves named in order of appearance. Language masks joke. Latin opaque to blacks.

"Dem names wuz gun ter 'em by ole Marse Dugal' McAdoo, w'at I use' ter b'long ter, en' dey use' ter b'long ter. Marse Dugal' named all de babies w'at wuz bawn on de plantation. Dese young un's mammy wanted ter

Note: last laugh. Blacks (mis) pronounce *secundus*. Secundus = Skundus. Black speech takes over —opaque to white—subverts original purpose of name. Language (black) makes joke. Skundus has new identity.

call 'em sump'n plain en' simple, like 'Rastus' er 'Casear' er 'George Wash'n'ton'; but ole Marse say no, he want all de niggers on his place ter hab diffe'nt names, so he kin tell 'em apart. He'd done use' up all de common names, so he had ter take sump'n else. Dem names he gun Skundus en' his brudders is Hebrew names en' wuz tuk out'n de Bible.''

I distinguish remarks from footnotes. Footnotes clarify specifics; they answer simple questions. You can always tell from a good footnote the question which it is answering. For instance: *The Short Fiction of Charles W. Chesnutt*, edited Sylvia Lyons Render, Howard Univ. Press, 1974: p. 47. Clearly someone wants to know, Where did this come from? How might I find it? Tell me where to look. Okay. Whereas remarks, at least my remarks, the ones I take the trouble to write out in my journal,* which is where the first long cogitation appears/appeared, [the ambiguity here is not intentional but situational, not imposed for irony's sake but necessary because the first long cogitation—*my remark*— being referred to both *appears* in the sense that every time I open my journal, as I did a few moments ago, as I am doing *NOW* to check for myself and to exemplify for you the accuracy of my statement—the remark *appears* as it does/did just now. (Now?) But the remark (original) if we switch to a different order of time, treating the text diacronically rather than paradigmatically, the remark *appeared*; which poses another paradox. How language or words are both themselves and *Others*, but not always. Because the negation implied by *appearance*, the so-called "shadow within the rock," is *disappearance*. The reader correctly anticipates such an antiphony or absence suggesting presence (shadow play) between the text as realized and the text as shadow of its act. The dark side paradoxically is the absence, the nullity, the white space on the white page between the white words not stated but implied. Forever.] are more complicated.

The story, then, having escaped the brackets can proceed. In this story, *Mine,* in which Chesnutt replies to Chesnutt, remarks, comments, asides, allusions, footnotes, quotes from Chesnutt have so far played a

---

Journal: unpaginated. In progress. Unpublished. Many hands.

disproportionate role, and if this sentence is any indication, continue to play a grotesquely unbalanced role, will roll on.

It is four o'clock on Sunday afternoon in the month of July. The air has been hot and sultry, but a light, cool breeze has sprung up; and occasional cirrus clouds (?) overspread the sun, and for a while subdue his fierceness. We were all out on the piazza (stoop?)—as the coolest place we could find—my wife, my sister-in-law and I. The only sounds that break the Sabbath stillness are the hum of an occasional bumblebee, or the fragmentary song of a mockingbird in a neighboring elm. . . .

The reader should know now by certain unmistakable signs (codes) that a story is beginning. The stillness, the quiet of the afternoon tells us something is going to happen, that an event more dramatic than bird-song will rupture the static tableau. We expect, we know a payoff is forthcoming. We know this because we are put into the passive posture of readers or listeners (consumers) by the narrative unraveling of a reality which, because it is unfolding in time, slowly begins to take up our time and thus is obliged to give us something in return; the story enacts word by word, sentence by sentence in "real" time. Its moments will pass and our moments will pass simultaneously, hand in glove if you will. The literary, storytelling convention exacts this kind of relaxation or compliance or collaboration (conspiracy). Sentences slowly fade in, substituting fictive sensations for those which normally constitute our awareness. The shift into the fictional world is made easier because the conventions by which we identify the real world are conventions shared with and often learned from our experience with fictive reality. What we are accustomed to acknowledging as awareness is actually a culturally learned, contingent condensation of many potential awarenesses. In this culture—American, Western, twentieth century—an awareness that is eye-centered, disjunctive as opposed to organic, that responds to clock time, calendar time more than biological cycles or seasons, that assumes nature is external, acting on us rather than through us, that tames space by man-made structures and with the I as center defines other people and other things by the nature of their relationship to the "I" rather than by the independent integrity of the order they may represent.

An immanent experience is being prepared for, is being framed. The experience will be real because the narrator produces his narration from the same set of conventions by which we commonly detect reality—dates, buildings, relatives, the noises of nature.

All goes swimmingly until a voice from the watermelon patch intrudes. Recall the dialect reproduced above. Recall Kilroy's phallic nose. Recall Earl and Cornbread, graffiti artists, their spray paint cans notorious from one end of the metropolis to the other—from Society Hill to the Jungle, nothing safe from them and the artists uncatchable until hubris leads them to attempt the gleaming virgin flanks of a 747 parked on runway N-16 at the Philadelphia International Airport. Recall your own reflection in the funhouse mirror and the moment of doubt when you turn away and it turns away and you lose sight of it and it naturally enough loses sight of you and you wonder where it's going and where you're going and the wrinkly reflecting plate still is laughing behind your back at someone.

                    The reader
here pauses stream a totally
irrelevant conversation:

. . . by accident twenty seven
double-columned pages by
accident

started yeah I can see starting curiosity whatever staring over somebodies shoulder or a letter maybe you
think yours till you see not
meant for you at all

and getting worse getting
finished when shit like this
comes down

Picks up in mid-

I mean it started that way

I'm not trying to excuse just understand it was not premeditated
your journal is your journal
that's not why I mean   I didn't
forget your privacy or lose respect
on purpose
                  it was just there
and, well we seldom talk and I
was desperate we haven't been
going too well for a long time

I wanted to stop but I needed
something from you   more than
you've been giving so when I saw
it there I picked it up   you understand   not to read but because it
was you you and holding it was
all a part of you

you're breaking my heart

please don't dismiss

dismiss dismiss what I
won't dismiss your prying
how you defiled   how you
took advantage

don't try to make me a criminal
the guilt I feel it   I know right
from wrong and accept whatever
you need to lay on me but I had
to do it   I was desperate for something, anything, even if the cost

was rifling my personal life
searching through my guts
for ammunition and did you
get any did you learn anything you can use on   me
Shit I can't even remember
      the whole thing is a
jumble I'm blocking it all
out my own journal and I
can't remember a word be-
cause it's not mine anymore

I'm sorry   I knew I shouldn't as
soon as I opened it I flashed on
the Bergman movie   the one
where she reads his diary I flashed
on how underhanded how evil a
thing she was doing but I couldn't
stop

A melodrama a god damned
Swedish subtitled melodrama you're going to turn it
around aren't you   make it
into

The reader can replay the tape at leisure. Can amplify or expand.
There is plenty of blank space on the pages. A sin really given the scar-
city of trees, the rapaciousness of paper companies in the forests which
remain. The canny reader will not trouble him/her self trying to splice
the tape to what came before or after. Although the canny reader would
also be suspicious of the straightforward, absolute denial of relevance
dismissing the tape.

Here is the main narrative again. In embryo. A professor of literature at a university in Wyoming (the only university in Wyoming) by coincidence is teaching two courses in which are enrolled two students (one
in each of the professor's seminars) who are husband and wife. They both
have red hair. The male of the couple aspires to write novels and is
writing fast and furious a chapter a week his first novel in the professor's creative writing seminar. The other redhead, there are only two
redheads in the two classes, is taking the professor's seminar in Afro-
American literature, one of whose stars is Charlie W. Chesnutt. It has
come to the professor's attention that both husband and wife are in-
veterate diary keepers, a trait which like their red hair distinguishes them
from the professor's other eighteen students. Something old-fashioned,
charming about diaries, about this pair of hip graduate students keeping
them. A desire to keep up with his contemporaries (almost wrote "peers"
but that gets complicated real quick) leads the professor, who is also a
novelist, or as he prefers novelist who is also a professor, to occasionally
assemble large piles of novels which he reads with bated breath. The
novelist/professor/reader bates his breath because he has never grown
out of the awful habit of feeling praise bestowed on someone else lessens
the praise which may find its way to him (he was eldest of five children
in a very poor family—not an excuse—perhaps an extenuation—never
enough to go around breeds a fierce competitiveness and being for four
years an only child breeds a selfishness and ego-centeredness that is only
exacerbated by the shocking arrival of contenders, rivals, lower than dog-
shit pretenders to what is by divine right his). So he reads the bait and
nearly swoons when the genuinely good appears. The relevance of this to
the story is that occasionally the professor reads systematically and because on this occasion he is soon to appear on a panel at a neighboring
university (Colorado) discussing "Surfiction," his stack of novels was
culled from the latest, most hip, most avant-garde, new *Tel Quel* chic,
anti, non-novel bibliographies he could locate. He has determined at
least three qualities of these novels. *One*—you can stack ten in the space
required for two traditional novels. *Two*—they are *au rebours* the present
concern for ecology since they sometimes include as few as no words at
all on a page and often no more than seven. *Three*—without authors
whose last names begin with *B*, surfiction might not exist. B for Beckett,
Barth, Burroughs, Barthes, Borges, Brautigan, Barthelme . . . (Which
list further discloses a startling coincidence or perhaps the making of a
scandal—one man working both sides of the Atlantic as a writer and
critic explaining and praising his fiction as he creates it: *Barth Barthes
Barth*elme.)

The professor's reading of these thin (not necessarily a dig—thin pancakes, watches, women for instance are *à la mode*) novels suggests to him that there may be something to what they think they have their finger on. All he needs then is a local habitation and some names. Hence the redheaded couple. Hence their diaries. Hence the infinite layering of the fiction he will never write (which is the subject of the fiction which he will never write). Boy meets Prof. Prof reads boy's novel. Girl meets Prof. Prof meets girl in boy's novel. Learns her pubic hair is as fiery red as what she wears short and stylish, flouncing just above her shoulders. (Of course it's all fiction. The fiction. The encounters.) What's real is how quickly the layers build, how like a spring snow in Laramie the drifts cover and obscure silently.

Boy keeps diary. Girl meets diary. Girl falls out of love with diary (his), retreats to hers. The suspense builds. Chesnutt is read. A conference with Prof in which she begins analyzing the multilayered short story "The Deep Sleeper" but ends in tears reading from a diary (his? hers?). The professor recognizes her sincere compassion for the downtrodden (of which in one of his fictions he is one). He also recognizes a fiction in her husband's fiction (when he undresses her) and reads her diary. Which she has done previously (read her husband's). Forever.

The plot breaks down. It was supposed to break down. The characters disintegrate. Whoever claimed they were whole in the first place. The stability of the narrative voice is displaced into a thousand distracted madmen screaming in the dim corridors of literary history. Whoever insisted it should be more ambitious. The train doesn't stop here. Mistah Kurtz he dead. Godot ain't coming. Ecce Homo. Dats all Folks. Sadness.

And so it goes.

RICHARD PERRY

Blues for My Father,
My Mother, and Me

On SATURDAY, MY MOTHER CALLS. Dudley Strong is ill. No, nothing serious, a little pleurisy in his side. But he is moodier than usual. He sleeps fitfully and has bad dreams. Twice in the last week he woke screaming for Marcus. Perhaps if I came, not long, she knows I'm busy.

I try to stay away from my parents. I saw them last nine months ago at my brother's funeral. My mother didn't talk to me when I was a kid. My father always preferred my brother. I used to believe it was because Marcus was the older, but whatever the reason, it hurts. Still, it hasn't stopped me from making a life for myself. I've got a job, an apartment, and a couple of friends. A woman or two seem to enjoy my company. Sometimes I get a little lonely, but show me some people who don't.

I'll leave to see my parents in the morning. I have not been out today. I stayed in the darkroom, processing film I shot a week ago in Soho. Only two of the photographs developed revealed a smiling face. The smell of chemicals lines my throat. I swallow hard and something opens up inside, and I'm missing my brother.

"It's been tough," Marcus said. "I'm not crying, but it seems like for a long spell now, I've just been marking time. I'm ready to devote myself to what I have to do. I see that lasting change takes lasting struggle."

We were having a drink in the West End Bar on Broadway. It was one of the few times he allowed me a glimpse of what his life was like then, in the summer of 1971. He said he was dreaming all the time of Bobby Johnson, of Schwerner, Chaney and Goodman. Mississippi had ripped something out of Marcus. He'd been so confident, so brash. Mississippi had found his soft spot, taught him the meaning of fear, self-doubt, and failure. For a long time after he came North he was disconnected, floated from Harlem to Newark to Greenwich Village searching for the "radical" solution. His eyes were empty and his shoulders slumped. I worried, but there was nothing I could do. Then he got a regular job and found a shrink, and I thought he'd turned the corner.

The last time I saw him was six months before he died. He'd joined a group that planned to blow up the Statue of Liberty and the Stock Exchange. I thought he'd given up on all of that; I said he was crazy. He said I was part of the problem. That there could be no revolution without risk. That it was men like him who offered a way out, and that if I insisted on standing in the middle, then the middle was where I'd fall.

At the end he was sounding just like my father, and we were shouting. It's not good to imagine that your brother died angry at you. For a while I blamed myself.

My parents are another story. All the way up on the bus from New York to Kingston, I turn it over in my head. Sure they make me guilty, like anybody's parents can, but my reasons for staying away are better than most. The air in my parents' house is laced with their mutual hate, and I can't breathe it. I can't even figure out if something happened to make them the way they are, or if each just grew into despising the other. Sometimes I go through my childhood week by month, trying to recall some word, some gesture or expression that would tell me. But I never find anything. The way they are just is, that's all.

But it's such a waste. What's more important than family? I look at young couples in the street and I talk under my breath to them, telling them not to blow it. Don't fuck up the children, I say. Love one another. I'll never have my own kids, so I get very touchy about the subject. Maybe that's why I miss Marcus so, because now I can't have him. And it eats me up that we parted the way we did. I hate guilt. I'm guilty because I've mostly stayed away from my parents the last eight years. They're seventy-seven and seventy-four. They'll die soon. I don't know how I'll handle it. I feel like there's something awful in me that their deaths will activate, some unprotected place that, once bruised, will never heal. But I don't want to think about that now. I settle back in my seat and try to let the bus wheels hum me to sleep. After a while I sit up, stare out the window at the bright December sky.

I stand in front of the house I grew up in. It's small, two storied, has a porch my father screened himself. I am remembering waiting here for him to come home from work, wondering if he'd be drunk or sober. The foods he wore on his waiter's uniform, his music. My mother holding silence to her shoulders like a shawl. My brother, sure of himself from the time he understood the meaning of self. And me, a stranger in this house, lost, really, until I discovered cameras and the magic of darkrooms.

But I don't live here anymore. I'm twenty-seven and I've got my own place. I go up the porch steps, through the living room. I'm met by the smell of baking, the figure of my mother at the kitchen sink.

"Mama?"

She turns: the broad nose, the impossibly angled cheekbones. "Jason?"

"How you doing?"

"Didn't expect you so soon."

I cross the room, take her in my arms. "You gain a few pounds, lady?"

"You know I ain't never been no size. Too old to get some now."

"Old? Come on. What's old?"

She pulls back from me, begins, as if I have violated her, to adjust her clothing needlessly. "Old," she says, "is what you get when you don't die."

There's a silence, building with a rush, that and the dull ache she triggers in my chest with distance. She has fully rearranged herself. "Dad upstairs?"

"Last I looked."

"Guess I'll go see him."

She doesn't look at me. It's as if I've come and gone already. I go back through the living room, climb the stairs.

At the top I pause in the door of the room I shared with my brother. Both beds are tightly made as if we would sleep in them again, as if we would lie again in darkness and share our dreams. I miss my brother. I turn down the hall toward my parents' door, open it enough to stick my head into the darkened room.

"Dad?"

"Marcus?"

"Jason." I step into the smell of menthol.

"I must have been dreaming," he says. "I keep dreaming about him."

"How you feeling?"

"Not too good." His head flops toward me, features forming in the dimness as my eyes grow accustomed to the dark. His face is withered and grizzled; he needs a haircut and a shave. "Got this cold in my side . . ."

"Want me to open a window?"

"The light," he grunts, "hurts my eyes. Sit. Rest yourself."

His guitar lies across the only chair. I lean the instrument against the wall, drag the chair to the bed. "Been playing?"

"Playing?"

"Guitar."

"Naw."

". . . Beautiful day outside."

"I guess so. When you seen your brother?"

Daylight leaks past the drawn shades, weak and tentative, the way light must enter the mausoleums of dead men. "Marcus is dead."

"I won't see another spring," he says. "I won't last the winter."

"Don't talk like that. Mama says it's only pleurisy."

"Your *mama*." He spits the word out and struggles to lift his head from the pillow. There's a charge in the room, electric; I recognize the hate. "Your mama," he says, eyes small and ugly in the dimness, "she the reason for me going to prison. She the one told." He is looking not at me, but at the window where the light creeps through. "She hated Garvey. Hated Black. All she care about is that lily white Jesus of her'n. He had the way. He had the plan. That's why they got him. He died for us," my father says fiercely, and for a moment I don't know if he's talking about the black Garvey or the white Christ.

"Dad, I don't believe Mama did that."

"Never did believe she could do nothing, did you? Ask her."

"Did you?"

"Didn't need to."

"Then how . . . ?"

"Because," my father says, "she told me."

I sit here, sinking beneath menthol and despair. A long time ago, my father worked for Marcus Garvey, had been his driver and personal gofer, and then my father left for a job in a meat-packing plant. When Garvey was sent to prison on charges of mail fraud, my father became part of a group that plotted to break him out. Someone had betrayed them, and my father spent three years in jail.

Now he is telling me that his wife had been the traitor. Was this the reason for the way they were? If so, why hadn't he left; was his punishment of her in the staying? Why hadn't he considered *his* life, his misery? My father was fifty when I was born, my mother forty-seven. Marcus was fourteen months my senior. Why had they had us then?

Why had my mother betrayed him?

Why is he telling *me*?

Had Marcus known?

I sit, disgusted, feeling sorry for myself, waiting for my father to continue. But it's as if I'm no longer here, as if he's slipped back into the half-demented world I've disturbed with my presence. I try not to be bitter, but I can't help it. He's probably, in the bright place of his memory, sitting on the porch, playing checkers with his oldest son, while I stand in the dark outside the circle they make, watching. I listen to the labored snarl of his breathing, and I am thinking that I should get up and leave this house, leave him, forever.

"And you know what?" my father says.

"What?"

"Marcus ain't dead."

"Dad . . ."

"Move out the way. Let me up."

"Dad . . ."

"*Move out the way, boy.*"

I move. It's the voice of his prime, full of power and authority, and I respond reflexively as I did when a child. He throws the blanket from his body, and then he looms above me, reeking of menthol. "Now where is my clothes?" he says, and, after a moment's indecision, makes his way like a drunken man to the closet. He is struggling to pull a pair of pants on over his pajamas. He is trying to put both feet into the same leg.

"Dad. Where you going?"

"Get my son."

"Where?"

"Want to come, come. Don't, don't."

I'm shaking. I cross to him, reach and grab his arm. "Come back to bed."

"Told you I'm going to get my son. Best let go of me." His voice is menacing, in his eyes a disbelief that I dare dictate to him, that I dare touch his body with impunity. I'm shaking. He is my father, no matter what he did to me, no matter how he felt about me, or feels now; he is my father. But I know what I have to do.

"Come back to bed. Marcus is dead."

"Ain't."

"He's dead," I shout. "I identified the body. They emptied shotguns in his face. Now come on back to bed."

"Going to see my son," he thunders. "Get out my way."

So it has come to this again. I watch him, towering above me, pants in a puddle at his feet. I think back nearly eight years to June, 1964, to the night before the morning Marcus and I left for Mississippi, when my father found out and waited up for Marcus and vowed to block Marcus' passage with his body, vowed to break his son's bones if need be, if that's what it took to keep him from going South. And Marcus coming into the room, frenzied, shaking my bed, and me awakening, thinking he my father finally come to seek revenge. *I didn't tell*, I said. The lamp turned over, the bulb exploded like a pistol shot and Marcus was astride me in the dark, screaming *traitor*, both fists flailing at my face. My father stood in the doorway, didn't move. So this is his revenge, I thought . . .

And all because, months before, when I saw them about to fight, I threw my body between my parents, and when my father, crazed with drink and rage, kept coming, I hit him. Not out of loyalty to my mother, but out of fear and a longing for peace. But I could never explain that to him; he wouldn't let me, only grunted when I tried. And now he was pushing me all the way out into the darkness by disconnecting me from my brother's love, his precious elder son who was going to Mississippi to risk his life for a thing as frail as freedom. My father's revenge was beautifully conceived and structured, the perfect poetry of a madman's shattered heart.

I was nineteen, but I understood this. I understood it in the way that young men suddenly realize that the earth does not exist to do their bidding, and that they are not immune to death. The understanding allowed me to accept when the policemen the neighbors called said that one of us, me or Marcus, had to cool off for the night in jail, and my father picked me. It also drove me from this house, all the way to Mississippi, with Marcus, who finally believed me. I hadn't planned to go. I thought my father was right, those folks would kill you. It didn't make any sense to me to risk my life like that. But I went because there was no place else to go and I learned to believe in nonviolence and I hoped and turned the other cheek until three men with axe handles beat between my thighs until my flesh was purple, until their daughters were safe, until what they'd done meant that I would have no children. I hate those men. But that I was there in the first place is still my father's fault.

He has accomplished the putting on of his pants, is struggling into a shirt, lurching for the door, the shirt unbuttoned, his feet bare. I grab his arm and spin him and slap him across the face.

The last time I hit my father he touched his face and stared at his fingers in disbelief. Now, with a growl, he cocks his fist and swings at my head. But my father is an old, sick man this morning, and I step inside the punch and embrace him. He is grunting, hammering at my back with both hands, but the blows don't hurt. I hold him tighter, his chin on my shoulder, and I feel the madness spending its strength. His hands fall to his sides; his knees buckle. I half carry, half drag him to the bed and lay him across it. I bump against the end table, setting in motion the empty vase which totters and falls, smashes against the floor. I leave it, peel the pants off, get him under the blanket. Then I just stand looking down at him, and I am frightened at what I feel: vengeance, pain, shame, love.

"You didn't," he says, "have to hit me." His face is turned, his eyes hidden.

"I'm sorry."

"Marcus . . ."

"I'm *Jason*. Not Marcus."

"He's dead," my father says. "And I won't last the winter."

Something wells in me. I would never have thought my father could make me cry. I reach and touch his shoulder. "Sure you will. You'll outlive all of us."

"I ain't got no quarrel. . . . I done lived a long time." He faces me, eyes alive with hurt. "You all I got left now. You the last Strong man. The name is yours. You got to carry on."

I don't trust myself to speak. My father doesn't know; I never told him. Marcus was the last Strong man.

"Mouth's dry. Could you get me some water?"

I'm shaking, spent, everything moving two ways inside me. I go downstairs. My mother sits at the table, eyes like a threatened bird's, shoulders hunched. "What was all that fuss?"

"Oh . . . Dad got upset. He'll be all right. He wants some water."

She stares at me, as if trying to discover what water has to do with it, and then her gaze veers toward the counter and the cooling bread. "Ain't him I'm worried about."

I sigh, abused by their mutual hate, their private drama. "What's wrong, Mama? What is it?"

"What's he saying about me?"

I wave away the question. "He's sick. You can't listen to everything he says."

"He told what I did?"

I nod.

"I didn't *mean* for him to go to prison," she wails. "I was scared, that's why I told. The man said nothing would happen if it got stopped in time."

"Mama . . ."

"I didn't *mean* it."

I close my eyes. "I know."

"And let me tell you something. My baby would've lived wasn't for him not being home. He the cause of my child dying."

The room begins to turn. I reach behind me for a wall; it's not there. I make it to the safety of the counter, hold to it with both hands. "What child?"

"It don't make no difference now."

"*Mama.* What child?" The room is turning, my mother's face the only still point. "Mama!"

She is rocking, holding herself, eyes fixed upon the floor. "We had a girl, your daddy and me. That's right. Was why he quit Garvey in the first place, we needed money. When Garvey went to jail for stealing, your daddy blamed himself as if his quittin' was the cause. Your daddy in prison and I'm left alone with a three-month baby, see? My milk went bad. From worrying. My baby died." She looks at me and blinks. "You had a sister. Been forty-seven had she lived. In August."

"Jesus, Mama. Did you tell him?"

"Tell him what?"

"How you *feel*," I whisper.

"Tell him? He knew."

She is curious, vaguely annoyed, and I hear the click as she dismisses my foolishness. "And then," she says, "to have him think I meant it. He had to have something on me, cause he know he the cause that baby dying. The way he know he the cause of Marcus ending up the way he did. It was what your daddy taught him. *Black* that, *black* this. He had to have something on me, to make us even."

It's more than she's spoken to me at one time in all my life. Winter sits on her face, gray and deadly, and when she speaks again her voice has lost its energy, gone flat. "This morning I went to take him his breakfast. He said he didn't like the way I looked at him. That I looked at him like he was a piece of dirt. And I told him . . . if the shoe fits, wear it."

"Maybe," I start, then say it anyway. "Maybe you shouldn't have said that."

Her eyes meet mine, then slide past to the window where the sun comes through. But I catch in the instant of our meeting her accusation, this and the knowledge that as she's suspected, nothing has changed. And as I begin to speak, to say that the path to peace did not lie in confrontation, I stop, thinking, who knew? Perhaps the *only* path to peace was confrontation, and my mother nods and says, almost triumphantly, "Sticking up for your father. Wasn't you, it was Marcus."

"I'm not taking sides. I just know he's suffering."

"Oh? *He's* suffering." And she looks at me and her face says I'm a grown man, yet stupid, have sight, but still can't see. "I birthed Marcus," she says, and blinks.

"I know. Listen. It'll be all right. He'll get over it."

"Maybe so. . . . But will I?"

I don't say anything. I move to the sink, fill a glass, then remember there is always a bottle of water in the refrigerator. Her voice arches behind me.

"Boy, let me tell you. You don't know the half. The *years*. But I won't cry no more. I won't."

I turn. Tears stream down her face. "Mama . . ." I step toward her; she holds her hands up.

"Go tend your father. He the one sick."

"What can I do? *Tell* me."

"Take your father his water."

I don't know where it comes from, but the thought explodes that someplace people are happy, someplace someone laughs. And all of it swells and bears down on me. The years of silence, of pain, and lost connections. I've had enough, not because I'm strong, but because I need and I'm grieving. I'm grieving for my parents, and for my brother, and I grieve for me. "There's nobody left but us now, Mama. Can't we make it better? Can't we try?"

She stares at me. If there's a feeling in her eyes, I can't read it. I look at her, all wrapped up in stubbornness and revenge, and I feel a sharp and searing rage. Then it drains, leaving me hollow, nothing to hold to. I wish my brother were here. I take a deep breath, try to get things to flow one way inside me. I go back upstairs, help my father to sit up, prop pillows behind his back.

"Did you dig a well?" he asks.

I consider strangling him. He drinks the water and smacks his lips. "Thankee, thankee. Now get me that guitar if you please."

I get the guitar. He picks a chord, tunes the instrument. "He really dead?"

"Dad," I say wearily.

"All right." He smiles a mocking, privileged smile. "What you want to hear?"

I want to say it doesn't matter. I want to say play a funeral dirge. Play the National Anthem. "Anything, Dad. Anything."

"You know 'Blues For The Boogie Man'?"

"No."

"How about 'I Have Had My Fun If I Don't Get Well No More'?"

"Yeah."

"Well, let's do it."

He begins to sing. I sit for a while, throat lined with menthol, feeling lost and tired and unconnected. I want to shout, to scream. I want to go to sleep in a sunlit room; I want to be held by someone who loves me. My father does something intricate on the guitar, makes it sound like laughing and crying at the same time, and I realize that though I've remembered the music, I've forgotten how good he is. Now I begin to focus on his song. It's an old song, one I recall from childhood; it is connected also to summer nights in Mississippi when I was afraid and wanted to leave there. Those voices in the South were deep and powerful, or high and sweet, and no matter how bad you felt they helped you make it through until the morning. My father's voice is thin, but not without strength, not without a stubborn desire to have the record show that although he was out there in the wilderness, half-mad, battered and barely alive, he was hanging tough. I'm feeling blue and washed out, but now at least I know. Everybody has a story; there's always a reason why. My parents had told their stories to me. I had seen the tales as burdens, dusty, unclaimed baggage whose weight they now insisted I should bear. But perhaps I am wrong. Perhaps each telling is a gift, a way of connecting to the only flesh they share.

I don't know, but as I listen to my father sing, I sense a developing of hope. And I realize that I will make it, that some of my parents' toughness is in me, that if they have never bestowed upon me a perfect love, they have bequeathed to me my spirit. My parents' lives were hard, but they were not wasted; they'd lived them the best way they knew. Neither was a life that I wanted to live, but I didn't have to. And I didn't have to let their lives color mine.

Even as I think this I feel something slip inside, go out of me, deepen the darkness of my father's room. None of what I want can be achieved without struggle. I'm tired, and more than a little afraid, and besides, there's all that history. I will always be my parents' child; some things I'll never forget. And I don't know if I'm strong enough to remember without yielding to bitterness and the urge to revenge, even when I know each prevents me from connecting.

My father sings. I hear steps on the staircase and my mother comes along the hall, stands in the doorway. She doesn't say anything, but she is here. As I am. My father sings. I go to my knees where the vase lies shattered, and I begin to pick up the pieces.

RITA DOVE

Second-Hand Man

Virginia couldn't stand it when someone tried to shorten
her name—like Ginny, for example. But James didn't. He set his twelve-
string guitar down real slow.

"Miss Virginia," he said, "you're a fine piece of woman."

Seemed he'd been asking around. Knew everything about her. Knew
she was bold and proud and didn't cotton to no silly niggers. Vir-gin-ee-a
he said, nice and slow. Almost Russian, the way he said it. Right then
and there she knew this man was for her.

He courted her just inside a year, came by nearly every day. First
she wouldn't see him for more than half an hour at a time. She'd send
him away; he knew better than to try to force her. Another fellow did
that once—kept coming by when she said she had other things to do. She
told him he do it once more, she'd be waiting at the door with a pot of
scalding water to teach him some manners. Did, too. Fool didn't believe
her—she had the pot waiting on the stove and when he came up those
stairs, she was standing in the door. He took one look at her face and
turned and ran. He was lucky those steps were so steep. She only got
a little piece of his pant leg.

No, James knew his stuff. He'd come on time and stay till she told
him he needed to go.

She'd met him out at Summit Beach one day. In 1921, that was the
place to go on hot summer days! Clean yellow sand all around the lake
and an amusement park that ran from morning to midnight. She went
there with a couple of girl friends. They were younger than her and a
little silly. But they were sweet. Virginia was nineteen then. "High
time," everyone used to say to her, but she'd just lift her head and go
on about her business. She weren't going to marry just any old Negro.
He had to be perfect.

There was a man who was chasing her around about that time, too.
Tall, dark Negro—Sterling Williams was his name. Pretty as a panther.

64

Married, he was. Least that's what everyone said. Left a wife in Washington, D.C. A little crazy, the wife—poor Sterling was trying to get a divorce.

Well, Sterling was at Summit Beach that day, too. He followed Virginia around, trying to buy her root beer. Everybody loved root beer that summer. Root beer and vanilla ice cream—the Boston Cooler. But she wouldn't pay him no mind. People said she was crazy—Sterling was the best catch in Akron, they said.

"Not for me," Virginia said. "I don't want no second-hand man."

But Sterling wouldn't give up. He kept buying root beers and having to drink them himself.

Then she saw James. He'd just come up from Tennessee, working his way up on the riverboats. Folks said his best friend had been lynched down there, and he turned his back on the town and said he was never coming back. Well, when she saw this cute little man in a straw hat and a twelve-string guitar under his arm, she got a little flustered. Her girl friends whispered around to find out who he was, but she acted like she didn't even see him.

He was the hit of Summit Beach. Played that twelve-string guitar like a devil. They'd take off their shoes and sit on the beach toward evening. All the girls loved James. "Oh, Jimmy," they'd squeal, "play us a *looove* song!" He'd laugh and pick out a tune:

> I'll give you a dollar if you'll come out tonight,
> If you'll come out tonight,
> If you'll come out tonight.
> I'll give you a dollar if you'll come out tonight
> And dance by the light of the moon.

Then the girls would giggle. "Jimmy," they screamed, "you oughta be 'shamed of yourself!" He'd sing the second verse then:

> I danced with a girl with a hole in her stockin',
> And her heel kep' a-rockin',
> And her heel kep' a-rockin';
> I danced with a girl with a hole in her stockin',
> And we danced by the light of the moon.

Then they'd all priss and preen their feathers and wonder which would be best—to be in fancy clothes and go on being courted by these dull factory fellows, or to have a hole in their stockings and dance with James.

Virginia never danced. She sat a bit off to one side and watched them make fools of themselves.

Then one night near season's end, they were all sitting down by the water, and everyone had on sweaters and was in a foul mood because the cold weather was coming and there wouldn't be no more parties. Someone said something about hating having the good times end, and James struck up a nice and easy tune, looking across the fire straight at Virginia:

> As I was lumb'ring down de street,
> Down de street, down de street,
> A han'some gal I chanced to meet,
> Oh, she was fair to view!
>
> I'd like to make dat gal my wife,
> Gal my wife, gal my wife.
> I'd be happy all my life
> If I had her by me.

She knew he was the man. She'd known it a long while, but she was just biding her time. He called on her the next day. She said she was busy canning peaches. He came back the next day. They sat on the porch and watched the people go by. He didn't say much, except to say her name like that.

"Vir-gin-ee-a," he said, "you're a mighty fine woman."

She sent him home a little after that. He came back a week later. She was angry at him and told him she didn't have time for playing around. But he'd brought his twelve-string guitar, and he said he'd been practicing all week just to play a couple of songs for her. She let him in then and made him sit on the stool while she sat on the porch swing. He sang the first song. It was a floor thumper.

> There is a gal in our town,
> She wears a yellow striped gown,
> And when she walks the streets aroun',
> The hollow of her foot makes a hole in the ground.
>
> Ol' folks, young folks, cl'ar the kitchen,
> Ol' folks, young folks, cl'ar the kitchen,
> O' Virginny never tire.

She got a little mad then, but she knew he was baiting her. Seeing how much she would take. She knew he wasn't singing about her, and she'd already heard how he said her name. It was time to let the dog in out of the rain, even if he shook his wet all over the floor. So she leaned back and put her hands on her hips, real slow.

"I just *know* you ain't singing about me."

"Virginia," he replied, with a grin would've put Rudolph Valentino to shame, "I'd *never* sing about you that way."

Then he pulled a yellow scarf out his trouser pocket. Like melted butter it was, with fringes.

"I saw it yesterday and thought how nice it would look against your skin," James said.

That was the first present she ever accepted from a man. Then he sang his other song:

> I'm coming, I'm coming!
> Virginia, I'm coming to stay.
> Don't hold it agin' me
> For running away.

> And if I can win ya,
> I'll never more roam,
> I'm coming Virginia,
> My dixie land home.

She was gone for him. Not like those girls on the beach: she had enough sense left to crack a joke or two. "You saying I look like the state of Virginia?" she asked, and he laughed. But she was gone.

She didn't let him know it, though, not for a long while. Even when he asked her to marry him, eight months later, he was trembling and thought she just might refuse out of some woman's whim. No, he courted her proper. Every day for a little while. They'd sit on the porch until it got too cold, and then they'd sit in the parlor with two or three bright lamps on. Her mother and father were glad Virginia'd found a beau, but they weren't taking any chances. Everything had to be proper.

He got down, all trembly, on one knee and asked her to be his wife. She said yes. There's a point when all this dignity and stuff get in the way of Destiny. He kept on trembling; he didn't believe her.

"What?" James said.

"I said yes," Virginia answered. She was starting to get angry. Then he saw that she meant it, and he went into the other room to ask her father for her hand in marriage.

But people are too curious for their own good, and there's some things they never need to know, but they're going to find them out one way or the other. James had come all the way up from Tennessee and that should have been far enough, but he couldn't hide that snake anymore. It just crawled out from under the rock when it was good and ready.

The snake was Jeremiah Morgan. Some fellows from Akron had gone off for work on the riverboats, and some of these fellows had heard about James. That twelve-string guitar and straw hat of his had made him pretty popular. So, story got to town that James had a baby somewhere. And joined up to this baby—but long dead and buried—was a wife.

Virginia had been married six months when she found out from sweet-talking, side-stepping Jeremiah Morgan who never liked her no-how after she'd laid his soul to rest one night when he'd taken her home from a dance. (She always carried a brick in her purse—no man could get the best of her!)

Jeremiah must have been the happiest man in Akron the day he found out. He found it out later than most people—things like that have a way of circulating first among those who know how to keep it from spreading to the wrong folks—then when the gossip's gotten to everyone else, it's handed over to the one who knows what to do with it.

"Ask that husband of your'n what else he left in Tennessee besides his best friend," was all Jeremiah said at first.

No no-good Negro like Jeremiah Morgan could make Virginia beg for information. She wouldn't bite.

"I ain't got no need for asking my husband nothing," she said, and walked away. She was going to choir practice.

He stood where he was, yelled after her like any old common person. "Mrs. Evans always talking about being Number One! It looks like she's Number Two after all."

Her ears burned from the shame of it. She went on to choir practice and sang her prettiest; and straight when she was back home she asked:

"What's all this Number Two business?"

He broke down and told her the whole story—how he'd been married before, when he was seventeen, and his wife dying in childbirth and the child not quite right because of being blue when it was born. And how when his friend was strung up he saw no reason for staying. And how when he met Virginia, he found out pretty quick what she'd done to Sterling Williams and that she'd never have no second-hand man, and he *had* to have her, so he never said a word about his past.

She took off her coat and hung it in the front closet. She unpinned her hat and set it in its box on the shelf. She reached in the back of the closet and brought out his hunting rifle and the box of bullets. She didn't see no way out but to shoot him.

"Put that down!" he shouted. "I love you!"

"You were right not to tell me," she said to him, "because I sure as sin wouldn't have married you. I don't want you *now*."

"Virginia!" he said. He was real scared. "How can you shoot me down like this?"

No, she couldn't shoot him when he stood there looking at her with those sweet brown eyes, telling her how much he loved her.

"You have to sleep sometime," she said, and sat down to wait.

He didn't sleep for three nights. He knew she meant business. She sat up in their best chair with the rifle across her lap, but he wouldn't sleep. He sat at the table and told her over and over that he loved her and he hadn't known what else to do at the time.

"When I get through killing you," she told him, "I'm going to write to Tennessee and have them send that baby up here. It won't do, farming a child out to any relative with an extra plate."

She held onto that rifle. Not that he would have taken it from her— not that that would've saved him. No, the only thing would've saved him was running away. But he wouldn't run either.

Sitting there, Virginia had lots of time to think. He was afraid of what she might do, but he wouldn't leave her, either. Some of what he was saying began to sink in. He had lied, but that was the only way to get her—she could see the reasoning behind that. And except for that, he was perfect. It was hardly like having a wife before at all. And the baby— anyone could see the marriage wasn't meant to be anyway.

On the third day about midnight, she laid down the rifle.

"You will join the choir and settle down instead of plucking on that guitar anytime anyone drop a hat," she said. "And we will write to your aunt in Tennessee and have that child sent up here." Then she put the rifle back in the closet.

The child never made it up to Ohio—it had died a month before Jeremiah ever opened his mouth. That hit James hard. He thought it was his fault and all, but Virginia made him see the child was sick and was probably better off with its Maker than it would be living out half a life.

James made a good tenor in the choir. The next spring, Virginia had her first baby and they decided to name her Belle. That's French for beautiful. And she was, too.

JOHN McCLUSKEY, JR.

The Best Teacher in Georgia

The Musing

AS DORA FELL OFF THE BACK PORCH, next door Miss Mary Lou Hunter was turning the selector to a rerun of "The Rockford Files." In her front room Miss Mary settled down in her favorite sitting chair, a steaming cup of sassafras tea, sweetened with two teaspoons of honey, resting on a carefully folded square of newspaper. To make sure that she did not miss a word of her favorite afternoon show, the set was turned up loud, so Dora's first shout for help, an embarrassed yelp more than anything else, was drowned in the twangy guitar crescendo of the opening theme. Then Miss Mary blew into her tea, took two sips, and set her cup down. Scratching down an arm, she sat back and waited for the first chase scene.

Dora had tried to catch herself on her hands, then her elbows, but had failed. Her knees and chin were the three points that absorbed the impact of her fall. She was as surprised at the lack of pain as she was by the fall itself, surprised even that her glasses stayed on. The world had been spinning when she stepped to the back porch. There were plenty of pecans under the great tree and she wanted to bring them in for a pie. That spinning that she had now been so accustomed to for the past eight months started again as the back door slammed and she had stopped at the edge of the porch and, already falling, was reaching for the railing. She heard a *crack* before the ground rushed up fast. The ground was still spinning as she lay there even now, the faint smell of packed dirt in her nostrils.

She tried to get up, but could not. She could not feel her arms, though she could see them tensing. It was as if they had fallen asleep during some nightmare and she was armless. She remembered screams in such dreams and knew that the one she recalled from just seconds ago was her own.

Her weight was on her neck now and she slid forward and to one side quickly to relieve the pain. But her shawl tightened deeply across a shoulder. She struggled to lessen the strain, but could not. Finally, she managed to turn just enough so that she could free one end of it. She let out a sigh. Again, she could compare this to only a bad dream. Occasionally there would be one—whether someone was chasing her or she was shut up in a closet didn't matter. She would be suffocating and one part of her could tell the other that she was face down in the pillow and all she had to do was roll over. The feeling was so strange, because there would be the great will to breathe again and the easy urge to lie like that as sweet resignation washed over her. And she would turn, in some mighty effort, just enough to breathe fresh air, then search back quickly for the episode in her dream that made her realize that she was suffocating. She could never find it.

Bunny had brought the shawl home from a trip to Philadelphia two years ago. Bunny and her husband had spent the Christmas away, so the gift was not presented until New Year's Eve. That was the day before the coming of the deer. New Year's Day was unseasonably warm and from the thick woods over a mile away a small band of deer found Dora's backyard. Fawns were frolicking about the pecan tree by the time Dora came to the back window. They played close to the porch while two larger does kept to the edge of the yard, watchful. With potato chips or soda crackers in their hands a few of the kids like little Calvin, Thomasina's loud boy, tried to tiptoe up on one of the fawns. When they saw a big buck step out of the woods and start digging at the ground with one of his front legs—well, those children just backed on off and went up to the porch to watch the show like everybody else. The deer stayed out there for ten, twenty minutes and then, one by one, they were gone. Just like ice storms in that part of Georgia, they appeared as swift and silencing miracles and then, with no trace, they left. That was the morning of the day Bunny and her husband returned. She brought the shawl over after dinner. It was in a deep-red box hidden beneath the wrapping paper, and inside the blue and cream shawl rested on crinkly paper. Dora had been connecting the shawl to the deer to ice storms ever since.

She reached down suddenly. A gust of wind had started up the back of her legs and she felt the hem of her skirt rising, then the skirt ballooning up from behind. She quickly smoothed down her skirt. Don't want that Mr. Leroy to look down here and see me with my bloomers showing to the sky. Just like him, too, to look out of his window and stay up there grinning like a fool and trying to see what all he could see while I'm down here rolling around. I've caught him a dozen times riding that old piece of bicycle he got, riding past the porches and trying to look up some woman's dress. He bends down like he cocking his head to say "hello" but he got something else on his mind. That man's got to be ninety if he's a day and still carrying on all sorts of foolishness. He's the loudest one in church on Sunday mornings and he shouts "amen" loud enough to shake the rooftop when the preacher starts in talking about the lust in some men's hearts. Yes, he'd see all he could see first before he would get over here to help out, nasty thing. She tried to push up, but failed.

"Lord, I've got to get up from here," she heard herself say.

What else might be going on? She thought of how some young fool could break right in the front door while she was out here and steal the television set or those pretty brass lamps that she had bought her mother on her seventieth birthday. Her mother would be in the bedroom humming to herself and not hear or see a thing. Then Dora let her body go limp. As the sound of her heavy breathing faded, she could hear a car or two passing out front. Before too long there would be the four o'clock whistle from the paper mill. She could hear now, as plain as the ticking of a clock coming closer, the wooden heels of someone walking past the house. She wanted to scream but decided against it. And what would that whistling somebody with the loud heels find? Just an old woman without her hair piece who fell off her back porch and could not get up again. About as bad as Humpty-Dumpty with all the king's men. She saw knights in dull grey armor attempt to pull her up, fail in their grunting, then mount their glorious black horses, liveried in silver, and move slowly off in single file. She laughed drily. "Well, I'm not that bad off and I want everyone to know it."

She thought that if she stayed still for just a short while longer the ground would stop spinning and she could roll to one side, then sit up. Last spring she had fallen and she had had several dizzy spells since then, spells which made her sit up for minutes until her head cleared. The first time she was in the backyard where she had finished hanging out some sheets to dry. From here, she could see the spot where she fell, and she remembered how she caught herself on her hands and waited there on all fours, her knees sinking into the soft ground, until the world stopped. She didn't tell her mother about that time. Would her mother have understood? She who, until her own blindness, never knew a sick day or a knock-down illness in her life?

At some time in her late years her mother must have fallen. But now with her cane, the fingers of her free hand walking the rough plaster walls, she knew every dangerous step, every corner, every table in the house. And Dora, twenty years younger and fading already, it seemed, was given to dizzy spells that a smart-aleck doctor with a beard could not cure. Her mother had already outlived a husband and son and it looked like she would outlast the only one she had left.

She gained an elbow about the time Miss Mary whooped when the private investigator, after hitting a lumbering goon on the chin, doubled up in pain, then blew across and kissed his aching knuckles. The giant merely blinked, rocked slightly on his heels, and chased Rockford off with a lead pipe. Miss Mary sipped again from her tea, then glanced to the window where the end of a branch was scraping. She could not hear it, however.

Still on one elbow, Dora concluded that her mother must be in the dim sitting room listening to the late afternoon symphony from a classical music station out of Atlanta. "The only colored woman in Spalding County, Georgia, to listen to the opera," she once boasted. But it was the news, the details of all events national and international, that kept her by the radio. She feared losing touch, feared not knowing the names of those who made the news. ("We as a people have got to get our heads out of the sand and realize there's a whole world out there. How come colored can't care about what's happening in India or Poland?")

Two squirrels skittered around the trunk of a burr oak in Mr. Leroy's yard. From somewhere a crow cawed and she could smell the smoke from someone's burning trash. At a two-year-old's height she could see the backyard. It was large enough for a child to run about, to feel small in. When she was growing up here, it always seemed that the yard was large enough for a dozen cows to graze in. The day she returned from Atlanta to live here she was shocked at the game her memory had played. It was still a large backyard dominated by one huge pecan tree at its center but three full-grown Herefords would have made it appear a pen.

Now she could only look. Just months earlier she had been hoeing in the garden which ran the length of the back fence. Now the green beans and most of the tomatoes had been picked. A few collards were left, but the sweet potatoes, somehow forgotten this year, might be a lost cause. Of course, as predictable as early November frost, there were the plentiful pecans. Each year, as an additional Christmas gift, she would send a large box of them to her daughter and her family in Milwaukee. The daughter would call on Christmas Day to thank her for the gifts, usually not mentioning the pecans. She called, too, after the arrival of flowery cards on Mother's Day and her birthday. Every two years the daughter with her family would visit and every other trip they would arrive in a new car. Dora would have appreciated a long letter on no special occasion and failed to convince herself that they were too busy adding on rooms, buying appliances, getting promotions on time. Had she as a mother failed to do something right when her daughter was six, or thirteen, or twenty? She wondered.

Adjusting her glasses, she tried to focus on the pecan tree now. During the late mornings of last August's brutal heat she would read in the shade of the great tree, its trunk cool along the length of her spine. Last summer she had stuck to poetry—Shakespeare's sonnets, the Brownings, and Countee Cullen. Six years before she retired she had been voted the best teacher in Georgia and she could recite Cullen poems with a voice pitched to the middle register of a flute: *These are no wind-blown rumors, soft say-sos/no garden-whispered hearsays, lightly heard . . .*

When she finished, her eyes often moist, the fifth-graders would look at one another in confusion. One or two might cover their mouths and roll their eyes, not knowing any better, and the silence would then beg for a snicker, a dry cough—anything to bring the room back to normal. How did she ever hope to successfully explain the weight behind the words she recited, the moons and suns those words created and softly landed upon? She hoped to merely provide them a form which their experiences would fill. In the all-white school where she taught during the last five years before her retirement, they would giggle. Somehow she would expect it there, though. She imagined they took the sight and her words home with them to be brought up over dinner. ("Mama, we got this strange colored woman for a teacher and she can stare out the window and say poems by heart. And sometimes she seemed to be about ready to cry over them.") Aside from screams barely audible over guitars, they had no stories, no songs. It was even getting that way for the black children. She confessed to herself many times that she pitied the young with their anthems of screaming guitars and runaway saxophones. Many gave them noise for music, but few gave them a poem.

She was almost up now, but, leaning too far forward, slipped and fell to her other side with a groan. ("Mama, Mama, don't come now and learn I'm like this!") A door slammed; Mr. Leroy's dog barked twice. Her view was once again that of a toddler's. She listened to the beating of her heart. It was not racing. Her breathing was normal. The ground had stopped spinning. She was relieved by at least that much. She managed to turn over on her back, not caring how her dress and sweater would look when she finally did get up. She relaxed and looked up through the limbs of the tree to the sky. She had not lain on her back looking at the sky for nearly fifty years.

Though it was summer that time, she could not remember the heat. Her high school friend Alphonso had introduced her to George, who attended Morehouse and visited town that summer after his junior year. With Alphonso's fiancée, they had all bicycled out to a small lake for a picnic. Then they walked, the couples separating, and she and George found a hill all their own. After they shared their future plans, they relaxed in a silence. She closed her eyes and saw red against the insides of her eyelids. Clover was sweet and she smelled his cologne, a faint lemon it was, before he kissed her lightly. The next day they returned alone and kissed many times, she recalled now. They made love quickly, awkwardly. Afterwards, briefly, she let the sunlight again paint the insides of her eyelids red. By the next summer he urged marriage, but she could not accept then. She would remember that hill, that red, those smells forever, but it had only been a few brief moments and she had imagined love to be a string of such moments, palpable, infinite in length.

Horace, however, was October, a vivid splash of color. She married him the year she found her first teaching job. It was a hard marriage. She grew to crave consistency. She fought for sameness, though it was the sudden peaks and valleys of emotions that raced her blood. He died fifteen years ago and she lived alone in Atlanta until she retired. Her daughter invited her to join her and her young family in Milwaukee. "Too cold," she had lied, not wanting to be a burden and, besides, her mother needed someone close by.

Perhaps it was the rush of those long ago moments, the slant of the afternoon light on this day, that had sent her to the back window before she decided that the fallen pecans were worth her trouble. Yes, perhaps that, before the porch started spinning. Resting on an elbow, she concluded once more that she would seek more moments, more vivid splashes of color. Just three days ago she had reserved a flight to New Orleans. She had planned the trip with Gladys, another retired teacher, but Gladys died suddenly in September. A local travel agency had made travel arrangements, reserved a seat at two plays, and was forwarding a listing of preferred restaurants with the ticket. ("You'll just love New Orleans, Mrs. Wright," said an agent over the phone, cool efficiency sugared by admiration. "We've got you a room in an elegant and quiet hotel on Royal. It's what we call a 'C and C,' clean and classy. All our clients just love the place. It's near everything in the Quarter. You're a mighty lucky lady.")

She and Horace had planned to visit New Orleans for two weeks around their fortieth anniversary. From the stories of clubwomen who had traveled there in groups or with their husbands, she knew all about the food, all about the balcony ironwork magically spun by slaves. This time of the year there would be no crowds and she would not be jostled on the sidewalks. But what if she had a spell there among strangers, collapsing on those ancient sidewalks before ancient cafés? She winced. Please hurry, ticket. With ticket and travel plans in hand, only then would she tell her mother. Another breeze swept up and terror was that sudden chill at the base of her neck.

And Fond Memory

She was sitting upright now. She could hear her mother working her way through the kitchen. She shook her shawl out and placed it around her shoulders. She brought her legs together and smoothed down her skirt and apron. After a glance at Mr. Leroy's window, she found a few pecans nearby and dropped them in her lap one by one, as she might drop stones in a pond.

"Dora? Dora child, where you at? I been calling you for the past ten minutes and can't get a word out of you."

"Out here, Mama. I'm out back."

"What you doing out there so long?" came her mother's voice.

"I'm just out here enjoying the weather."

Her mother pushed through the back door and came onto the porch. She tapped her cane against a chair, then against the wooden pillar that supported the railing. "You going to catch a cold out there. This fall weather can fool you."

She smiled. Over a long checkered dress her mother wore a faded brown sweater. She was a neat woman who dressed up and wore small gold earrings every day.

"I want to get supper started and I need you to slice a little of that ham off. Come on now. You ain't getting no younger and too much of this sitting around on the wet ground can give you arthritis. I know what I'm talking about."

"I'm on my way, Mama."

As her mother started to turn, the sleeve of her sweater caught a nail on the back post. In trying to pull away and misjudging her own strength, she pulled a hole in the sweater sleeve and, losing her balance, fell backward against, then through, the railing.

"Mama! Mama, the rail . . . !"

The old woman fell on her side, no scream, and her body made a dull sound when it landed, like that of a hundred-pound bag of seed.

"Mama, you all right?" She tried to inch forward on her elbows and stomach. "Mama, say something!"

Her mother was bleeding from the elbow and the forehead, a trickle of blood snaking between the eyebrows already. Her eyes wide—though her daughter felt the stare of such eyes long past fear—she looked to the sound of her daughter's voice as a child would. The blood, a thin crooked line, found the bridge of her nose.

"Oh, I'm all right. Just a scratch, child." She patted her own cheek.

"Still . . . no, you're bleeding, Mama!" She was close now, close enough to touch her. Then with the hem of her skirt she wiped the blood from her mother's face, dabbed at the cut lip she had just noticed.

Her mother shook her head as if to push her away, the way an embarrassed child anticipates a rough kiss.

"Help me up, Dora."

"I can't."

"What do you mean 'you can't'?"

"I can't. Mama, I can't get up my own self."

Her mother bowed her head as if in prayer. "Dora, how long you been out here like this?"

"Fifteen, twenty minutes maybe. My arms and legs just went numb for awhile . . ."

Her mother's soft shriek came as if she had been hit suddenly. Then her face tightened. Dora thought she was going to cry.

"Well, I'll be. How come you didn't call me, Dora?"

"There wasn't any need. It's happened to me once before and I got right up, quicker than a cat. If it keeps happening, I better learn to pull up some kind of way."

"You better to see a doctor is what you 'better' do. Why, you could just drop down at the shopping center or at church or anywhere. Whatever it is, you better not play with it."

"I have seen a doctor. He just gave me some pills. He said if they didn't do any good to come back around Thanksgiving for some tests." She glanced off. By Thanksgiving she would have been to New Orleans. Maybe the trip would cure her. She had heard of spells that just went away mysteriously after coming on once or twice.

Her mother was silent for a moment, then spoke softly to no one in particular. "You ain't getting no younger. You can't all the time be hoping to pull yourself up." Then to her daughter: "Can you see anybody around? Let's call somebody over."

"Mama, just give me a minute. I'll have both of us up."

"Well, just one minute then. This cold ground cause arthritis sure as we sittin' here." She snorted, patted a thigh. "At least I ain't broke nothing. Women fallin' at my age break a hip the same way you break a toothpick. Remember Lila's girl, Hattie, slipped and fell on her steps that time and broke her hip in two places? That's been what—two, three years, ain't it? You ain't broke nothing, did you?"

"I better not break anything. Can you imagine me on crutches?"

"There's worse things than crutches," her mother said.

Then Dora chuckled. "We must look quite the pair. Two women plopped down in the backyard and can't even get up."

"It won't be funny an hour from now and we still sittin' here."

"Just another min . . . the front door locked? You sure everything's off the stove?" Dora suddenly imagined the house on fire, smoke billowing from the kitchen. Sirens before loud-talking, heavy-booted firemen intruding, crashing through the kitchen to find them in the backyard.

"Nothing's on the stove and I 'spect the front door is still fastened. I locked it right back after the mailman done handed me the mail." (The ticket! The ticket!)

Dora turned to her side, pushing, but her arms were numb, muscleless. She sighed. She wanted to laugh. She wanted to cry.

"This telling me I'm getting old," Dora said.

"You got to use your common sense, Dora. You got to fall off the porch to find out you ain't thirty no more? Or even sixty?"

She looked at her mother's sightless eyes. They were hazel. Younger, Dora felt that when she looked directly at her mother the light eyes gave the impression of pools that you looked into. Her own eyes, dark brown and like most of her features, were those of her father. She fidgeted.

"Well, I don't like this. I don't like this feeling where you can't control what your body's going to do the next minute."

"What you gon' do about it? I don't like it either, but ain't nothing neither one of us can do about it. You gon' stop the clock?"

"I mean I'm scared, Mama. I been scared for a long time, but it took this to make it plain."

She brushed dirt from her mother's shoulders, then dabbed again at her forehead. The trickle of blood had slowed.

"Scared?" her mother asked. "I tell you what scared is. I'm talking after the change of life and after your teeth go bad and your hair thin. I do have to thank the good Lord my hair stayed thick as it was when I was fifty. But then your hearing go on you and you get tired of bothering folks all the time, asking them to repeat what they say. So you just shake your head at them and go ahead and say something to what you think they be saying. And you remember how it was early morning when you hear the birds just starting up, just before daybreak? Well, you get so you can hardly make out the sounds. 'Bout the only thing you can catch is some big ole crow or Mr. Leroy's loud rooster. Then before you get used to not hearing as good as you used to, your smell give out on you. Oh, you can still make out cabbage all right, but what happened to cinnamon and thyme and just plain ole coffee? You see something that could be a rose or a apple, but unless it's right up against your nose, it might as well be plastic. Dora, you hear what I'm telling you?"

"I can hear you."

Her mother cleared her throat. "Then if all that ain't enough to make you scared and mad at the same time, you might get some real bad luck and get the cataracts on your eyes so bad that even after operations . . ."

"Mama, I know about what happened. You don't . . ."

". . . listen good, now—after the operations you still can't see and over months you can't see nothing, not one blessed thing. You can tell light from dark, but you see things like they was ghosts or something and you know you'll be that way—even if you believe every jack-leg preacher between here and Nashville who say he got the cure for you—know you'll be seeing ghosts for the rest of your life. And all the while your bones drying out and getting like . . . like chalk. Every little bump you pay for, every fall. You and me gon' feel this fall clear into next week."

Dora was shaking her head. She tried to see herself in ten years, fifteen, twenty. Wondered what her luck would be. Would she be able to see the morning light sparkling on heavy frost? Would she be able to see her amaryllis in bloom? Would she be able to do for herself alone? But her mother continued, reaching to pat her arm.

"Ain't no time to be scared, child. We just got to get on up from here before we have everybody laughing at us out here. They'll laugh first, then come running over here asking if they can help."

"They're not that bad."

"I tell you I know them, I know how they do."

She wanted to tell her mother that it was not just the embarrassment and confusion of a body failing, growing stranger. It was death, of course, that frightened her, that chilled her again that afternoon with terror. And when she finally brought herself to say it, she was alarmed at how still her mother became. A truck rumbled down the street out front.

"Don't be so scary, will you? You talk like you got one foot in the grave already. Plus, it ain't too late for a woman like you to have men to come calling."

Dora snickered. "Only eligible men 'way out here are not doing so well, in and out of the hospital every day. You talking about them calling and they can barely make it back and forth from the bedroom to the kitchen table to the bathroom . . ."

Her mother threw up her hands. "There you go again talking like you too good."

"I'm not too good. Don't you think I'd like to have a man to talk to, to have dinner with and dance with, all these years?"

"All I'm saying is that a woman like you—educated and who think about things—a woman like you need friends, educated friends. I know there ain't much here for you. Maybe for somebody like myself, when I was your age, there were one or two. You remember I used to see that Mr. Coates? Now he was a nice decent man to come courting and like me he just barely finished high school."

"Mama, college by itself doesn't mean a person's nice or decent or even educated."

Her mother talked on, low. Dora didn't know whether her mother heard her this time. Softening, she pitied her in that instant, pitied them both. After Horace's death, there had been a special friend once and, now, the sun flooding the yard with its dying light, she spoke of him. She had promised herself never to tell.

He had been five years younger and his wife was in poor health. Downtown Atlanta had only recently opened up for blacks and three nights a week they would meet at a small restaurant off Peachtree. They kept to the side streets, hand in hand. Once even they checked into a downtown hotel, avoiding the popular Paschal's Motel, as husband and wife. As excited as teenagers, they had been. But their affair lasted only three months. Except for her award, it was the most exciting time of her last fifteen years.

Her mother's face had registered curiosity when she first started. By the end of Dora's confession, however, her face revealed horror. Her head snapped once, as one shakes from a sudden chill or as if slapped from a trance.

"Shame on you, running around like some hot-blooded Jezebel! Rochelle Louise Fields didn't raise no child to run around with married men. Taking advantage of some sick woman that way and you a respectable schoolteacher and all. I bet you got plenty of secrets."

Dora's shoulders sagged under a heavy load. She saw herself in New Orleans alone on Rue Royal. The knocking of her shoes was the loudest noise in the world as she walked. She stepped into a puddle of light, scattering pigeons. There was a spring in her step as she moved on. The background music was not Dixieland, but Ella Fitzgerald's "A Tisket-A Tasket." Lilac was strong in the air, though it was autumn.

"I was lonely, Mama. He was, too. That was all it was." She dared not tell her that for six of those ten daring weeks it had been much, much more. Then as if some bright monarch butterfly skimming the tops of grass and grain, love had skipped away.

"You don't know how lonely I've been these last fifteen years. There have been times I've wanted to walk over to the woods and just scream like some crazy woman. You hear that clock ticking, cars passing out front with people on their way to . . . to something—work, a family, somebody to touch and talk to. And you know all you can do is sit or dress up to walk downtown or around the mall. Crowds make you feel even more lonely so you come back home and sit. Maybe you find a book every once in awhile to take your mind off things. Even then you want to share it."

"That don't mean you take up with a married man," her mother said. "They're plenty of folks lonely—I can tell you a thing or two 'bout loneliness—but they ain't dabblin' in no other folkses' home business. And you don't have to talk about me on the sly, talking about what I didn't learn. I only got past high school. I know I never got the chance to go to college or nothing. My folks barely had enough to send one off and that was your uncle who just wasted his time and your grandpa's money . . ."

Dora clapped both hands to her ears, for she had heard many times the tale of the ungrateful son who had gone up to Fisk to be a doctor and had ignored his studies. He had been dismissed and worked in Nashville over a year before he found the nerve to tell the family what had happened. Meanwhile Rochelle had worked and bought second-hand books to know the worlds she thought only available to the formally educated. She learned manners from books of etiquette and from the languid gestures of young white women she served during lawn parties. Grew defensive, then rigid about what she learned in solitude. So when her brother returned to confess his failure, she wanted to throw a pot at him. She, not he, should have been the one to go to college. Later her carpenter husband would stand mute before her monologues on good manners.

How quickly we forget! Rochelle's own daughter took her own good fortune in stride. Why, even after she had been voted Teacher of the Year for the entire state and shifted to a formerly all-white school as something of a reward, Dora was not pleased. Dora's hands came down quickly when she heard.

"Mama, how many times I have to tell you that I made my way teaching among my own? I was happy at Phillis Wheatley. I didn't need white folks to tell me I was good. My students and other teachers and principal nominated me. That made me the proudest."

But her mother was convinced that such matter-of-factness before so astounding an achievement—she had been voted best out of the "colored" and the white!—was unnatural. Was vanity.

Dora now thought of the plaque, a gold-plated square on a walnut-stained shield, hanging on the front room wall where no one could miss it. Her mother had insisted that it be hung there. Dora thought of the telegram that she tore open with trembling hands and the long, flowery letter that followed. This, before the award ceremony and the plaque.

"Oh, Mama, remember how you came to Atlanta with Miss Mary and everybody? How I wore my best dress—it was the baby-blue one with the lace at the collar and sleeves, remember?—I put on so much rosewater I bet they could smell me clear to Macon. And, when that skinny man with the big belly announced my name, how I walked up—I don't know 'til this day how my legs carried me up there—and I had to practically tear the plaque away from him."

Her mother nodded and managed a smile. "He acted like you was taking gold." It was one of her mother's last sights. In a brief silence they sat. That night in an auditorium in downtown Atlanta had been one of the last genuinely happy moments they had shared. Now her mother cleared her throat.

"Dora, we ain't got all day. The past is dead and gone."

"Maybe." In two weeks, her ticket clutched against one side, she would board a gleaming silver jet with royal blue trim. Two stewardesses would flash smiles and point her to her seat. Her mother would be here in this house where she would be cared for by Miss Mary until Dora returned. By then she would understand why Dora needed the trip. By then all her questions would be exhausted.

She got to her knees and leaned on her mother. "Mama, just stay still. I need your shoulder here to help me up." Trying to put as little weight on the shoulder as she could, she pressed down and gained one foot, then the other.

"Glory," she sighed. "Mama, I'm up. I'll come from behind you and pull you up."

Slipping her arms inside her mother's, she pulled her up in one mighty effort. Then she brushed the dirt from both of them and led her mother to the porch.

"You smell good today, Mama."

"You saying I don't always smell good?"

"No, I'm just saying you smell special. It's that new Avon you ordered? You got somebody special to come calling?"

"Don't sass," her mother said.

Smiling, Dora did not look back as they opened the door. The pecans were still scattered behind. She would come back for them soon. Right now there was a supper to start.

Miss Mary turned off the set as the last of the theme song died out. She climbed upstairs to her bedroom and walked to the window. She heard the back door slam next door at the Fields's. Their backyard seemed to float up toward her. There was a spot just beyond the porch that was favored by the sun. Pecans had rained there. The yard looked like a meadow left shimmering after a morning mist had just lifted. She recalled that years ago a flock of pink flamingoes had played near that very same spot.

Or was it peacocks or rabbits or . . . deer?

KATHY ELAINE ANDERSON

Louisiana Shade

Sterling

RAINS HAVE COME. The air told me it was time. The down-turning of leaves. The hissing rain makes. I place my fingers palms up on leaves receiving the wetness.

The rain air whips my pants, then pulls them like breath in a balloon. My feet seek roots that stream across the path. A trickle of a path. I touch the tree trunks that line the way. I have discovered faces in these trunks. One, narrow and lean, the bark rough and patchy. Another with knots I can hold onto, hollows I explore with cautious fingers. Wet and pungent, the few remaining pine trees are sticky to the touch. The oak holds the lace of a spider web, wet with dew and the soft warmth of decomposing wood.

There are trees that have elbows. Indians tied them down when the trees were saplings—they learned to grow horizontal. When released, the center stayed parallel to the ground, the rest of the trunk continued seeking sun. They make a trail. I follow my hand as it finds them. They lead me to the spring.

The ground instead of yielding to my feet, ever so slightly, has become rocky. And here I sit and have sat, dangling the dark legs I pretend shadow the underworld.

LeRoy

It's hot. That little bit of rain didn't do nothin'. I'm in the middle in bed and even with the covers off it's hot. Wish I could draw on the ceiling. Give me something to look at some nights. I can't stand it no more. It's about time I go to the window, I love wigglin' down to the bed bottom. I guess I better wash the windowsill tomorrow before Momma sees this dark place where I've been putting my chin.

Woods and stars. Everybody sleep or pretending to be. The woods be dark but there's this clear space right at the edge of town. It's almost time. There, there he go, standing like Moses in that picture in the Bible. And he just stand there.

He lives in the woods. Grandma say it was thirty years the house he live in was empty. His daddy would come back every year when his granddaddy died to make sure everythin' was alright—nothin' broken into. He paid Mr. Culver to watch it and keep it up when he was gone. Mat Sterling's momma never came back. I wish I could of seen them. We wait every Saturday for him, the son who came back thirty years later. We wait for him to go to the general store.

He real tall, only Mr. Culver come close. And he got this big stick carved with all this stuff we never get close enough to see what of. And black! Billy Lee say if he walked around at night you wouldn't know the difference unless he spoke to you. I know better.

He don't stay long, just look like he be looking right at me. Then he turn around and go back. He must be wanting to talk sometime. Me too. I wants to go away like in one of those dreams I have sometime. He be in my dreams and we sit and talk. Remind me of Daddy but I can never remember what we talk about. Shoot, it's my secret—watchin' him standin' there three or four of the seven nights in the week. Just watchin' his face let me know he ain't gonna hurt me. His comin' say to me he want to talk. I look at my bandana in the moonlight. Squint real good. Yeah.

I wish it didn't happen. I wish I wasn't there last Saturday. I wish I didn't have to do what I got to do before this Saturday.

Grandma

Child, why are you fidgeting so? LeRoy, if those ain't ants in your pants, they must surely be fleas. Have you been out in the woods with that dog? Stop swinging on that porch rail before you end up fixing it! Come down here and keep Grandma some company in the garden. Here, start turning that soil up, that's right, right there."

"Grandma, are you really the oldest deaconess in the church?"

"That's right. My momma and your daddy's granddaddy started working this land when it was just trees rising back till you can't see no more."

"Do you remember when they came?"

"They who?"

"You know, the Sterlings."

"You been asking about that man all summer, ever since you children knew you did wrong. I don't care if *you* didn't say anything. You all should be shamed, calling that man Mr. Sterling names. All of you should have been whipped in the middle of town, as it is, there was many a daddy with a sore arm from switching brown behinds. That Sterling family . . . my momma always said they brought more than forty acres and a mule. They had seven wagons piled high. He built the house totally by himself, almost. The rest of them helped a little. She said they were real friendly. They all were, cause we all were trying to make a space for ourselves after the war. We just didn't want to bother white folk—moved as far back as possible so as not to disturb them. Actually, to say the truth, so they wouldn't disturb us. We heard about some white folk trying to keep their slaves, telling them the war wasn't over and they weren't emancipated. Humph. It worked moving back here, 'cause we each had our little gifts for doing things so we didn't have to go to them for nothing.

"The first Mat Sterling must of got his name cause his work was so good. At sunset there would be a battle between his furnace and the sun right through the trees. Nearly anything iron around here still standing he forged into something beautiful. I knew the second Mat Sterling and you know the third. The third Mat Sterling's daddy went up North to go to college (people didn't see why, we got good Negro colleges right here) and then came back and didn't keep the furnace burning. Maybe it was because he wasn't named Mat Sterling. It was little Mat who got that love of fire and iron from his granddaddy. I sat down with his granddaddy, the second Mat Sterling, and he said his father and his father's father was a blacksmith. It's such a shame that house stayed empty thirty years after the accident.

"Child, that row could use some straightening. Those are very good. Now, why do you keep asking me about the Sterlings?"

"Grandma, I got to go. I'm supposed to meet everybody. I'll be back. I did my chores already."

"Well, I guess it's alright. Come give me some sugar and go ahead and play while you still got some play left and I'll tell your momma."

Sterling

The night is escaping slow. Wisps cling to the edges of trees. The wooden floor is still slightly warm from the first heat since the rains. I stand in the sun mornings before my work inside is begun. Do you know I have returned to your forge? Stand silent, touching each tool—the instruments you played six days of every week. The woods would sing with the sound.

For ten years, the ten years remaining to you, I did not see you, I was only able to speak to you over telephone wire. Over and over you said it wasn't right that you couldn't see the third Mat Sterling, that my mother was wrong stealing me away.

It was an accident. I was going to learn your trade—what my father wouldn't. I return Mat Sterling. You are here still in the quiet of the mornings. I think of when I would slip out of bed and you would be waiting for our walk. I return with my own instruments. I can't use yours but mine continue to play the songs you began long ago.

LeRoy

It was Mr. Culver who knowed he was coming. We were waiting for him but our folks said we weren't supposed to stare. Trying to be respectful—we just made sure we had work to do outside that day.

When he came walking down the street, I peeped at Grandma, Momma and Daddy. They were wondering too. They were just better at hiding it. Grandma started patting her foot and humming a little and that always means somethin' special was about to happen. She was thinking somethin' but that day she wasn't sayin'.

He walked into town with this carved stick taller than him. The elders said it was somethin' from their mommas' and daddies' time. It was all carved up and pretty. He walked like he knew where he was going. That was when Grandma said he was blinded at his granddaddy's forge when he was five years old.

Grandma

"Boy, you awfully quiet. What's on your mind?"

"Oh, I was just thinkin' about the day when Mat Sterling came to town. Hey, Grandma, has anyone ever visited Mr. Sterling?"

"Young man, hay is for horses and by now you should know the good Lord didn't put me here in the shape of a horse. I don't know of anyone visiting him. I guess nobody's been invited. His daddy wasn't like that or his momma. His daddy would come asking all kinds of questions and then disappear into that house for days. The tap-tap-tap of that machine would come out of the woods at night.

"They say he got his degree in something called folklore. He was studying us, real friendly, but studying all the while. He said our great,

great-grandchildren are going to want to know about us. That we got to record our ways cause the white folk who were weren't doing us no justice. Well, we tried to help him best we could, him being from here and all and his family helping to start this town. And boy, why do you want to know?"

"Oh, I was just wondering. Nobody really talks to him except 'how do you do' and I keep thinkin' what's it like to have nobody to talk to and nobody to see either. I wonder if he gets lonely. Nobody knows if he can speak, huh? He's been away two times more than I been alive. Did his momma make them go back North?"

"I see you have been paying attention to your math. No child, nobody has heard him speak and his momma sure did snatch him up quick and take him up North. She was a schoolteacher and never seemed to get used to our ways. And when little Mat was blinded, well, she just went crazy. LeRoy, I don't know how to answer your other questions. But it hurts me to my heart to see him so. You know, we make our own choices in this life, and the least we can choose is what we do with what we got. Now, your daddy's coming home and you better get ready for supper."

Sterling

I thought I could return and work in peace. I thought within this wood, the fold of my family home, I could just disappear, become stone. The children, first with taunts, then with a fragment of the stone I have become, demand recognition.

They did not accept my offerings, what I have been able to give of myself—left on the trees where they have found them, each their own nature, a gift.

The children know, they won't accept my silence. They mock me, I do not hear their voices, I hear the chorus of ancestors through them, a chorus that becomes louder each time we meet, the chorus dark without face, just voice—my work must be shared—they are coming for me. I must face them this Saturday.

LeRoy

We shouldn't of called him names. Our butts wouldn't of been tore up and I wouldn't be standing on this road with all the boys mad, all quiet, makin' the air thick and mean. I tried to open my mouth but everybody stared me down. I feel sick every Saturday morning. I try to get out of coming but they call me "chicken" and "blind man junior." Why doesn't he say somethin'? Why don't he do somethin'?

Week after week, after we got our butts beat we stood on the road before town. It was Billy Lee who got beat worst of all. He started it. As soon as Sterling got close Billy Lee started mumbling softly making no sense. They all caught on and made this sound that got louder, raspy and ugly until he went past. And oh how they'd laugh! We wouldn't get in trouble cause hey, we didn't say nothin'—did we?

He didn't do nothin'! Didn't say a word. He be crazy or stupid. Why did he want and go do that for? So, every Saturday we'd be waitin'.

I tried to meet him on the road by myself. I'd watch him. He'd touch the trees and sometimes he'd just stand with his face lifted no matter if it was rain or sun touchin' it. I never got the nerve to speak and he was so hard in his thinkin' I don't even know if he knew I was there.

I'm not sure when we noticed the bandanas. Week after week he said nothin'. I noticed that each time he came to town he got a different bandana hangin' out his back pocket. They'd be all different colors. They ain't nothin' store-bought. They never be the same cause one day we done compared the ones we got. And when he came back from town they wasn't there no more. I found the first one, like some strange bird off a tree.

And whoever finds one has to be treated like a king all that week. Everybody got to do what the king say then . . . and if you don't get it, well, the old king keeps on bein' king until somebody gets it. I was hopin' everybody would stop botherin' him but they didn't. They thought it was fun and scary and somethin' to do cause it was so hot.

But now, cause of last Saturday, nobody goes up that road on Saturday mornings anymore and I got to see Mat Sterling at his house.

Last Saturday it was so dry and hot. There was a silence that made you forget that the forest had animals and birds and bugs. If you looked down the road the air looked wavy. Everybody was cross. For the last time I said, let's leave him alone. Boy, then everythin' bust wide open. They started shoutin', "Blind man junior! Blind man junior! Go ahead and be with him—you look like him too—black and stinky. We're not going to be your friend anymore. You stand there and look stupid, see if we care. Shh! he's coming!"

They started that hum, this time standin' at different points on the road. They started kickin' pebbles. And he didn't do nothin'. I couldn't stand it. I started shoutin', "Why don't you do somethin'? Why do you let us take your bandanas? Why do you stand at the edge of town at night? I see you, I see you, I see you. You think you better? You think we stupid? Tell us to stop—we'd stop, honest. You, you . . ." and I took a rock and threw it. You ask me why and I can't tell you. It hit him. I swear, it hit him. He stopped. Shook his head and turned around to face us. None of us said anything or breathed. There he stood in the middle of the road lookin' like Moses like he do at the edge of town at night. He stood there with his head a little to one side as if trying to see. And for the first time, he had somethin' to say.

"Names may never hurt me but that rock you threw did. I think it is about time we all had a talk. I suppose if I had spoken with you earlier, it may not have come to this. I suppose you wonder what I do all day and night and why you and your parents have not been invited to my house. My grandfather saw your families often. Fixed your families' gates, shod your horses, reforged broken axles. I can't do that but I do have some things to show you. Next Saturday I invite the young man who threw the rock to my house and anyone else who would like to accompany him. Your parents need not be concerned—I will not harm you. They are invited too; I will tell them so on this trip to town. It will be an open house—light up my home as you have never seen—a beacon. Oh, was that LeRoy Washington who spoke? If so tell your grandmother I have something to give her."

That's all he said. Everyone looked at each other and then they all had somethin' to say to me.

"Boy, you went and done it now and you're gonna get it. Oh brother, I'm glad I ain't you. Nobody's gonna want to go with you. He might strangle you and hang you over the river to rot. He might burn your eyes out and eat them for dinner."

All I could say was, "Oh, shut up!"

Grandma and LeRoy

"Boy, I'm not answering another question about Mat Sterling, not a single one. I do know I'm going to visit. I don't care if the rest of the town act a fool.

"Just imagine, he came to town, opened his mouth and spoke so clear—his voice is deeper than the preacher Michael's. Folks are having a hard time deciding. Not me. You say he got something for me? Goodness, I didn't think he'd remember me, he was so small."

"Remember what, Grandma?"

"Don't start me lying. Baby, now you know Grandma don't lie if she can help it. This will be our secret. Don't you tell a soul. Come here close. That's right. Now.

"Sometimes real early in the morning me, Mat Sterling and his grandfather would go for a walk in the woods. That's after his wife died and I was married to your granddaddy. Oh, I was bold in those days. If anyone would of found out, I would have been marked a scandal—me a married woman walking in the woods with a widower and his grandchild at that time in the morning. But it was good times and the little Mat would chatter like a squirrel. Real good times . . ."

"Grandma. Grandma, I have a secret to tell you too. I'll tell Momma and Daddy and I'm going to get punished, but please, I got to go see Mr. Sterling first. I, I threw a rock at him and it hit him and I want to say I'm sorry. I got to go to his house before tonight. Grandma, can I go? Please?"

"Child, why did you throw a rock at Mr. Sterling?"

"Grandma, I don't know but I got to go see him."

"What is this world coming to that my baby is throwing rocks at a blind man? At any man. You're right. You are going to get punished but I'm proud that you know to go pay your respects, say you're sorry, and face the consequences of your acts. Yes, LeRoy, you go and I won't breathe a word of what you got to tell your momma and daddy. Now go on, you hear?"

LeRoy and Sterling

I only know where his house is cause Daddy showed me where we are goin' to start huntin' next year when I get my first gun. Those trees look funny, all bent over. Maybe that's what I'm goin' to look like when I get home. But he didn't sound mad at me. He even said that I should tell Grandma he had something for her.

There it is and there he is standing with his face in the sun.

"Yes? Who is there?"

"It's me, LeRoy Washington. I come to say I'm sorry, I didn't mean to hit you with that rock. I just wanted you to make them stop and every Saturday you didn't say nothin'. You just let us do it. I didn't mean to tell about you at the edge of town. I kind of thought that was our secret, except you didn't know I saw you, did you?"

"No, I didn't. Well, seeing that is the case, I think you should be the first to enter my house. Don't stand back; I won't bite you and my porch steps don't creak so you don't have to step so gingerly."

"What does my steppin' have to do with ginger?"

"That simply means carefully."

"Excuse me Mr. Sterling, how come your door look like that?"

"Well, when I was a little older than you, when my family moved up North I met two African carvers and they taught me how to carve. I carved a yam knife first, then a bowl and other things. Doors were a challenge. Where they came from people of high rank had special doors made that told the story of their strength and wisdom. This door has its story too."

"Hey, Grandma was right! She said your great-granddaddy came with seven wagons piled high and here up at the top is a man with seven wagons! How come the bottom half don't have nothin'?"

"I haven't lived it yet. Come inside."

"Mr. Sterling, what are those pictures up there where your wood walls stop? They don't look like nothin' I ever seen before. And how come your walls are like that—half thick, thick wood and then walls like ours? And why you got these wood things where most of us put our livin' room furniture? Did you do all this?"

"Yes."

"But you're blind! You can't see to paint no picture. How can you paint when you can't see?"

"I always liked the coolness of rain. Often I try to put it on canvas. The coolness, the rain, the wet sound. Sometimes, I try to paint what is behind my eyelids. See, my canvasses are large. I need to be able to swing my hands over their surfaces. I paint when I can't say anything with my hands directly. I paint when I want to see. This first one is called *Louisiana Shade*. Isn't it the shape and texture of the soft warmth under a tree in a Louisiana summer? I was trying somehow to capture that space under a large tree but I am certain that's not the definite shape of a tree. And these are *Midnight's Last Call, The Close Wind Speaks, Tree Talk, Black Man Carving, Black Folk, The Ways of Some Gifted Ancestors* and *Phantasmagoria*.

"My walls touch you back. There are three paths carved into these walls. Close your eyes and you will feel the story. Your hand will find a lone figure standing in front of three portals, three entrances. They lead to the same place but each path is different. You must feel the story, not see it.

"And so my carvings in clay and wood are where you put furniture? They are large because each has its own spirit, its own opening into space.

"Come, follow me upstairs, I will show you where this all comes from."

"Can I touch . . . ?"

"Yes."

"Up here, facing East, the sun finds this room first. This is where I paint."

"It sure is bare. What's that?"

"It's my easel and that row of cans in the rack in front are my paints. I believe the colors are a little like a rainbow."

"Why you got a brush at both ends? Do you paint with both brushes at the same time?"

"Yes, sometimes I do. Both hands have something to say."

"Hey, those are our bandanas!"

"That's right. All the children don't have one yet, so I am making the remaining ones.

"In the first light I paint here. Then the light changes and moves. In this next room I carve. I made the door here and the panels of the walls downstairs."

"What is that big hunk of wood goin' to be?"

"I don't know yet. Sometimes it takes awhile for a piece to take shape.

"This final room is my clay room. I am here in the evening when it is cool and in shadow. I face the forge here. My grandfather was a great blacksmith and I think of him sometimes, particularly in this room. Come, the time has passed quickly and you must go home.

"Here, give this to your grandmother."

"Oh, she's goin' to like this! She told me a secret and here it is. You made it out of wood. Here you all are walkin' in the woods—you a little boy, Grandma and your granddaddy, and nobody'll know 'ceptin' us!"

"That's right. You go on home. Thank you for coming by and please, come back."

Grandma

"He's been carrying a weight too long and he done spun it into something precious.

"It sounds like a dream to me. Precious."

"That weight—he done spun to gold."

DAVID BRADLEY

Looking Behind Cane

I

I WAS INTRODUCED to Jean Toomer in the spring of 1970 when I was a student at the University of Pennsylvania, taking a course in "Black Literature." I had enrolled in the course under duress; 1970 was a year of tension in the black consciousness movement, and American blacks everywhere—especially those on college campuses—were under pressure from their peers, black and white as well, to, as Roberta Flack sings, "Be Real Black For Me." One of the things you were supposed to do—along with drinking sweet wine, listening to cool jazz, and attending boring discussion sessions—was to take courses which were "relevant to the struggle" and/or which "explored Black Culture." I preferred beer and classical music, and refused to attend meetings; I was under some pressure to conform to the fourth norm.

I had, however, enrolled in the Black Literature course for deeper reasons, although I doubt I could have articulated them at the time. I was an English major then, reading a lot of books, and was constantly plagued by a mild irritation at the way black people were presented in literature, even—or perhaps I should say, especially—"modern" and "contemporary" literature. Few characters—the only truly notable exceptions were Twain's Jim and Faulkner's Lucas Beauchamp—seemed to have any real humanity. I suspected that black authors would write about black people with a little more empathy than most white writers apparently could—or would.

I had no real proof to support that suspicion, which was another reason I enrolled in the course. It was bad enough, although easily explainable, that I had gotten to college without ever having read a book-length work of literature which I knew to have been written by a black person; but I considered it robbery—although again, easily explainable (if you happen to be cynical)—that I had gotten through two years as an

English major without having to read such a book either. The simple, sad fact was that writing by blacks was mostly unrepresented in basic literature courses, and if I wanted to study it—not just read it, but study it with the same sort of professional guidance I got when I confronted Faulkner or Hemingway—then I had to do it in a special course segregated for black literature.

Those were my stated reasons for taking the course. But there was something clandestine going on, too. I was calling myself an English major and even making noises about graduate school, but the truth was I meant to be a writer, and I needed to know if black people wrote—or ought to write—any differently from white people, not only about black characters, but about everything. The dogma of the times insisted that there was a "black aesthetic," that blacks had different artistic problems and different ways of solving them. In liberal circles, the alleged difference was assumed to be an unrelievedly positive thing. The trouble was that when I compared my writing to that of the authors I most admired, the only difference I saw was that they knew what they were doing and I did not. But perhaps, I reasoned, I was being too hard on myself. Perhaps I wasn't bad at all; I was just measuring myself by the wrong standards. Maybe the harder I worked to measure up to those standards, the farther I would get from what I should really be trying to be.

And so I came to English 289, Readings in Black Literature, in search of literature that would help me define myself in a number of ways. I did not expect to love the whole of "Black Literature" anymore than I loved the whole of "Seventeenth-Century Literature." I was hoping merely to stumble on one author in whose work I could immediately and instinctively recognize a paradigm for my own.

The less said about the course, the better. It was as good as any course can be when the subject material is selected with reckless disregard for genre, period and social context; no critic in his right mind would design a seminar that considered the poetry of Anne Bradstreet, the novels of Upton Sinclair and the drama of David Rabe, yet this course combined the poetry of Phillis Wheatley, the novels of Richard Wright and the drama of Amiri Baraka. By the third week of the course I realized that the instructor was every bit as much a victim of political pressure as I was; by the fourth week I knew that that exhilarating moment when you look at the material and perceive the pattern that ties it all together would, in this course, never come. But along about the ninth week I read a recent reprint of a book first published forty years before. It was called *Cane*, by someone named Jean Toomer.

In some ways, *Cane* made about as much sense as the course. It was a hodge-podge of genres—poems, sketches, a novella, a short play. It lacked, in many instances, the kind of polish and unified intention that I had come to admire in and expect from great literature. Some of the characters were barely developed, and the plots . . . well, even the narrator admitted that one tale was "crudest melodrama." And that narrator! I had learned by then that the defining of narration was one of the basic concerns in modern criticism, but *Cane*'s narrative voice was impossible to define in critical terms, like "restriction," "point of view" or "ironic distance." In a lot of ways, *Cane* was not only a hodge-podge, but an amateurish one.

But God, it was beautiful! It dealt with passions and people, not mindless emotion and stereotypes, as did most books that purported to speak of black people (and by now I realized that a lot of "Black Literature" fit into that scruffy category). There was sensuality, religious ecstasy, rage, humor—vibrant expressions not of "blackness" but of the humanity of people who were black. I appreciated that, sometimes, it was wanting in terms of technique. But the strength of the emotion made me realize for the first time what technique was *for*. And Toomer, as author, was frankly and joyously connected, not with some abstract "Black History" but with the earthy realities of a Black past. Toomer didn't explore it, he *believed* in it. *Lived* it. *Loved* it. And I loved him.

Cane inspired me; I wanted to talk about it. Unfortunately I tried to open discussion with a young lady in the class whose "black consciousness" was in a highly advanced state. At the mention of Toomer, she glared. "*You* would like him," she snapped. "He denied his blackness." This was, in 1970, a capital offense. As she stalked angrily away I realized that once again I was responding to the wrong standards. I began to wonder if there was any hope for me.

For more than a decade I lived with the confusion occasioned by that exchange. How, I wondered, could a writer accept so completely in his work what he repudiated in his life? At last I decided to look into the matter—to look behind *Cane*.

II

Nineteen seventy was a critical year—the year when the backlash response to the social upheaval of the sixties had become as visible as a distinct and powerful ideology. While back in 1968 the doves may have forced Lyndon Johnson to give up the Presidency, the electorate had given a warm response to George Wallace and had elected Richard Nixon. The liberals may have passed the 1968 Civil Rights Act, but the conservatives had tacked on the "Rap Brown" Amendment, making it a federal crime to cross state lines with intent to incite a riot.

This backlash, although later defined in nonradical, almost Cromwellian terms, as "hardhat" response to "longhaired" radicalism, was in large measure racist. George Wallace's 1963 vow, "Segregation now! Segregation tomorrow! Segregation forever!" had been a subliminal hum behind the buzzwords of his 1968 campaign, and Nixon's "Law and Order" was an easily decoded slogan endorsing brutalization of blacks by urban police forces. By 1970 there was a growing sense of bewilderment and beleaguerment among liberals, white and, especially, black, who saw the battles fought and won in the sixties rejoined, refought and this time lost. The danger on the right seemed to justify extreme measures: the injection of essentially political concerns into the study of American culture—i.e., Black Studies courses; the use, and at times misuse, of the facts of history to support liberal views.

Ironically, the publishing industry, traditionally conservative but notoriously ponderous, was only then beginning to respond to the liberal impulses that had gathered momentum in the first two-thirds of the decade. While as late as 1966 most of the various manifestos, statements and declarations of liberal or radical groups, many of which enjoyed a great popularity with the liberal intelligentsia and would therefore have been highly profitable for commercial publishers, were being issued by small, occasionally *ad hoc*, often noncommercial presses; in that year Glad Day Press published Stokely Carmichael's *Toward Black Liberation* and the perennial avant-garde Grove Press issued *The Autobiography of Malcolm X*. But by the late sixties, while most of America seemed to be leaning right, some of the most reputable and, in some cases, conservative houses were taking over the publication of radical statements. The venerable Dial Press published Julius Lester's *Look Out Whitey! Black Power's Gon' Get Your Mama* in 1968, followed by a book by H. Rap Brown in 1969. Random House, at that time a subsidiary of blue-chip RCA, took Carmichael from Glad Day, issuing *Black Power* (co-authored with Charles Hamilton) in 1967 and *Stokely Speaks* in 1971, giving him Bobby Seale (*Seize the Time*, 1970), Amiri Baraka (*Raise, Race, Rays, Raze*, 1971) and Huey Newton (*To Die for the People*, 1972) as stablemates.

Nor were the publishers limiting the product to polemics; fiction writing was affected as well. While it had been the fashion for some time to publish novels about blacks written, usually in paternalistic idiom, by whites, often southerners—*To Kill a Mockingbird*, Harper Lee's sentimental rehash of Faulkner's *Intruder in the Dust; The Liberation of Lord Byron Jones*, Tennessean Jesse Hill Ford's tale of a southern black undertaker who dares file for divorce; *The Confessions of Nat Turner*, Virginian William Styron's perversion of history, in which the black leader of one of the most significant rebellions in American history is supposedly motivated by love of a white girl—the late sixties saw an upsurge of novels about blacks written by blacks, many of them first novels: Ishmael Reed's *The Free Lance Pallbearers* (1967); John Edgar Wideman's *A Glance Away* (1968); Toni Morrison's *The Bluest Eye* (1970); Alice Walker's *The Third Life of Grange Copeland* (1970). At the same time the publishers began to search their vaults—and anybody else's—in search of old books by black authors which, whatever their intrinsic merit, might have enough historical significance to be adopted by black studies courses. One of these re-publications was *Cane*.

In many ways the conditions that surrounded *Cane*'s second publication were reminiscent of those that surrounded its first. Nineteen twenty-three was a crucial year in an increasingly conservative era that followed a time of relative liberality. The social sentiments that gave rise to Wilsonian Progressivism, the "New Freedom," and female suffrage came to an end in 1919 when Attorney General A. Mitchell Palmer, formerly a Wilsonian Progressive, launched a series of raids on the increasingly violent radical groups. The "Red Scare" climate was evidenced by events like the arrest of more than six thousand persons, the two indictments of John Reed, the trial of Sacco and Vanzetti, the deportation of 250 to Russia, the three-year incarceration of Eugene V. Debs, the expulsion of five duly elected Socialists from the New York State Legislature, and the decision of the United States Supreme Court in 1924, in *Gitlow vs. New York*, that it was within the powers of the State to suppress revolutionary utterances regardless of their actual effect, since "a single revolutionary spark may kindle a fire that, smouldering for a time, may burst into a sweeping conflagration. It cannot be said that the State is acting arbitrarily or unreasonably when it . . . seeks to extinguish the spark without waiting until it has enkindled the flame. . . ."

As was the case in 1970, the conservatism of the twenties was essentially racist, although the twenties-brand racism was so laughably extreme as to be virtually subtle. Madison Grant had articulated its terms in 1916, when he declared in *The Passing of the Great Race in America* that the inferior "races" represented by Jews and even Mediterranean and Alpine Europeans were attenuating the moral and cultural superiority of Nordic stock. This philosophy was reiterated and popularized by Kenneth Roberts who, in 1922, wrote a series of articles for the *Saturday Evening Post*. By the year of *Cane*'s initial publication, the

Ku Klux Klan had reached the height of its resurgence and was claiming 2.5 million members, and crowds of five and six hundred were reported to be watching lynchings. Nineteen twenty-four saw the legal confirmation of this broadly racist tendency: the passage of the Johnson-Reed Act, an immigration law designed to "purify" the racial preponderance of the basic strain by basing immigration quotas on the population not as it existed, but as it *had* existed a third of a century—and four censuses—previous.

Publishing, too, followed a pattern similar to that which it would follow in the sixties, issuing books, especially novels, about blacks written by whites, notably Waldo Frank's *Holiday* (1923) and Carl Van Vechten's *Nigger Heaven* (1926), then by the end of the decade moving to books about blacks by blacks (many of them first novels), notably Rudolph Fisher's *The Walls of Jericho* (1928), and Wallace Thurman's *The Blacker the Berry* (1929)—books which years later would be linked to the so-called "Harlem Renaissance." But at least one publisher had been ready to make this move earlier: in 1923 Boni & Liveright had published a book which it publicized as "a book about negroes by a negro," despite the author's bald assertion that he was not a Negro at all—that book was *Cane*.

III

"Dear Mr. Toomer:
For some time we, and by we I mean a group of three friends, the other two of whom are literary men, one colored and one white, have wondered who and what you are. . . ."

Thus began a letter to Jean Toomer, written in 1923 by one Claude Barnett, a black newspaper editor. The question—blunt, almost impolite—expresses a dichotomously dichromic way of thinking that has for six decades tainted public perception of Toomer and of *Cane*. For what Claude Barnett was asking Toomer was not in any way philosophical; all he wanted to know was, was Toomer black. "There have been several arguments," Barnett wrote, "the literary men contending that your style and finish are not negroid, while I . . . felt certain that you were—for how else could you interpret 'us' as you do . . . ?" This was an expression of the assumptions basic to the time, namely that blacks were pretty much incapable of artistic expression (hence the newsworthy nature of the Harlem Renaissance) and the notion that blacks—almost like Orientals—were so mysterious that no one who was not a black could truly understand them, although they could and did portray them—to great profit in the cases of Eugene O'Neill (*The Emperor Jones, All God's Chillun Got Wings*), Marc Connelly (*Green Pastures*), and DuBose Heyward (*Porgy*). The latter assumption—despite fame, profits and prizes to the contrary—was at the basis of the Toomer revival of the sixties; ironically blacks, who had become aware of white America's tendency to stereotype for political and economic purposes, accepted the twenties' stereotype of Toomer, in part because it confirmed the ideology of the sixties. What the sixties wanted were stories of blacks who had been held back by racism, making them heroes if they overcame it, victims if they did not. Toomer's story, vaguely known as it was, seemed to be such a moral tale. What was glossed over whenever possible was Toomer's apparent repudiation of blackness, the accusation that, as one white critic, David Littlejohn, put it, Toomer "suddenly declared himself white." The twenties, for reasons equally political, were not minded to ignore the matter. Identifying him as a Negro, as Liveright did, threw up a challenge to the popular notion that blacks were barely literate, as Barnett's letter implies. Moreover, the intellectual community was still a little embarrassed over the case of Charles Chesnutt, whose stories about "simple blacks" seen through the eyes of a white assumed a far more ironic meaning when it was belatedly learned that the author was black.

Cane's publication resulted in the same kind of "misunderstanding." Bruno Lasker graced his joint review of Frank's *Holiday* and Toomer's *Cane* with the assertion that the men were one and the same when referring to *Cane*: "In this medley of poems, sketches, and short stories, Frank—for is not 'Jean Toomer' a polite fiction?" The chagrin Lasker must have felt was made explicit by John Bennett, a founder of the Poetry Society of South Carolina, who discovered that a nonresident member of the Society named Jean Toomer was publishing a book called *Cane* that the Society was about to announce as a book by a member, and that was being advertised in items "running all over the *Times*" (meaning the *New York Times Book Review*) as "a book about negroes by a negro." Wrote Bennett: "It is to laugh! Eh? Or not to laugh?"

The Poetry Society decided to ignore Toomer and made no announcement of books by members that year. *Time* magazine did not ignore him, unfortunately, even nearly a decade after *Cane* was published, running an article on him in March of 1932. The occasion for such renewed attention was the surfacing of a rumor that the new husband of the novelist Margery Bodine Latimer, a gentleman who had been identified by the local press as "Nathan Jean Toomer," author of *Essen-*

tials: Definitions and Aphorisms, was none other than Jean Toomer, who had been identified by the *New York Times Book Review* as the author of *Cane,* a "book about negroes by a negro." This was of interest to *Time* because Miss Latimer, a reputed descendant of the New England poetess Anne Bradstreet, was not a Negro. Responding to the crushing significance of the event, *Time* sent a reporter to the couple's home in Carmel, California.

The story that resulted was a marvel of journalistic objectivity. "No Negro," it began, "can legally marry a white woman in any Southern State. But Wisconsin does not mind, nor California." Toomer was described as a "Negro philosopher," Latimer as a "Novelist." The piece was titled "Just Americans," an irreverent reference to Toomer's assertion that America was spawning a new race of people who "will achieve tremendous works of art, literature and music. They will not be white, black or yellow—just Americans." Toomer thus, wittingly or unwittingly, articulated the antithesis to Madison Grant's and Kenneth Roberts' thesis of degenerate mongrelization.

The *Time* article had its most immediate effect not on Toomer's career, but on Latimer's—the sales of her novels declined. Toomer felt compelled to write a pamphlet, "A Fact and Some Fictions," which he had printed and circulated to his friends, an interesting course of action, since if *Time* was so fascinated, one wonders why another magazine would not have published Toomer's response. Or perhaps, given Toomer's ideas, it is not curious. In any event, the pamphlet represents the strongest evidence that Toomer did, in fact, "declare himself white," for in it Toomer wrote of his grandfather, P.B.S. Pinchback: "Whereas others would have thought it to their disadvantage to claim Negro blood, Pinchback thought it to his advantage. So he claimed it. . . . Thus it happened that he and his family became associated with the Negro. . . . With me, however, there is neither reason nor motive for claiming to have Negro blood. So I do not claim it. . . . Others have, however, occasionally seen fit to claim it for me. . . . I have neither claimed to have or disclaimed having Negro blood. . . . As for being a Negro, this of course I am not—neither biologically nor socially."

Thus, in 1932, Toomer seemed to contradict the assertion made in a letter to Claude McKay (who, like Barnett, was interested in Toomer's biography), written in 1923: "Racially, I seem to have (who knows for sure) seven blood mixtures: French, Dutch, Welsh, Negro, German, Jewish, and Indian," and through this contradiction, to have testified to his own guilt of the charge Littlejohn would later make.

Nor was this the only action of Toomer's that could be—and has been—interpreted as declaring himself white, or, as Horace Liveright apparently put it, trying to "deny his race." He did, apparently, change his name on the application for his marriage to Latimer—although he was born with the name Nathan Eugene Toomer—and had obviously changed the Eugene to Jean previously and publicly. He may have failed to mention his authorship of *Cane* to the local press—although that may have been a ruse to avoid the kind of publicity that eventuated. His own writings do attest that he was irritated with Horace Liveright's determination to advertise *Cane* as being written by a Negro, and that he told Liveright that, "as I was not a Negro, I could not feature myself as one." It is also true that, in 1932, he wrote, "Since the publication of 'Cane' there have unfortunately arisen certain misunderstandings. . . . Though I am interested in and deeply value the Negro, I am not a Negro." And it is certain that, by the time he was rediscovered by the sixties, he had committed three other sins that implied he was denying his blackness; he had sent his child to a private school that would not accept blacks, he had failed to identify himself with any of the movements for Civil Rights, and he had married a white woman—had done it twice, in fact. Thus was Toomer tried and convicted in two eras in which the issue of race was of great importance.

Was Jean Toomer a Negro? For if he was not, then he could hardly be accused of trying to pass for white. If, as Toomer claimed and as appears to be the case, the black blood he possessed came from his grandfather, who bore such meager resemblance to a black that blacks were impressed that he claimed to be black, it is unlikely that Toomer himself was more than one-eighth black, possibly only one-sixteenth. Even during the antebellum era, this would not have made Toomer legally black. No state had, at that time, adopted the doctrine that a single drop of black blood made one black. Virginia, in 1849, established the color line at one fourth. South Carolina's Court of Appeals went so far as to rule that there had to be a "visible mixture," and that social factors should be considered: "It may appear that a man of worth . . . should have the rank of a white man," using the same combination of criteria that Toomer did in "A Fact and Some Fictions." Of course by the time *Cane* was published, antebellum practicality had been replaced by rabid irrationality. South Carolina, in the late nineteenth century, changed the definition to "one-eighth Negro blood" and, in the twentieth century, to "any ascertainable trace." Nevertheless, the answer to the question of whether Toomer was black would have been answered differently in different times. Clearly, at some times and places he would have been white. Clearly, too, he had as much right as anybody to define himself that way if he chose. But in fact, he never did.

Toomer's actions and statements reveal a curious pattern for one intent on declaring himself white. In his various autobiographical writings, including portions of the pamphlet, Toomer claimed that he did not know how much black blood, if any, had flowed in his grandfather's veins. This is not the same as saying there wasn't any. In fact, Toomer speculated that "Pinchback's mother possibly had some dark blood. It might have been Negro or Indian or Spanish or Moorish or some other." He characterized his mother's complexion as "Italian-olive" and his father's as that "of an Englishman who has spent time in the tropics," surely not exaggerating their darkness, but certainly not hiding it. Nor did he hide his own, as when he wrote to Waldo Frank of the necessary procedures for a planned journey south: "At whatever town we stay, I'll have to be known as a Negro. First, only because by experiencing white pressure can the venture bear its fullest fruit. Second, because the color of my skin (it is nearly black from the sun) at the present time makes such a course a physical necessity." Moreover, he associated himself for some years with publications that had a decidedly black orientation, submitting an essay to Alain Locke for *The New Negro*, allowing Locke to use his drama *Balo* in *Plays of Negro Life* (1927), and allowing himself to be listed in the 1927 edition of *Who's Who in Colored America*. And he wrote to McKay, at a time when he was virtually an unknown quantity, that he had, possibly, some Negro blood, shortly thereafter responding to Barnett, a journalist who could hardly be counted on to keep the matter confidential, that "In so far as the old folk songs, syncopated rhythms, the rich sweet taste of dark-skinned life, in so far as these are Negro, then I am body and soul, Negroid. . . ."

Jean Toomer was not denying his race; that is clear. And in the grammatical precision of his response to Barnett, the clear distinction between adjective forms is clear indication of what Toomer was doing: resisting the all-encompassing and expectation-laden label Negro, something no era apparently has been able to accept or comprehend.

In the twenties Toomer was a "Negro writer"; he was never allowed by commentators, black and white, to be anything else—although the labels surely changed with the times. In 1932, *Time*'s "Negro philosopher" was also described as the product of "cultured Negroes of old Creole stock" by Eugene Holmes. In 1948, Hugh M. Gloster made him a "colored writer," and a decade later Robert F. Bone made him "the only Negro writer of the 1920's who participated on equal terms in the creation of the modern idiom." In 1966, Toomer, in the hands of Arna Bontemps, "faded completely into white obscurity." By 1971, he was "the first Negro writer" to be dedicated to "writing as an art, not a Negro art," according to Frank Durham. By 1980, according to Brian Benson and Mabel Dillard, Toomer had had "no desire to perpetuate the traditions common to black authors"—whatever they were. What is tragic about this rather bizarre preoccupation with labeling Toomer as black —an effort that is doomed, as Toomer noted ("They can pile up records and labels a mile high, and in the end they will find, pinned under that pile, not me but their own intelligence.")—is that it has interfered with the process of understanding "who and what" Toomer really was.

Toomer, for example, has often been presented as the leading edge of the Harlem Renaissance, despite the fact that he apparently spent little time in Harlem and did not mention the place in his autobiographical writings, instead characterizing his New York experience: "In New York, I stepped into the literary world. Waldo Frank, Gorham Munson, Kenneth Burke, Hart Crane, Matthew Johnson, Malcolm Cowley, Paul Rosenfeld, Van Wyck Brooks, Robert Littell—*Broom*, the *Dial*, the *New Republic*. . . . I lived on Gay Street. . . ." And, moreover, he disclaimed artistic connection with the "New Negro" in an essay that Alain Locke, in his book on the "New Negro," refused to publish—while nevertheless publishing sections of *Cane*.

But the worse effect of this obsession with Toomer's blackness, or lack of it, has been to conceal what he was trying to achieve—a different, but equally important kind of unity. "I have strived," he wrote McKay, "for a spiritual fusion analogous to the fact of racial intermingling. Without denying a single element in me, with no desire to subdue one to the other, I have sought to let them function in harmony." This striving found expression, in the twenties, in poetry: "My style, my aesthetic, is nothing more nor less than my attempt to fashion my substance into works of art," he wrote to Barnett in 1923. "My poems," he wrote to James Weldon Johnson seven years later, "are not Negro poems, nor are they Anglo-Saxon or white or English poems. My prose likewise. They are, first, mine. And second . . . they spring from the result of racial blending here in America." To read *Cane* as the expression of a black consciousness is therefore, inevitably, to misread it. But it has been so read. This has lost us some understanding.

The fact that *Cane* was so misread in the twenties lost us more than that; it lost us Toomer. For, though *Cane* is flawed and the man who wrote it had a lot to learn about craft, he clearly possessed instincts and sensitivities and intelligence that would have brought him to the forefront of American letters. But Toomer became frustrated with the insistence that he be one race or the other. He has been accused of denying his blackness; in fact, he was guilty of refusing to deny everything else.

Toomer understood that there was a certain self-protectiveness in the insistence of some that he was black, for he wrote to Frank: "Sherwood Anderson has doubtless a very deep and beautiful emotion by way of the Negro. Here and there he has succeeded in expressing this. But he is not satisfied. He wants more. He is hungry for it. I come along. I express it. It is natural for him to see me in terms of this expression." But understanding did not lead to acceptance: "He limits me to Negro. As an approach, as a constant element (part of a larger whole) of interest Negro is good. But to tie me to one of my parts is to lose me."

Not everyone lost him. Waldo Frank seemed to understand what Toomer was about before Toomer did, for he wrote in his preface to the first edition, "A poet has arisen in the land who writes, not as a Southerner, not as a rebel against Southerners, not as a negro, not as an apologist or priest or critic: who writes as a poet," and, in varying his parallel construction, indicated that he shared Toomer's belief in a "non-racial" future: "The simple slave Past, the shredding Negro Present, the irridescent passionate dream of the Tomorrow. . . ." And Paul Rosenfeld, in *Men Seen, Twenty-four Modern Authors* (1925), wrote that the characters of *Cane* "are prophetic not only for men of negro blood. They throw forward much in America; for they are symbols of some future America of which Jean Toomer by virtue of the music in him is a portion. He looks two ways. Through this recognition of the beauty of a doomed simplicity, sensuosity, passionateness not of the South or of the past asserts, cries out, comes conscious of itself: some America beyond the newspapers, regimented feelings, edgeless language . . . drawing more imminent."

But most did lose Toomer. The Establishment determined to make him a Negro expert on Negroes ignored his essays on race. His 1925 "The Negro Emergent" went unpublished. His "Race Problems in Modern Society," published in 1928, apparently attracted little attention. Frustrated, Toomer wrote: "My writing . . . the very thing that should have made me understood was being so presented and interpreted that I was not much more misunderstood in this respect than at any other time in my life."

By 1932, Toomer had decided to adopt a new tactic and so declined to participate in the preparation of a volume on race in America and refused to have his work included in *The Book of American Negro Poetry*, or to have a copy of his privately published *Essentials* (1931) placed in the Schomberg Collection at the New York Public Library (all actions that later were used to support the "passing" accusation). "In order to establish my view," he wrote, "I have had—for a time—to swing into a rather extreme position which has not allowed me to be associated with any race other than what we call the American race."

It is hard to say what Toomer thought was going to happen after " a time." Perhaps he thought that sanity would assert itself. In this he was sadly wrong. For this tactical decision, made out of anger or frustration or perhaps real calculation, was nothing less than a turning away from the source of his art. "Within the last two or three years, however," he had written to McKay in 1922, "my growing need for artistic expression has pulled me deeper into the Negro group. And as my powers of receptivity increased I found myself loving it in a way I could never love the other. It has stimulated and fertilized whatever creative talent I may contain within me. Now I cannot conceive of myself as aloof, and separated. My point of view has not changed; it has deepened, it has widened."

And so, in the end, this is the tragedy of Jean Toomer—a tale of oppression that the "liberal" sixties not only ignored, but perpetuated. Some have said Toomer denied his self and turned away from greatness. In fact he was driven away from the source of that greatness. And the saddest thing, perhaps, is that he knew it. "We are," wrote finally the man who had once so joyously celebrated his connection with the Negro past, "split men, disconnected from our own resources, almost severed from our *Selves*, and therefore out of contact with reality."

ARNOLD RAMPERSAD

The Origins of Poetry in Langston Hughes

IN HIS STUDY *The Life of the Poet: Beginning and Ending Poetic Careers* (1981) Lawrence Lipking asks three main questions, one of which concerns me here in the case of Langston Hughes: "How does an aspiring author of verses become a poet?" In the case of John Keats, for example, how did the poet arrive at "On First Looking Into Chapman's Homer," that great leap in creative ability in which Keats, sweeping from the legend of "the realms of gold" toward modern history, "catches sight not of someone else's dream but of his own reality? He stares at his future, and surmises that he may be a poet. The sense of possibility is thrilling, the moment truly awesome. Keats has discovered Keats." Or in the well-known words of Keats himself: "The Genius of Poetry must work out its own salvation in a man: It cannot be matured by law & precept, but by sensation & watchfulness in itself—That which is creative must create itself."

Can one ask a similar question about the origins of poetry in Langston Hughes, who in June 1921, at the age of nineteen, began a celebrated career when he published his own landmark poem "The Negro Speaks of Rivers" in W.E.B. Du Bois' *Crisis* magazine? Like Keats before "Chapman's Homer," Hughes had written poems before "The Negro Speaks of Rivers." Much of the poetry before "Rivers" is available for examination, since Hughes published steadily in the monthly magazine of his high school in Cleveland, Ohio. Certain aspects of this verse are noteworthy. It has nothing to do with race; it is dominated by images of the poet not as a teenager but as a little child; and, in Hughes's junior year, he published his first poem in free verse, one that showed the clear influence of Walt Whitman for the first (but not the last) time. Revealing an increase in skill, Hughes's early poetry nevertheless gives no sign of a major poetic talent in the making. At some point in his development, however, something happened to Hughes that was as mysterious and as wonderful, in its own way, as the miracle that overtook John Keats after the watchful night spent with his friend Charles Cowden Clarke and a copy of Chapman's translation. With "The Negro Speaks of Rivers" the creativity in Langston Hughes, hitherto essentially unexpressed, suddenly created itself.

In writing thus about Hughes, are we taking him too seriously? With a few exceptions, literary critics have resisted offering even a modestly complicated theory concerning his creativity. His relentless affability and charm, his deep, open love of the black masses, his devotion to their folk forms, and his insistence on writing poetry that they could understand, all have contributed to the notion that Langston Hughes was intellectually and emotionally shallow. One wonders, then, at the source of the creative energy that drove him from 1921 to 1967 to write so many poems, novels, short stories, plays, operas, popular histories, children's books, and assorted other work. As a poet, Hughes virtually reinvented Afro-American poetry with his pioneering use of the blues and other folk forms; as Howard Mumford Jones marveled in a 1927 review, Hughes added the verse form of the blues to poetry in English (a form that continues to attract the best black poets, including Michael Harper, Sherley Anne Williams, and Raymond Patterson). One wonders, too, in his aspect as a poet, why this apparently happy, apparently shallow man defined his creativity in terms of unhappiness. "I felt bad for the next three or four years," he would write in *The Big Sea* about the period beginning more or less with the publication of "The Negro Speaks of Rivers," "and those were the years when I wrote most of my poetry. (For my best poems were all written when I felt the worst. When I was happy, I didn't write anything.)"

Hughes actively promoted the image of geniality to which I have alluded. Wanting and needing to be loved, he scrubbed and polished his personality until there was no abrasive side, no jagged edge that might wound another human being. Publicly and privately, his manner belied the commonly held belief that creativity and madness are allied, that neuroses and a degree of malevolence are the fair price of art. His autobiographies, *The Big Sea* (1940) and *I Wonder As I Wander* (1956), made no enemies; to many readers, Hughes's mastery of that form consists in his ability to cross its chill deep by paddling nonchalantly on its surface. And yet in two places, no doubt deliberately, Hughes allows the reader a glimpse of inner turmoil. Both appear in the earlier book, *The Big Sea*. Both involve personal and emotional conflicts so intense that they led to physical illness. Because of their extreme rarity, as well as their strategic location in the context of his creativity, these passages deserve close scrutiny if we hope to glimpse the roots of Hughes's originality as a poet.

The first of these two illnesses took place in the summer of 1919, when Hughes (at seventeen) saw his father for the first time in a dozen years. In 1903, James Hughes had gone to Mexico, where he would become a prosperous property owner. In a lonely, impoverished, passed-around childhood in the Midwest, his son had fantasized about the man "as a kind of strong, bronze cowboy, in a big Mexican hat, going back and forth from his business in the city to his ranch in the mountains, free—in a land where there were no white folks to draw the color line, and no tenements with rent always due—just mountains and cacti: Mexico!" Elated to be invited suddenly to Mexico in 1919 at the end of his junior year in high school, Langston left the United States with high hopes for his visit.

The summer was a disaster. James Hughes proved to be an unfeeling, domineering, and materialistic man, scornful of Indians and blacks (he was himself black) and the poor in general, and contemptuous of his son's gentler pace and artistic temperament. One day, Langston could take no more: "Suddenly my stomach began to turn over and over. And I could not swallow another mouthful. Waves of heat engulfed me. My eyes burned. My body shook. I wanted more than anything on earth to hit my father, but instead I got up from the table and went back to bed. The bed went round and round and the room turned dark. Anger clotted in every vein, and my tongue tasted like dry blood." But the boy, ill for a long time, never confessed the true cause of his affliction. Having been moved to Mexico City, he declined to help his doctors: "I never told them . . . that I was sick because I hated my father." He recovered only when it was time to return to the United States.

Hughes's second major illness came eleven years later. By this time he had finished high school, returned to Mexico to live with his father for a year, attended Columbia University for one year (supported grudgingly by James Hughes), dropped out of school, and served as a messman on voyages to Africa and to Europe, where he spent several months in 1924 as a dishwasher. All the while, however, Hughes was publishing poetry in a variety of places, especially in important black journals. This activity culminated in books of verse published in 1926 (*The Weary Blues*) and 1927 (*Fine Clothes to the Jew*) that established him, with Countee Cullen, as one of two major black poets of the decade. In 1929, he graduated after three and a half years at black Lincoln University, Pennsylvania. In 1930, Hughes published his first novel, *Not Without Laughter*.

This book had been virtually dragged out of him by his patron of the preceding three years, "Godmother" (as she wished to be called), an old, white, very generous but eccentric woman who ruled Hughes with a benevolent despotism inspired by her volatile beliefs in African spirituality, folk culture, mental telepathy, and the potential of his genius. But the result of her largesse was a paradox: the more comfortable he grew, the less Hughes was inclined to create. Estranged by his apparent languor, his patron finally seized on an episode of conflict to banish him once and for all. Hughes was devastated. Surviving drafts of his letters to "Godmother" reveal him deep in self-abasement before a woman with whom he was clearly in love. Ten years later, he confessed in *The Big Sea*: "I cannot write here about that last half-hour in the big bright drawing-room high above Park Avenue . . . because when I think about it, even now, something happens in the pit of my stomach that makes me ill. That beautiful room . . . suddenly became like a trap closing in, faster and faster, the room darker and darker, until the light went out with a sudden crash in the dark, and everything became like . . . that morning in Mexico when I suddenly hated my father.

"I was violently and physically ill, with my stomach turning over and over. . . . And there was no rationalizing anything. I couldn't." For several months, according to my research (Hughes erroneously presents a far briefer time frame in *The Big Sea*), he waited in excruciating hope for a reconciliation. As in Mexico, he wasted time and money on doctors without revealing to them the source of his chronic illness (which one very ingenious Harlem physician diagnosed as a Japanese tapeworm). Rather than break his silence, Hughes even agreed to have his tonsils removed. Gradually it became clear that reconciliation was impossible. Winning a prize of four hundred dollars for his novel, Hughes fled to seclusion in hot, remote Haiti. When his money ran out some months later, he returned home, healed at last but badly scarred.

Although they occurred more than a decade apart, the two illnesses were similar. Both showed a normally placid Hughes driven into deep rage by an opponent, a rage which he was unable to ventilate because the easy expression of personal anger and indignation was anathema to him. In both cases, he developed physical symptoms of hyperventilation and, eventually, anemia. More importantly, both were triggered in a period of relatively low poetic creativity (as when he was still a juvenile poet) or outright poetic inactivity (as with his patron). In each instance, Hughes had become satisfied with this low creativity or inactivity. At both times, a certain powerful figure, first his father, then "Godmother," had opposed his right to be content. His father had opposed any poetic activity at all; "Godmother" had opposed his right to enjoy the poetical state without true poetical action, or writing. In other words, a powerful will presented itself in forceful opposition to what was, in one sense, a vacuum of expressive will on Hughes's part. (Needless to say, the *apparent* absence of will in an individual can easily be a token of the presence of a very powerful will.) The result on both occasions, which was extraordinary, was first Hughes's endurance of, then his violent rebellion against, a force of will that challenged his deepest vision of the poetic life.

I use the term "will" knowing that to many people it is an obsolete concept, in spite of the revival of interest in Otto Rank, or continuing critiques of Freud's use of the term as, for example, Harold Bloom's excellent essay "Freud's Concepts of Defense and the Poetic Will." But I am referring here mainly, though not exclusively, to the will as a function of consciousness, as in the case of "Godmother's" will, or that of Hughes's father, or—far less demonstrably—Hughes's own volition. And what do I mean by Hughes's "vision of the poetic life"? I refer to what one might call unshaped or amorphous poetic consciousness, poetry not concretized or written down, but the crucial element (when combined with poetic "material") out of which written or oral poetry is made. In an old-fashioned but still significant way, the poet Richard Eberhart has written of "Will and Psyche in Poetry" (in Don Cameron Allen's *The Moment of Poetry*, 1962). Poems of the will value the body, activity, struggle, and the things of this world; poems of the psyche endorse spirit, "an uncontaminated grace," and the "elusive, passive, imaginative quality" of the world beyond this world. A poem of will, such as Marvell's "To His Coy Mistress," might involve a man calling a woman to bed; for an exemplary poem of psyche, Eberhart chose Poe's "To Helen," where desire leads directly away from sexuality toward spirit.

The notorious placidity of surface in Hughes, as I see it, bespeaks the extent to which he was a poet who preferred his poems unwritten—a poet, like his great mentor Walt Whitman, who saw his life itself as a poem greater than any poem he could possibly write. Hughes's greatest poetical instinct was to preserve his unformed or dormant poetic consciousness as the highest form of poetry. Such an instinct may suggest infantilism; one remembers Freud's unfortunate words about the link between creative writing and daydreaming. Infantilism would be wrong as an explanation. But, in Hughes's case, I suspect, the instinct had something to do with the youthfulness of the self he clearly regarded as his authentic, or most cherished, self. Placidity of surface, anxiety to please and to be loved, apparent asexuality (the most consistent con-clusion—rather than that of homosexuality, for which there is no evi-dence—about his libido among people who knew him well), and the compulsion against concretized or written poetry reflect a sense of self as prepubescent, or apubescent; in other words, a sense of self as an eternal child. At some level, Hughes saw himself ideally as a child—a dreamy genius child, a perfect child, a princely child, a loving child, even a mothering and maternal child—but first and foremost as a child (almost never is he the destructively rebellious child, in spite of his radical poetry).

It must be stressed that such a sense of self, although it modulates art (as does every other factor of comparable importance), is by no means an inherent handicap to a creative person. In any event, Hughes teetered between a sense of confidence (a sense of being loved by a particular person to whom he was emotionally mortgaged) and a rival, harrowing sense, born in his own childhood, of abandonment and despair. The latter was closer to the origins of his poetry. Release Hughes as an artist from the stabilizing social context and he flies almost immediately toward themes of nihilism and death. For example, take his poem "Border Line":

> I used to wonder
> About living and dying—
> I think the difference lies
> Between tears and crying.
>
> I used to wonder
> About here and there—
> I think the distance
> Is nowhere.

Or "Genius Child":

> *. . . Nobody loves a genius child.*
>
> Can you love an eagle,
> Tame or wild?
>
> Wild or tame,
> Can you love a monster
> Of frightening name?
>
> *Nobody loves a genius child.*

Kill him—and let his soul run wild!

Or "End":

> There are
> No clocks on the wall,
> And no time,
> No shadows that move
> From dawn to dusk
> Across the floor.
>
> There is neither light
> Nor dark
> Outside the door.
>
> *There is no door!*

In Hughes's writing, there is precious little middle ground between such verse and that for which he is far better known (and deservedly so), the poems steeped in race and other social concerns. Nature as flora and fauna bored the man who preferred Harlem in hot summer to the cool New England woods, as he once joked, because "I prefer wild people to wild animals." Hughes understood wherein his salvation rested.

This bleakness, almost always ignored in critical treatments of Hughes, evolved out of the saturation of his dormant poetical consciousness by the powerful will toward death stimulated in him by his loneliness as a child. But Hughes did not surrender passively to the force of his father and "Godmother" when they turned against him. These attacks, in fact, elicited in him a massive retaliatory display of willfulness, at first (while he was ill) as uncontrolled and uncontrollable as the right to the passive poetic consciousness it defended. The invocation of will in such massive degree could easily have remained as toxic as it was while he was sick with his silent rage. Only the modification of will, a compromise between passive poetic consciousness and the purposefulness needed to defend that consciousness, could prevent the consummation of poetry (amorphous or concrete) by rage. And only an appeal to a third force that was neither Hughes nor his enemy could allow him to fashion a balance between will and his unformed poetical consciousness.

Both in the experience with his father in Mexico and in the struggle with "Godmother," the third force was represented by the black race. Hughes's attitude to the black masses is too complicated to detail here. But my argument depends on the crucial understanding that Hughes was virtually unique among major black writers not so much because of the considerable depth of his love of black people, but because of *the depth of his psychological dependence on them.* Hughes became dependent because of a relatively complicated set of circumstances in his youth, when he was reared by his poor but very proud grandmother, the aged, wrinkled, and laconic Mary Langston, whose first husband had died at Harpers Ferry with John Brown. But Mary Langston's zeal to defend the rights of her race was offset for her grandson by her personal remoteness both from him and the race, and by the severity of her pride —a pride compounded by her very light skin, her Indian rather than predominantly African features, her Oberlin education, and her high-toned religion, which all kept her distant from the black masses. She did not attend black churches, did not sing black spirituals (much less the blues); she spoke in a clipped manner, rather than a folksy drawl, and she detested popular culture—as Hughes spelled out partially in *The Big Sea*, but more completely in an unpublished portrait prepared in 1943.

What Mary Langston offered in the abstract, however, was made wonderfully concrete to young Hughes by two persons with whom he lived from time to time (when his grandmother was forced to rent out her house, and after she died) and whom he described in an Arcadian paragraph in *The Big Sea*—"Uncle" and "Auntie" Reed. "Uncle" James Reed, who dug ditches for the city, smoked his pipe and stayed home on Sundays. "Auntie" Reed (later Mrs. Mary J. Reed Campbell) took Langston to St. Luke's A.M.E. church (a church apparently not good enough for his grandmother) and taught the Sunday School there in which the boy was the brightest star. Through the childless Reeds, who clearly adored the boy, he learned how to love the race, its church ways and folk ways, and its dreams and aspirations, of which the handsome, scrubbed, light brown boy, the grandson of "Colonel" Charles Langston (whose brother John Mercer Langston had served in the U.S. Congress and as an ambassador of the U.S.), was the shining embodiment. And it was a lie he told to the Reeds (that Jesus had come to Hughes at a revival meeting, after "Auntie" Reed had prayed that this would happen) that led to the major trauma of his childhood, as related in *The Big Sea*—a long weeping into the night (the second to last time he cried, Hughes wrote) because he had waited for Jesus, who had never come, then had lied to the people who loved him most. In *The Big Sea* Hughes would admit to hating his father; he would partly ridicule his mother; he would admit that he did not cry when his grandmother died. The Reeds, however, were different: "For me, there have never been any better people in the world. I loved them very much."

In his bitter struggles with his mother and "Godmother," Hughes turned to the black race for direction. But one needs to remember that this appeal in itself hardly gave Hughes distinction as a poet; what made Hughes distinct was the highly original manner in which he internalized the Afro-American racial dilemma and expressed it in poems such as "When Sue Wears Red," "The Negro Speaks of Rivers," "Mother to Son," "Dream Variations," and "The Weary Blues," poems of Hughes's young manhood on which his career would rest. Of these, the most important was "The Negro Speaks of Rivers."

> I've known rivers.
> I've known rivers ancient as the world and older
>   than the flow of human blood in human veins.
>
> My soul has grown deep like the rivers.
>
> I bathed in the Euphrates when dawns were young.
> I built my hut near the Congo and it lulled me to sleep.
> I looked upon the Nile and raised the pyramids above it.
> I heard the singing of the Mississippi when Abe Lincoln
>   went down to New Orleans, and I've seen its muddy
>   bosom turn all golden in the sunset.
>
> I've known rivers:
> Ancient, dusky rivers.
>
> My soul has grown deep like the rivers.

Here, the persona moves steadily from dimly starred personal memory ("I've known rivers") toward a rendezvous with modern history (Lincoln going down the Mississippi and seeing the horror of slavery that, according to legend, would make him one day free the slaves). The death wish, benign but suffusing, of its images of rivers older than human blood, of souls grown as deep as these rivers, gives way steadily to an altering, ennobling vision whose final effect gleams in the evocation of the Mississippi's "muddy bosom" turning at last "all golden in the sunset." Personal anguish has been alchemized by the poet into a gracious meditation on his race, whose despised ("muddy") culture and history, irradiated by the poet's vision, changes within the poem from mud into gold. This is a classic example of the essential process of creativity in Hughes.

The poem came to him, according to Hughes (accurately, it seems clear), about ten months after his Mexican illness, when he was riding a train from Cleveland to Mexico to rejoin his father. The time was sundown, the place the Mississippi outside St. Louis. "All day on the train I had been thinking of my father," he would write in *The Big Sea*. "Now it was just sunset and we crossed the Mississippi, slowly, over a long bridge. I looked out of the window of the Pullman at the great muddy river flowing down toward the heart of the South, and I began to think what that river, the old Mississippi, had meant to Negroes in the past—how to be sold down the river was the worst fate that could overtake a slave in bondage. Then I remembered reading how Abraham Lincoln had made a trip down the Mississippi on a raft, and how he had seen slavery at its worst, and had decided within himself that it should be removed from American life. Then I began to think of other rivers in our past—the Congo, and the Niger, and the Nile in Africa—and the thought came to me: 'I've known rivers,' and I put it down on the back of an envelope I had in my pocket, and within the space of ten or fifteen minutes, as the train gathered speed in the dusk, I had written this poem."

Here, starting with anguish over his father, Hughes discovered the compressed ritual of passivity, challenge, turmoil, and transcendence he would probably have to re-create, doubtless in variant forms, during the great poetic trysts of his life. Even after he became a successful, published poet, the basic process remained the same, because his psychology remained largely the same even though he had become technically expert. In his second major illness, caused by his patron "Godmother," Hughes wrote poetry as he struggled for a transcendence that would be long in coming. The nature of that interim poetry is telling. When he sent some poems to a friend for a little book to be printed privately, she noticed at once that many spoke of death—"Dear lovely Death/That taketh all things under wing—/Never to kill...." She called the booklet *Dear Lovely Death*. In "Afro-American Fragment," unlike in "The Negro Speaks of Rivers," Africa is seen plaintively:

> ... Subdued and time-lost
> Are the drums—and yet
> Through some vast mist of race
> There comes this song
> I do not understand,
> This song of atavistic land,
> Of bitter yearnings lost
> Without a place—
> So long,
> So far away
> Is Africa's
> Dark face.

But when Hughes returned home, scarred but healed, after months in seclusion in Haiti, he no longer thought of loss and death. Instead, he plunged directly into the life of the black masses with a seven-month tour of the South in which he read his poetry in their churches and schools. Then he set out for the Soviet Union, where he would spend more than a year. Hughes then reached the zenith of his revolutionary ardor with poems (or verse) such as "Good Morning Revolution," "Goodbye Christ," and "Put One More 'S' in the USA."

"Good Morning Revolution," for example, and "The Negro Speaks of Rivers" are very different poems. The former is the polar opposite of the poetry of nihilism; the latter blends aspects of existential gloom with the life-affirming spirit of the black race. Together, the poems illustrate the wide range of possibility in the mixture of will and passivity which characterizes Hughes's art (although one can argue that "Good Morning Revolution"—by far the lesser poem—marks an overreaction of will, and thus is not truly representative of Hughes's poetic temperament in that it contains no element of passivity). But the creative process has remained the same. The right to amorphous poetic consciousness is challenged. The will is aroused in defense of that consciousness. Illness (an extreme version of Wallace Stevens' "blessed rage for order"?) marks the struggle of will against opposing will. The long-endured illness, in silence, gradually allows the mutual fertilization of will and poetic consciousness that is needed for concrete art. Illness ends when that ratio is achieved or perceived, and writing begins. Creativity, in Keats's term, has created itself. A poet, or a poem, is born.

To some extent, this process is nothing more than Wordsworth's definition of poetry as the final recollection "in tranquility" (a phrase often underplayed or even ignored in quoting Wordsworth's definition) of emotion that had once spontaneously overflowed. What is different, of course, is that Wordsworth (and Keats and Stevens) did not have to contend with race as a factor in his creativity. For many writers, perhaps even most, race is a distracting, demoralizing force. Hughes's genius, or his good fortune, consisted in his ability to accommodate race harmoniously within the scheme of creativity common to all major poets, and to turn it from an anomaly into an intimate advantage.

HOUSTON A. BAKER, JR.
AND
CHARLOTTE PIERCE-BAKER

PHOTOGRAPHS BY ROLAND L. FREEMAN

Patches: Quilts and Community in Alice Walker's "Everyday Use"

> During the Depression and really
> hard time, people often paid their
> debts with quilts, and sometimes
> their tithe to the church too.
> —*The Quilters*

A PATCH IS A FRAGMENT. It is a vestige of wholeness that stands as a sign of loss and a challenge to creative design. As a remainder or remnant, the patch may symbolize rupture and impoverishment; it may be defined by the faded glory of the already gone. But as a fragment, it is also rife with explosive potential of the yet-to-be-discovered. Like woman, it is a liminal element between wholes.

Weaving, shaping, sculpting, or quilting in order to create a kaleidoscopic and momentary array is tantamount to providing an improvisational response to chaos. Such activity represents a nonce response to ceaseless scattering; it constitutes survival strategy and motion in the face of dispersal. A patchwork quilt, laboriously and affectionately crafted from bits of worn overalls, shredded uniforms, tattered petticoats, and outgrown dresses stands as a signal instance of a patterned wholeness in the African diaspora.

Traditional African cultures were scattered by the European slave trade throughout the commercial time and space of the New World. The transmutation of quilting, a European, feminine tradition, into a black women's folk art, represents an innovative fusion of African cloth manufacture, piecing, and appliqué with awesome New World experiences—and expediencies. The product that resulted was, in many ways, a double patch. The hands that pieced the master's rigidly patterned quilts by day were often the hands that crafted a more functional design

119

in slave cabins by night. The quilts of Afro-America offer a *sui generis* context (a weaving together) of experiences and a storied, vernacular representation of lives conducted in the margins, ever beyond an easy and acceptable wholeness. In many ways, the quilts of Afro-America resemble the work of all those dismembered gods who transmute fragments and remainders into the light and breath of a new creation. And the sorority of quiltmakers, fragment weavers, holy patchers, possesses a sacred wisdom that it hands down from generation to generation of those who refuse the center for the ludic and unconfined spaces of the margins.

Those positioned outside the sorority and enamored of wholeness often fail to comprehend the dignity inherent in the quiltmakers' employment of remnants and conversion of fragments into items of everyday use. Just as the mysteries of, say, the blues remain hidden from those in happy circumstances, so the semantic intricacies of quiltmaking remain incomprehensible to the individualistic sensibility invested in myths of a postindustrial society. All of the dark, southern energy that manifests itself in the conversion of a sagging cabin—a shack really—into a "happy home" by stringing a broom wire between two nails in the wall and making the joint jump, or that shows itself in the "crazy quilt" patched from crumbs and remainders, seems but a vestige of outmoded and best-forgotten customs.

To relinquish such energy, however, is to lose an enduring resourcefulness that has ensured a distinctive aesthetic tradition and a unique code of everyday, improvisational use in America. The tradition-bearers of the type of Afro-American energy we have in mind have always included ample numbers of southern, black women who have transmuted fragments of New World displacement into a quilted eloquence scarcely appreciated by traditional spokespersons for wholeness. To wit: even the perspicacious and vigilant lion of abolitionism Frederick Douglass responded as follows to Monroe A. Majors' request for inclusions in his book *Noted Negro Women*:

> We have many estimable women of our variety but not many famous ones. It is not well to claim too much for ourselves before the public. Such extravagance invites contempt rather than approval. I have thus far seen no book of importance written by a negro woman and I know of no one among us who can appropriately be called famous.

Southern black women have not only produced quilts of stunning beauty, they have also crafted books of monumental significance, works that have made them appropriately famous. In fact, it has been precisely the appropriation of energy drawn from sagging cabins and stitched remainders that has constituted the world of the quiltmakers' sorority. The energy has flowed through such women as Harriet Brent Jacobs, Zora Neale Hurston, and Margaret Walker, enabling them to continue an ancestral line elegantly shared by Alice Walker.

In a brilliant essay entitled "Alice Walker: The Black Woman Artist as Wayward," Professor Barbara Christian writes: "Walker is drawn to the integral and economical process of quilt making as a model for her own craft. For through it, one can create out of seemingly disparate everyday materials patterns of clarity, imagination, and beauty." Professor Christian goes on to discuss Walker's frequently cited "In Search of Our Mothers' Gardens" and her short story "Everyday Use." She convincingly argues that Walker employs quilts as signs of functional beauty and spiritual heritage that provide exemplars of challenging convention and radical individuality, or "artistic waywardness."

The patchwork quilt as a trope for understanding black women's creativity in the United States, however, presents an array of interpretive possibilities that is not exhausted by Professor Christian's adept criticism of Walker. For example, if one takes a different tack and suggests that the quilt as metaphor presents not a stubborn contrariness, a wayward individuality, but a communal bonding that confounds traditional definitions of art and of the artist, then one plays on possibilities in the quilting trope rather different from those explored by Christian. What we want to suggest in our own adaptation of the trope is that it opens a fascinating interpretive window on vernacular dimensions of lived, creative experience in the United States. Quilts in their patched and many-colored glory, offer not a counter to tradition, but in fact, an instance of the only legitimate tradition of "the people" that exists. They are representations of the stories of the vernacular natives who make up the ninety-nine percent of the American population unendowed with money and control. The class distinction suggested by "vernacular" should not overshadow the gender specificity of quilts as products of a universal woman's creativity—what Pattie Chase in *The Contemporary Quilt* calls "an ancient affinity between women and cloth." They are the testimony of "mute and inglorious" generations of women gone before. The quilt as interpretive sign opens up a world of *difference*, a nonscripted territory whose creativity with fragments is less a matter of "artistic" choice than of economic and functional necessity. "So much in the habit of sewing something," says Walker's protagonist in the remarkable novel *The Color Purple*, "[that] I stitch up a bunch of scraps, try to see what I can make."

The Johnson women, who populate the generations represented in

Walker's short story "Everyday Use," are inhabitants of southern cabins who have always worked with "scraps" and seen what they could make of them. The result of their labor has been a succession of mothers and daughters surviving the ignominies of Jim Crow life and passing on ancestral blessings to descendants. The guardians of the Johnson homestead when the story commences are the mother—"a large, big-boned woman with rough, man-working hands"—and her daughter Maggie, who has remained with her "chin on chest, eyes on ground, feet in shuffle, ever since the fire that burned the other house to the ground" ten or twelve years ago. The mood at the story's beginning is one of ritualistic "waiting": "I will wait for her in the yard that Maggie and I made so clean and wavy yesterday afternoon." The subject awaited is the other daughter, Dee. Not only has the yard (as ritual ground) been prepared for the arrival of a goddess, but the sensibilities and costumes of Maggie and her mother have been appropriately attuned for the occasion. The mother daydreams of television shows where parents and children are suddenly—and pleasantly—reunited, banal shows where chatty hosts oversee tearful reunions. In her fantasy, she weighs a hundred pounds less, is several shades brighter in complexion, and possesses a devastatingly quick tongue. She returns abruptly to real life meditation, reflecting on her own heroic, agrarian accomplishments in slaughtering hogs and cattle and preparing their meat for winter nourishment. She is a robust provider who has gone to the people of her church and raised money to send her light-complexioned, lithe-figured, and ever-dissatisfied daughter Dee to college. Today, as she waits in the purified yard, she notes the stark differences between Maggie and Dee and recalls how the "last dingy gray board of the house [fell] in toward the red-hot brick chimney" when her former domicile burned. Maggie was scarred horribly by the fire, but Dee, who had hated the house with an intense fury, stood "off under the sweet gum tree . . . a look of concentration on her face." A scarred and dull Maggie, who has been kept at home and confined to everyday offices, has but one reaction to the fiery and vivacious arrival of her sister: "I hear Maggie suck in her breath. 'Uhnnnh,' is what it sounds like. Like when you see the wriggling end of a snake just in front of your foot on the road. 'Uhnnnh.'"

Indeed, the question raised by Dee's energetic arrival is whether there are words adequate to her flair, her brightness, her intense colorfulness of style which veritably blocks the sun. She wears "a dress so loud it hurts my eyes. There are yellows and oranges enough to throw back the light of the sun. I feel my whole face warming from the heat waves it throws out." Dee is both serpent and fire introduced with bursting esprit into the calm pasture that contains the Johnsons' tin-roofed, three-room, windowless shack and grazing cows. She has joined the radical, black nationalists of the 1960s and 1970s, changing her name from Dee to Wangero and cultivating a suddenly fashionable, or stylish, interest in what she passionately describes as her "heritage." If there is one quality that Dee (Wangero) possesses in abundance, it is "style": "At sixteen she had a style of her own: and knew what style was."

But in her stylishness, Dee is not an example of the indigenous rapping and styling out of Afro-America. Rather, she is manipulated by the style-makers, the fashion designers whose semiotics the French writer Roland Barthes has so aptly characterized. "Style" for Dee is the latest vogue—the most recent fantasy perpetuated by American media. When she left for college, her mother had tried to give her a quilt whose making began with her grandmother Dee, but the bright daughter felt such patched coverings were "old-fashioned and out of style." She has returned at the commencement of "Everyday Use," however, as one who now purports to know the value of the work of black women as holy patchers.

The dramatic conflict of the story surrounds the definition of holiness. The ritual purification of earth and expectant atmosphere akin to that of Beckett's famous drama ("I will wait for her in the yard that Maggie and I made so clean and wavy yesterday afternoon.") prepare us for the narrator's epiphanic experience at the story's conclusion.

Near the end of "Everyday Use," the mother (who is the tale's narrator) realizes that Dee (a.k.a., Wangero) is a *fantasy* child, a perpetrator and victim of: "words, lies, other folks's habits." The energetic daughter is as frivolously careless of other peoples' lives as the fiery conflagration that she had watched ten years previously. Assured by the makers of American fashion that "black" is currently "beautiful," she has conformed her own "style" to that notion. Hers is a trendy "blackness" cultivated as "art" and costume. She wears "a dress down to the ground . . . bracelets dangling and making noises when she moves her arm up to shake the folds of the dress out of her armpits." And she says of quilts she has removed from a trunk at the foot of her mother's bed: "Maggie can't appreciate these quilts! She'd probably be backward enough to put them to everyday use." "Art" is, thus, juxtaposed with "everyday use" in Walker's short story, and the fire goddess Dee, who has achieved literacy only to burn "us with a lot of knowledge we didn't necessarily need to know," is revealed as a perpetuator of institutional theories of aesthetics. (Such theories hold that "art" is, in fact, defined by social institutions such as museums, book reviews, and art dealers.) Of the two quilts that

she has extracted from the trunk, she exclaims: "But they're 'priceless.' "
And so the quilts are by "fashionable" standards of artistic value, standards that motivate the answer that Dee provides to her mother's question: " 'Well,' I said, stumped. 'What would *you* do with them?' " Dee's
answer: "Hang them." The stylish daughter's entire life has been one
of "framed" experience; she has always sought a fashionably "aesthetic"
distance from southern expediencies. (And how unlike quilt frames that
signal social activity and a coming to completeness are her *frames*.) Her
concentrated detachment from the fire, which so nearly symbolizes her
role vis-à-vis the Afro-American community (her black friends "worshipped . . . the scalding humor that erupted like bubbles in lye"), is
characteristic of her attitude. Her goals include the appropriation of exactly what *she* needs to remain fashionable in the eyes of a world of pre-
tended wholeness, a world of banal television shows, framed and insti-
tutionalized art, and polaroid cameras—devices that instantly process and
record experience as "framed" photograph. Ultimately, the framed polaroid photograph represents the limits of Dee's vision.

Strikingly, the quilts whose *tops* have been stitched by her grandmother from fragments of outgrown family garments and quilted after
the grandmother's death by Aunt Dee and her sister (the mother who
narrates the story) are perceived in Dee's polaroid sensibility as merely
"priceless" works of an institutionally, or stylishly, defined "art world."
In a reversal of perception tantamount to the acquisition of sacred
knowledge by initiates in a rite of passage, the mother/narrator realizes
that she has always worshiped at the altars of a "false" goddess. As her
alter ego, Dee has always expressed that longing for the "other" that
characterizes inhabitants of oppressed, "minority" cultures. Situated in
an indisputably black and big-boned skin, the mother has secretly admired the "good hair," full figure, and well-turned (i.e., "whitely trim")
ankle of Dee (Wangero). Sacrifices and sanctity have seemed in order.
But in her epiphanic moment of recognition, she perceives the fire-
scarred Maggie—the stay-at-home victim of southern scarifications—in a
revised light. When Dee grows belligerent about possessing the quilts,
Maggie emerges from the kitchen and says with a contemptuous gesture
of dismissal: "She can have them, Mama. . . . I can 'member Grandma
Dee without quilts." The mother's response to what she wrongly interprets as Maggie's hang-dog resignation before Dee is a radical awakening
to godhead:

> When I looked at her . . . something hit me in the top of my head
> and ran down to the soles of my feet. Just like when I'm in church

and the spirit of God touches me and I get happy and shout. I did something I never had done before: hugged Maggie to me, then dragged her on into the room, snatched the quilts out of Miss Wangero's hands and dumped them into Maggie's lap.

· Maggie is the arisen goddess of Walker's story; she is the sacred figure who bears the scarifications of experience and knows how to convert patches into robustly patterned and beautifully quilted wholes. As an earth-rooted and quotidian goddess, she stands in dramatic contrast to the stylishly fiery and other-oriented Wangero. The mother says in response to Dee's earlier cited accusation that Maggie would reduce quilts to rags by putting them to everyday use: " 'She can always make some more,' I said. 'Maggie knows how to quilt.' " And, indeed, Maggie, the emergent goddess of New World improvisation and long ancestral memory, does know how to quilt. Her mind and imagination are capable of preserving the wisdom of grandmothers and aunts without material prompts: "I can 'member . . . without the quilts," she says. The secret to employing beautiful quilts as items of everyday use is the secret of crafty dues.

In order to comprehend the transient nature of all wholes, one must first become accustomed to living and working with fragments. Maggie has learned the craft of fragment weaving from her women ancestors: "It was Grandma Dee and Big Dee who taught her how to quilt herself." The conjunction of "quilt" and "self" in Walker's syntax may be simply a serendipitous accident of style. Nonetheless, the conjunction works magnificently to capture the force of black woman's quilting in "Everyday Use." Finally, it is the "self," or a version of humanness that one calls the Afro-American self, that must, in fact, be crafted from fragments on the basis of wisdom gained from preceding generations.

What is at stake in the world of Walker's short story, then, is not the prerogatives of Afro-American women as "wayward artists." Individualism and a flouting of convention in order to achieve "artistic" success constitute acts of treachery in "Everyday Use." For Dee, if she is anything, *is* a fashionable denizen of America's art/fantasy world. She is removed from the "everyday uses" of a black community that she scorns, misunderstands, burns. Certainly, she is "unconventionally" black. As such, however, she is an object of holy contempt from the archetypal weaver of black wholeness from tattered fragments. Maggie's "Uhnnnh" and her mother's designation "Miss Wangero" are gestures of utter contempt. Dee's sellout to fashion and fantasy in a television-manipulated world of "artistic" frames is a representation of the *complicity of the clerks*. Not "art," then, but use or function is the signal in Walker's fiction of sacred creation.

Quilts designed for everyday use, pieced wholes defying symmetry and pattern, are signs of the scarred generations of women who have always been alien to a world of literate words and stylish fantasies. The crafted fabric of Walker's story is the very weave of blues and jazz traditions in the Afro-American community, daringly improvisational modes that confront breaks in the continuity of melody (or theme) by riffing. The asymmetrical quilts of southern black women are like the off-centered stomping of the jazz solo or the innovative musical showmanship of the blues interlude. They speak a world in which the deceptively shuffling Maggie is capable of a quick change into goddess, an unlikely holy figure whose dues are paid in full. Dee's anger at her mother is occasioned principally by the mother's insistence that paid dues make Maggie a more likely bearer of sacredness, tradition, and true value than the "brighter" sister. "You just don't understand," she says to her mother. Her assessment is surely correct where institutional theories and systems of "art" are concerned. The mother's cognition contains no categories for framed art. The mother works according to an entirely different scale of use and value, finally assigning proper weight to the virtues of Maggie and to the ancestral importance of the pieced quilts that she has kept out of use for so many years. Smarting, perhaps, from Dee's designation of the quilts as "old-fashioned," the mother has buried the covers away in a trunk. At the end of Walker's story, however, she has become aware of her own mistaken value judgments, and she pays homage that is due to Maggie. The unlikely daughter is a *griot* of the vernacular who remembers actors and events in a distinctively black "historical" drama.

Before Dee departs, she "put on some sunglasses that hid everything above the tip of her nose and her chin." Maggie smiles at the crude symbolism implicit in this act, for she has always known that her sister saw "through a glass darkly." But it is the mother's conferral of an ancestral blessing (signaled by her deposit of the quilts in Maggie's lap) that constitutes the occasion for the daughter's first "real smile." Maggie knows that it is only communal recognition by elders of the tribe that confers ancestral privileges on succeeding generations. The mother's holy recognition of the scarred daughter's sacred status as quilter is the best gift of a hard-pressed womankind to the fragmented goddess of the present.

At the conclusion of "Everyday Use," which is surely a fitting precursor to *The Color Purple*, with its sewing protagonist and its scenes of sisterly quilting, Maggie and her mother relax in the ritual yard after the dust of Dee's departing car has settled. They dip snuff in the manner of African confreres sharing cola nuts. The moment is past when a putatively "new" generation has confronted scenes of black, everyday life. A change has taken place, but it is a change best described by Amiri Baraka's designation for Afro-American music's various styles and discontinuities. The change in Walker's story is the "changing same." What has been reaffirmed at the story's conclusion is the value of the quiltmaker's motion and strategy in the precincts of a continuously undemocratic South.

But the larger appeal of "Everyday Use" is its privileging of a distinctively woman's craft as *the* signal mode of confronting chaos through a skillful blending of patches. In *The Color Purple*, Celie's skill as a fabric worker completely transmutes the order of Afro-American existence. Not only do her talents with a needle enable her to wear the pants in the family, they also allow her to become the maker of pants par excellence. Hence, she becomes a kind of unifying goddess of patch and stitch, an instructress of mankind who bestows the gift of consolidating fragments. Her abusive husband Albert says: "When I was growing up . . . I use to try to sew along with mama cause that's what she was always doing. But everybody laughed at me. But you know, I liked it." "Well," says Celie, "nobody gon laugh at you now. . . . Here, help me stitch in these pockets."

A formerly "patched" separateness of woman is transformed through fabric craft into a new unity. Quilting, sewing, stitching are bonding activities that begin with the godlike authority and daring of women, but that are given (as a gift toward community) to men. The old disparities are transmuted into a vision best captured by the scene that Shug suggests to Celie: "But, Celie, try to imagine a city full of these shining, blueblack people wearing brilliant blue robes with designs like fancy quilt patterns." The heavenly city of quilted design is a form of unity wrested by the sheer force of the woman quiltmaker's will from chaos. As a community, it stands as both a sign of the potential effects of black women's creativity in America, and as an emblem of the effectiveness of women's skillful confrontation of patches. Walker's achievement as a southern, black, woman novelist is her own successful application of the holy patching that was a staple of her grandmother's and great-grandmother's hours of everyday ritual. "Everyday Use" is, not surprisingly, dedicated to "your grandmama": to those who began the line of converting patches into works of southern genius.

VALERIE SMITH

The Quest for and Discovery of Identity in Toni Morrison's Song of Solomon

IN HER FIRST THREE NOVELS, *The Bluest Eye* (1970), *Sula* (1973), and *Song of Solomon* (1977), Toni Morrison explores the interplay between self-knowledge and social role. Her characters, like Ralph Ellison's Invisible Man, inhabit a world where inhospitable social assumptions obtain. But Morrison does not provide her people with the option of living underground, in isolation, beyond community. Those whom social relations exclude (like Pecola Breedlove of *The Bluest Eye* or Sula) lack self-knowledge and are destroyed by themselves or by others. My analysis here centers on *Song of Solomon*, the only one of Morrison's novels in which her protagonist completes successfully his/her search for psychological autonomy. Yet, no discussion of the search for identity in *Song of Solomon* would be complete without some mention of Morrison's two earlier novels. The structure and thematic concerns of these two works establish a framework in terms of which we may understand the meaning and status of Milkman's discovery.

I

The black characters in Morrison's early novels are especially vulnerable to the defeats that accompany isolation; in *The Bluest Eye* and in *Sula*, she examines the complex economic, historical, cultural and geographic factors that problematize their relations within the black community and the world beyond. Pecola Breedlove, on whom *The Bluest Eye* centers, typifies Morrison's outsiders. Her story illustrates the destructive potential of a culture that recognizes only one standard of physical beauty and equates that standard with virtue. Ostensibly, Pecola is driven mad by her inability to possess blue eyes. But her insanity really results from the fact that she serves as the communal scapegoat, bearing not only her own self-loathing, but that of her neighbors and family as well. Soaphead Church's failure to provide her with blue eyes is thus simply the proverbial back-breaking straw.

The Bluest Eye does not address the hard questions directly. The book does not undertake to explain, for example, why black Americans aspire to an unattainable standard of beauty; why they displace their self-hatred onto a communal scapegoat; how Pecola's fate might have been averted. The metaphors of Claudia MacTeer that frame and image Pecola's story, and the very structure of the novel itself, suggest that such considerations are irresolvable. "This soil is bad for certain kinds of flowers," Claudia remarks. "Certain seeds it will not nurture, certain fruit it will not bear." Claudia accepts as a given the fact that certain "soils" will reject both marigolds and plain black girls. To her, the reasons for this incompatibility are structural, too intricately woven to distinguish. She therefore believes that any attempt to explain Pecola's deterioration will be fruitless and concludes that *"There is really nothing more to say—except why. But since why is difficult to handle, one must take refuge in how."*

I would argue that not only Claudia, but the novel itself, avoids "why," taking refuge instead in "how." Claudia, the narrator of the primer, and the ostensibly omniscient narrator all tell stories—tell "how" fast and furiously. These stories, in general, demonstrate what it means to find inaccessible the possessions and attributes that one's culture values. Their thematic similarity reveals the representative nature of Pecola's story: self-loathing leads inevitably to some form of destruction. Perhaps more importantly, the remarkable number of stories symbolizes the complex sources and effects of this cycle of self-loathing. The form is therefore a figure for the cultural condition the novel addresses.

The structure of *The Bluest Eye* underscores the proliferation of stories and of narrative voices within the novel. The body of the text is divided into four chapters which are, in turn, subdivided. Each begins with an episode, usually involving Pecola, told from the point of view of Claudia the child but shaped by her adult reflections and rhetoric. Claudia's stories then yield place to one or two stories told by an apparently objective, omniscient narrator. This narrator usually recalls information to which Claudia would not have had access: he/she tells stories from Pecola's life that involve other characters and weaves flashbacks from the lives of these other characters (Polly or Cholly Breedlove, Geraldine, or Soaphead Church, for example) into Pecola's story. In addition, in each chapter several garbled lines from the primer separate Claudia's voice from that of the omniscient narrator.

The chapters counterpoint three moments in time: a past before the narrative present (the flashbacks), the eternal present of the primer, and the narrative present of Pecola's story as told by Claudia. The different narratives in each chapter provide variations on a specific theme. This technique demonstrates here and throughout Morrison's fiction the interconnectedness of past and present. The form implies that the meaning of Pecola's story may only be understood in relation to events that predated her birth.

The cacophony of voices in *The Bluest Eye* demonstrates that Pecola is inextricably linked to the linguistic community that forms the novel. Yet she is clearly denied a place in the world the text purports to represent; her involuntary isolation from others leads to her psychological disintegration. *Sula* as well features a scapegoat-protagonist, although Sula clearly cultivates those qualities that distinguish her from her neighbors. Here, too, Morrison's plot relies on a multiplicity of narratives to implicate Sula in the very community from which she is alienated. Although Sula, unlike Pecola, chooses her isolation, it is precisely that distance that destroys her.

Sula centers on a character who believes that she can create for herself an identity that exists beyond community and social expectations. "An artist with no art form," Sula uses her life as her medium, "exploring her own thoughts and emotions, giving them full reign, feeling no obligation to please anybody unless their pleasure pleased her." She thus defies social restraints with a vengeance. She disavows gratuitous social flattery, refusing to compliment either the food placed before her or her old friends gone to seed, and using her conversation to experiment with her neighbors' responses. As the narrator remarks: "In the midst of pleasant conversation with someone, she might say, 'Why do you chew with your mouth open?' not because the answer interested her but because she wanted to see the person's face change rapidly." Worst of all in her neighbors' judgment, she discards men, black and white, as rapidly as she sleeps with them, even the husband of her best friend, Nel.

There are moments when the text seems to validate Sula's way of life; the narrator suggests, for example, that Sula's independence has bestowed upon her a kind of immortality:

Among the weighty evidence piling up was the fact that Sula did not look her age. She was near thirty and, unlike them, had lost no teeth, suffered no bruises, developed no ring of fat at the waist or pocket at the back of her neck. It was rumored that she had had no childhood diseases, was never known to have chicken pox, croup or even a runny nose. She had played rough as a child—where were the scars?

But by interweaving Sula's story with Shadrack's and Nel's, Morrison demonstrates structurally the collective nature of human identity.

Sula's story stands in analogous relation to Shadrack's, symbolic evidence that her situation, like Pecola's, is hardly unique. The communal response to Sula is identically Shadrack's response to the unexpected. Shadrack, the insane World War I veteran whose story opens the novel, exemplifies in the extreme this need to explain or find a place for the inexplicable. By creating National Suicide Day, he finds a way of controlling his fear: "If one day a year were devoted to [death], everybody could get it out of the way and the rest of the year would be safe and free."

The people of the Bottom of Medallion, Ohio, ridicule Shadrack's holiday, but their survival, like his, depends upon finding ways of controlling their terrors. Superstitions, which recur in the narrative and in their collective discourse, help them explain disturbing disruptions. When Hannah, Sula's mother, dies suddenly, Eva, Sula's grandmother, reflects that she would have been prepared for the tragedy if she had read properly the omens she had received. Likewise, the denizens of the Bottom remark that they should have anticipated Sula's deleterious effect on their community, because her return was accompanied by a plague of robins. Like Eva, the townspeople find a sign or a reason for their trouble after the fact. Their retrospective justifications are finally no different from Shadrack's.

And just as they must find a way of controlling the unexpected evils that beset them, so do they find a place for Sula. Since they do not understand her, they call her evil and hold her responsible for the injuries and deaths that befall their community. As the narrator notes, the townspeople actually become more generous when they shun Sula because they assign to her their own baser impulses. For all her efforts to transcend the community, then, Sula remains an integral part of it.

Morrison also undercuts Sula's aspirations to originality by characterizing her as only half a person. As several critics have argued, Sula and Nel complement each other psychologically, and neither is fully herself after geography, and Sula's relation to Jude, separate them.

Sula and Nel are products of two different styles of childrearing:

their friendship grows out of their fascination with their dissimilarities. Sula's family is the source of her independence of mind and sexual nonchalance. Her mother is known especially for her sexual generosity; her grandmother, Eva, for selling her leg to support her children. Eva's home provides a figure for her family, replete with an ever-changing cast of boarders, gentleman callers, and foundlings:

> Sula Peace lived in a house of many rooms that had been built over a period of five years to the specifications of its owner, who kept on adding things: more stairways—more rooms, doors and stoops. There were rooms that had three doors, others that opened out on the porch only and were inaccessible from any other part of the house; others that you could get to only by going through somebody's bedroom.

Nel, on the other hand, is raised in a well-ordered but repressive household, and is thus prepared to choose a life of limited options such as the one she shares with Jude. Haunted by the image of her own mother, a prostitute, Nel's mother tries to launder the "funk" out of her daughter's life. During their childhood and adolescence, Nel provides Sula with restraints, and Sula offers Nel license. More importantly, they offer each other a kind of security that neither finds in her own family. Together they begin to discover the meaning of death and sexuality. As the narrator remarks:

> Because each had discovered years before that they were neither white nor male, and that all freedom and triumph were forbidden to them, they had set about creating something else to be. Their meeting was fortunate, for it let them use each other to grow on. Daughters of distant mothers and incomprehensible fathers (Sula's because he was dead; Nel's because he wasn't), they found in each other's eyes the intimacy they were looking for.

Their relationship is permanently destroyed when Sula sleeps with Jude, although Sula reflects that she never intended to cause Nel pain. Without Nel, "the closest thing to both an other and a self," Sula is cut off from the only relation that endowed her life with meaning, and she drifts to her death. Nel, too, is rendered incomplete when her friendship with Sula ends. She may think that her inescapable grief is the result of having lost her husband, but as she realizes at the end of the novel, what she had missed for so many years was not Jude, but Sula.

The descendant of a line of relatively autonomous women, Sula attempts to go them one better and create herself outside of the collective assumptions of women's behavior. Morrison denies the feasibility of such a choice most obviously by killing off her protagonist. But the narrative structures she employs in *Sula* further undercut Sula's aspirations. By characterizing her as both a scapegoat and the second self of her more conventional best friend, Morrison denies Sula the originality she seeks.

II

Song of Solomon centers on Milkman Dead's unwitting search for identity. Milkman appears to be doomed to a life of alienation from himself and from others because, like his parents, he adheres to excessively rigid, materialistic, Western values and an attendant linear conception of time. During a trip to his ancestral home, however, Milkman discovers his own capacity for emotional expansiveness and learns to perceive the passage of time as a cyclical process. When he incorporates both his familial and his personal history into his sense of the present, he repairs his feelings of fragmentation and comprehends for the first time the coherence of his own life.

Milkman's father, Macon Dead, Jr., is a quintessential self-made man. Orphaned and disinherited in his adolescence, he wheeled and dealt his way into his position as the richest black man in town. Milkman can therefore brag about his father's houses, cars, assets and speculations, to the delight of the Reverend Mr. Cooper and his Danville companions. The avid materialism and rugged individualism that made Macon financially successful have exacted their price from him in other ways, however. Macon has come to believe that money, property and keys are what is real in the world; his financial success has thus cost him his capacity for communication and emotion. As he advises his son:

> "Come to my office; work a couple of hours there and learn what's real. Let me tell you right now that one important thing you'll ever need to know: Own things. And let the things you own own other things. Then you'll own yourself and other people too."

The Macon Deads exemplify the patriarchal, nuclear family that has been traditionally a stable and critical feature not only of American society, but of Western civilization in general. The primary institution for the reproduction and maintenance of children, ideally it provides the individual with the means for understanding his/her place in the world. The degeneration of the Dead family, and the destructiveness of Macon's rugged individualism, symbolize the invalidity of American, indeed Western values. Morrison's depiction of this family demonstrates the incompatibility of received assumptions and the texture and demands of life in black American communities.

Macon, Jr. believes that a successful businessman cannot afford to be compassionate. Reflecting that his first two keys to rental units would never have multiplied had he accommodated delinquent accounts, he sees his tenants as only so much property. Moreover, he objectifies his family. He brutalizes his wife Ruth both subtly and overtly because he suspects her of incestuous relations with her father and son. Despite his concern for Milkman, he only speaks to him "if his words [hold] some command or criticism." And by refusing to acknowledge Pilate as his sister, Macon denies her humanity as well. His resentment is based in part on his belief that she stole the gold that the two of them should have shared. More significantly, though, he eschews her company because he considers her deportment to be socially unacceptable. He fears that the white bankers will cease to trust him if they associate him with a woman bootlegger.

Weak and pathetic as she is, Ruth finds subtle methods of objectifying the members of her family as well. She retaliates against her husband's cruelty by manipulating him. Since she cannot attract his attention in any other way, she demeans herself until, out of disgust, he lashes out at her. Similarly, she remarks that her son has never been "a person to her." Before he was born, Milkman was "a wished-for bond between herself and Macon, something to hold them together and reinstate their sex lives." After she realizes that her husband will never again gratify her sexually, she uses Milkman to fulfill her yearnings by breastfeeding him until he is old enough to talk, stand up and wear knickers.

Pilate Dead, Macon's younger sister, provides a marked contrast to her brother and his family. Like Macon, Pilate presides over a household which is predominantly female. But while Macon's love of property and money determines the nature of his relationships, Pilate's sheer disregard for status, occupation, hygiene and manners enables her to affirm spiritual values such as compassion, respect, loyalty and generosity.

If the Macon Deads seem barren and lifeless, Pilate's family bursts with energy and sensuality. Pilate, Reba and Hagar engage ceaselessly in collective activity, erupting spontaneously into harmonious song. On his way to his own emotionally empty house one evening, Macon, Jr.

peeks through the window of his sister's home in search of spiritual nourishment. He hears the three women sing one song, Pilate stirring the contents of a pot, Reba paring her toenails and Hagar braiding her hair. Macon is comforted both by the soothing and unending motion of each character in the vignette and by the harmony and tranquillity of the music they make together.

As Pilate introduces vitality into her brother's life, so does she introduce a magical presence into the otherwise spiritually lifeless world of Part I of the novel. The circumstances of her birth make her a character of larger-than-life dimensions—one who has transcended the limitations of her historical moment and milieu. Pilate delivered herself at birth and was born without a navel. Her smooth stomach isolates her from society, since those who know of her condition shun her. Moreover, her physical condition symbolizes her thorough independence of others; even as a fetus she did not need to rely on another person for sustenance. Her isolation and self-sufficiency enable her to "throw away every assumption she had learned and [begin] at zero." She is therefore neither trapped nor destroyed by decaying values as her brother's family is. Like Macon she is self-made, but her self-creation departs from, instead of coinciding with, the American myth. Pilate decides for herself what is important to her, and instead of appropriating collective assumptions, she remakes herself accordingly. After cutting her hair:

> [Pilate] tackled the problem of trying to decide how she wanted to live and what was valuable to her. When am I happy and when am I sad and what is the difference? What do I need to stay alive? What is true in the world?

Quintessential self-made man that he is, Macon predicates his behavior on a linear conception of time. To his mind, future successes determine identity and justify one's actions in the past and in the present. Macon's futuristic, linear vision of time and of identity is evidenced by his failure to consider his past as part of himself. He denies the importance of his relationship with his sister and of their shared past. Moreover, as he remarks while telling Milkman about his days in Lincoln's Heaven, he does not even allow himself to think about his past:

> He had not said any of this for years. Had not even reminisced much about it recently. . . . For years he hadn't had that kind of time, or interest.

Macon's linear vision of time is also partly responsible for his sense of family and of morality. Because he believes that the coherence and significance of his identity lie in his future, he cares only about his relationship to his son. To his patriarchal mind, it is in that connection that the most important genealogical transfer occurs. But Macon has no time whatsoever for any connection that would cause him to exercise his capacity for horizontal or (what would be to him) peripheral vision.

Macon's ability to see the world only in linear, exclusive terms explains his lack of sympathy in yet other ways. He believes that the ends justify any means; as a result, he excuses his own corruption by considering only the financial profits it brings him. He feels no need to offer Mrs. Bains (one of his tenants) charity because charity will not increase his wealth. And he encourages Milkman and Guitar to steal what he thinks is Pilate's gold, despite the kindness she has shown them all.

In contrast to Macon's, Pilate's vision of time—indeed, of the world —is cyclical and expansive. Instead of repressing the past, she carries it with her in the form of her songs, her stories and her bag of bones. She believes that one's sense of identity is rooted in the capacity to look back to the past and synthesize it with the present; it is not enough simply to put it behind one and look forward. As she tells Macon:

> "You can't take a life and walk off and leave it. Life is life. Precious. And the dead you kill is yours. They stay with you anyway, in your mind. So it's a better thing, a more better thing to have the bones right there with you wherever you go. That way it frees up your mind."

Before Milkman leaves Michigan, he perceives the world in much the same way that his father does. His steadiness of vision and lack of compassion allow him to abuse remorselessly and unself-consciously the people around him. For instance, his letter to Hagar reveals his inability to understand her feelings and psychology despite their years of intimacy. He fails to accept responsibility for ending their relationship: instead, he writes little more than a business letter suggesting that he leave her for her own best interest. Moreover, his sister Lena tells him that he has "urinated" on the women in his family. That is, he has demanded their service and shown them no consideration. He has presumed to know what is best for them without knowing them at all.

Milkman's search for gold indicates further the similarity between his father's vision of the world and his own. He thinks that leaving his hometown, his past and his responsibilities will guarantee him a sense of his own identity. As he becomes increasingly implicated in the scheme to retrieve Pilate's gold, Milkman acquires a clearer but equally false sense of what freedom means. He believes that gold will provide him with a "clean-lined definite self," the first sense of identity he has ever known.

Milkman's assumption that the key to his liberation may be found in Danville and Shalimar is correct, although it is not gold that will free him. In his ancestors' world, communal and mythical values prevail over individualism and materialism; when he adopts their assumptions in place of his own, he arrives at a more complete understanding of what his experience means. When Milkman arrives in the South he wears a "beige three-piece suit, button down light-blue shirt and black string tie, [and] beautiful Florsheim shoes." He ruins and loses various articles of clothing and jewelry as he looks first for gold and then for the story of his people. Indeed, just before his epiphanic moment in the forest, he has changed from his cosmopolitan attire to overalls and brogans. Similarly, the people he meets in Shalimar force him to throw off his pretenses before they offer him the help and information he needs. Only when he ceases to flaunt his wealth and refer to their women casually do they admit him into their community. Until he sheds the leaden trappings of materialism, Milkman is like the peacock he and Guitar see: too weighted down by his vanity to fly.

While in Michigan, Milkman believes that when he finally achieves his freedom, he will no longer need to submit to the claims of others. In the woods, away from the destructive effects of "civilization," he realizes that human connection—horizontal vision—is an inescapable part of life:

> It sounded old. Deserve. Old and tired and beaten to death. Deserve. Now it seemed to him that he was always saying or thinking that he didn't deserve some bad luck, or some bad treatment from others. He'd told Guitar that he didn't "deserve" his family's dependence, hatred, or whatever. That he didn't even "deserve" to hear all the misery and mutual accusations his parents unloaded on him. Nor did he "deserve" Hagar's vengeance. But why shouldn't his parents tell him their personal problems? If not him, then who?

While previously he had dehumanized his friends and relations, he now empathizes with his parents and feels shame for having robbed Pilate:

... the skin of shame that he had rinsed away in the bathwater after having stolen from Pilate returned. But now it was as thick and as tight as a caul. How could he have broken into that house—the only one he knew that achieved comfort without one article of comfort in it. No soft worn-down chair, not a cushion or a pillow. . . . But peace was there, energy, singing, and now his own remembrances.

In keeping with this new awareness of others and of his personal past, Milkman, insensitive to Hagar and unwilling to accept responsibility for her in life, understands her posthumously and assumes the burden of her death. He acknowledges the inappropriateness of his letter to her and realizes that he has used her. Moreover, he knows without being told that she has died and he is to blame. As Pilate has carried with her the bones of the man she believes she has murdered, so too does Milkman resolve to carry with him the box of Hagar's hair: a symbol of his newly acquired cyclical vision of a past he no longer needs to escape.

Macon, Sr., Milkman's grandfather, was an American Adam, a farmer who loved the land and worked it profitably. Moving north cost Macon, Jr. some of the talent he had inherited from his father; still able to manipulate cold cash, he lost his father's organic connection to the soil. In the South, Milkman, too, seems disconnected from nature. Graceful in the "civilized" world, he is clumsy and obtuse when he enters the wilderness. However, he becomes increasingly attuned to nature's rhythms as he grows in self-awareness. During the bobcat hunt he senses through the contact between his fingertips and the ground beneath him that someone is about to make an attempt on his life. And as he returns to the town, Milkman feels as if he is part of the "rock and soil" and discovers that he no longer limps.

Finally, however, Milkman's discovery of his identity lies not so much in his connection with the earth, or in his ability to understand his own past; these accomplishments only attend his greater achievement—learning to complete, to understand and to sing his family song. Milkman comes to know fully who he is when he can supply the lyrics to the song Pilate has only partially known. Throughout his life, Milkman has had an inexplicable fascination with flight. Robert Smith's abortive attempt to fly from the hospital roof precipitated his birth. Riding backward makes him uncomfortable because it reminds him of "flying blind, and not knowing where he [is] going." And as he approaches Circe's house, he recalls his recurring childhood fantasy of being able to take flight. When Milkman knows the entire song, however, and can sing it to Pilate as she has sung it to others, he can assume his destiny. Flight is no longer a fancy that haunts him, appearing unsummoned in his consciousness. He now understands it as a significant action from his ancestral past. Indeed, the ultimate sign of his achievement of identity is his ability to take flight in the way his grandfather did. In the process of assuming himself, Milkman discovers that his dreams have become attainable.

Milkman acquires a sense of identity when he immerses himself in his extended past. He comes full round from the individualism his father represents and advocates. Assuming identity is thus a communal gesture in this novel, as, indeed, Morrison suggests in her two earlier novels. Knowing oneself derives from learning to reach back into history and horizontally in sympathetic relationship to others. Milkman bursts the bonds of the Western, individualistic conception of self, accepting in its place the richness and complexity of a collective sense of identity.

CHARLES H. ROWELL

The Quarters: Ernest Gaines and the Sense of Place[*]

> Beyond the trees was the road that led you down into
> the quarters. At the mouth of the road was the main
> highway, heading toward Bayonne, and just on the
> other side of the highway was the St. Charles River. A
> light breeze had just risen up from the river, and I
> caught a faint odor from the sweet-olive bush which
> stood in the far right corner of the garden.
> —*A Gathering of Old Men*

I*F YOU DRIVE WEST out of Baton Rouge on U.S. 190, you
eventually cross the Mississippi River, Mechesebe, "Father of Waters."
If you by-pass Port Allen and take the Alexandria exit about three miles
up the road, you soon come to Pointe Coupée Parish. As you enter the
parish, you immediately recognize its four geographical distinctions:
the same oppressive heat you encountered in Baton Rouge—if you are
traveling between late spring and early fall; live oaks, standing like pre-
historic giants with hair of Spanish moss; flat, fertile soil which once,
with abundance, supported the agricultural empire of the South; and
False River, a lake whose shape forms the illusion of a river.*

*You are driving along False River; you are coming into New Roads,
the seat of the parish, its major town, whose power belongs to a few
whites of a decided gentility—families who have held sway over the*

[*]I want to thank the administration and staff of the Carter G. Woodson Institute of the University of Virginia for their cordiality and support when I was writing
and preparing this article for publication. Special thanks to Julie Saville who directed
me to various historical sources, including those on slavery and the plantation. In my
discussion of *Catherine Carmier*, I have drawn upon Thadious M. Davis' article "Head-
lands and Quarters: Louisiana in *Catherine Carmier*," *Callaloo*, VII (Spring–Summer,
1984), 1–13.

146

people and land of the parish since the Louisiana Purchase. The many outlying hamlets, such as Morganza, Oscar, Lavonia and Lakeland, are no more than sprawling plantations owned by white families. Inquiries in the right places will tell you that these families once, through the exploitation of blacks and Cajuns, transformed this land into high-yielding crops of sugar cane and cotton.

As you move around in the parish, you discover that its architecture reflects the history, past and present, of the social classes and racial groups of the parish: mansions or "big houses," some with two-tiered verandas, evoking memories of the Spanish and French settlers; modest homes of a simple but severe design, known in Louisiana as Cajun architecture; and then cabins or shanties, sometimes grouped in what is known as "quarters," where blacks live. Although you drove west and slightly north at the beginning of your trip, you realize that the Mississippi River, twisting southward, declares itself at the eastern boundary of the parish. And to the north and west the Red River and the Atchafalaya River make their presences known.

I

Pointe Coupée Parish, Louisiana. St. Raphael Parish, as Ernest Gaines renames it in his fiction, in honor of his stepfather, Raphael Norbert Colar. Here Gaines was born and spent the first fifteen years of his life; and here he frequently returns from California (where he moved in 1948) to be with the people and "the land in different seasons, to travel the land, to go into the fields, to go into the small towns, to go into the bars, to eat the food, to listen to the language . . . to absorb things" (*Callaloo #3*). This is the parish Gaines chose for his fiction—a collective fable exploring the conditions of modern humanity in the throes of traditions and values that forever threaten to stifle its will to live.

The action in Gaines's fiction takes place in the quarters, homes, jails, saloons, stores, yards and fields; in the city of New Roads (named Bayonne and St. Adrienne for Gaines's mother, Adrienne Gaines Colar) and on False River (St. Charles River, for his brother Charles); at gates and public gatherings; and on the roads and in other places. In its infinite details, the world of the fiction of Ernest Gaines encompasses the countryside, the villages, and the town of New Roads in Pointe Coupee Parish.

Explaining his motive for using rural Louisiana in his fiction, Gaines tells us that he wanted to smell that Louisiana earth, feel that Louisiana sun, sit under the shade of one of those Louisiana oaks, search for pecans in that Louisiana grass in one of those Louisiana yards next to one of those Louisiana bayous, not far from a Louisiana river. I wanted to see on paper those Louisiana black children walking to school on cold days while yellow Louisiana buses passed them by. I wanted to see on paper those black parents going to work before the sun came up and coming back home to look after their children after the sun went down. I wanted to see on paper the true reason why those black fathers left home—not because they were trifling or shiftless—but because they were tired of putting up with certain conditions. I wanted to see on paper the small country churches (schools during the week), and I wanted to hear those simple religious songs, those simple prayers—that true devotion. . . . And I wanted to hear that Louisiana dialect—that combination of English, Creole, Cajun and Black. For me there's no more beautiful sound anywhere—unless, of course, you take exceptional pride in "proper" French or "proper" English. I wanted to read about the true relationship between whites and blacks—about the people . . . I had known.

Gaines concentrates on Pointe Coupée/St. Raphael Parish as a center of meaning in order to "record" the lives of the people he knew as he saw them, and to use their experiences to construct a myth that articulates the struggles of a static world fiercely resistant to change. St. Raphael Parish is like William Faulkner's Yoknapatawpha and James Joyce's Dublin: it equals the modern world. To understand the Gaines canon, we must explore its symbolic geography. We can begin with the quarters, the focal place and central metaphor of his parish. To examine the quarters community as a phenomenon in southern history, and as a physical, social, and political entity in Gaines's work is to tell much about the symbolic, temporal reality of his fictional world.

II

He sat in the car looking into the yard at the house. The yard was clean and bare, except for a mulberry tree on the left side of the walk and a rose bush on either side of the steps. The house itself was exactly like every other one in the quarters. They all had the same rusted corrugated tin roofs with a brick chimney sitting in the center. They all had the same long, warped porches, with

three or four steps leading up to the porch. Every
house had two doors facing the road. All had been
whitewashed at the same time, twenty-five or thirty
years ago—none had been painted since—and the
weather had turned all of them the same ashy gray
color.

—In My Father's House

The quarters, as a southern phenomenon, has a long history which
goes back to the days of slavery in the American South. Originally, the
quarters referred to the housing or living area—the physical community—of the slaves, which essentially "consisted of rows of cabins
near the Big House or the overseer's residence" (*The Reshaping of
Plantation Society*). In B. A. Botkin's *Lay My Burden Down*, Charley
Williams, who grew up as a slave on a plantation in Louisiana, recalls
that the slave cabins ran "along both sides of the road that go to the
fields. All one-room log cabins. . . ." The group arrangement and architecture of the slave cabins obviously varied from plantation to plantation, from state to state. The first significant matter for us here, then,
is that the slave master crowded the slaves into confined space in order
to observe, break, and control them. The slaves, however, did not allow
the confinement of the quarters to destroy their humanity. Instead
they transcended the designs of those who wished to control their minds
and bodies, bonding together as a community through friendship and
mutual protection.

According to Thomas L. Webber, the world of the quarters was
the slaves' primary source of education; here the slaves acquired and
developed "the knowledge, attitudes, values, and skills with which they
learned to view the world and make sense of their relationship to it"
(*Deep Like the Rivers*). Although they were continuously in view of
the master and his overseer in their quarters community, the slaves
made a world there. That is to say, they created and developed a culture, society, and world view that persisted, however modified, into
the twentieth century. It is important for us to remember that a large
measure of what we refer to as Black South folk culture originated in
the quarters or from experiences with restrictions and forms of oppression not unlike those of the quarters.

The quarters community, as a physical, social, and political entity,
continued into the 1970s. After Emancipation and Reconstruction a
majority of the freed-men/women in the South returned to labor and
economic conditions that were similar to those during slavery. Many

149

became sharecroppers and tenant farmers who owned their own persons but were bound to the land on which they worked. Like the slaves, they, too, were clustered into quarters communities. In testimony before the federal Industrial Commission on Agriculture and Agricultural Labor in 1901, William Carter Stubbs reported that the houses in quarters on Louisiana plantations were "arranged in rows, probably 30 to 40 cabins together . . . on both sides of the street [i. e., the road]." During the first half of the twentieth century, a large number of people occupied the quarters, but the different waves of the Great Migration gradually diminished the community's population. Opportunities unheard of in the rural South attracted millions of black southerners to cities beyond the region. By the 1890s, with farming as a corporate enterprise, the quarters as a community has virtually disappeared.

In its representation of the quarters, the Gaines canon covers a period of just over one hundred years. Its chronological time in plot dating begins with the Civil War in *The Autobiography of Miss Jane Pittman* (1971) and ends with the late 1970s in *A Gathering of Old Men* (1983). *Miss Jane Pittman* alone covers a hundred years, up until the Civil Rights Movement of the 1960s, which reaches its height in Bayonne with Reverend Phillip Martin's activism in *In My Father's House* (1978). *Catherine Carmier* (1964) and some of the stories in *Bloodline* (1968), notably "Just Like a Tree" and "Bloodline," are also set in the 1960s, but most of the action in *Of Love and Dust* (1967) takes place during the 1940s. The quarters in the Gaines canon is a slowly changing entity whose social and political activities recall the evolving Black South.

III

> We was already in the quarters. Far as you could see was nothing but this long road of white dust. It hurt your eyes to look at so much dust, so much whiteness, so much heat rising up from it. It was the hottest part of the day—between one thirty and two—and there wasn't another person anywhere in sight. The tall blood weeds on both sides of the road made the place look hotter. We was coming up to 'Malia's house. I could see two chairs on the gallery. They wasn't there when I came down the quarters the first time.
>
> —"Bloodline"

Felix's description of the quarters as a physical entity in "Blood-line" should not escape the reader's attention. When he goes there in the morning, Felix tells the reader that " 'Malia's house was the first one in the quarters, a little gray house that hadn't been painted in ages." His descriptions of Amalia's trees and the importance of the shade they provide from the intense heat in the buildings are all that he tells us about the Laurent Quarters. When he later recounts the events of his afternoon trip with Frank Laurent to Amalia's home for a meeting with Copper (Christian Laurent), Felix offers a similar description. He concentrates on the natural elements of the quarters: the dust, the heat, the weeds and the weathered houses. These images recur throughout Gaines's fiction. Whenever they appear, we know they represent the quarters and the human activities which take place there. In St. Raphael Parish, the reader's attention is frequently directed, for example, toward the giant trees in Raoul Carmier's front yard, the intense heat of the sun beating down on Marcus in the field, the encompassing white dust which follows Marshall Hebert's speeding car, the weeds growing all over the quarters on Candy Marshall's plantation. And the reader soon realizes that these elements of nature are not simply descriptions of setting.

One element of the natural scene Gaines never allows his reader to forget is the weather, which functions variously in different scenes of the novels. Except for the cold, rainy weather of *In My Father's House* and the different seasons that pass during the many years *The Autobiography of Miss Jane Pittman* covers, the main seasonal setting of Gaines's novels is the summer that oppresses the inhabitants of the quarters working in the fields, moving up and down the dusty roads, standing by or passing through gates, or sitting on their front porches. The people of the quarters never cease complaining about the heat. "This is the hottest place in the world," the returning Lillian Carmier tells her sister Catherine, who uses the heat as an excuse to meet secretly with Jackson from time to time. "It was hot" out in the fields, says the narrator in *Of Love and Dust*, "it was burning up. You could see little monkeys dancing out there in front of you." The weather, along with dust, is the recollective image that Miss Jane Pittman uses to open her narrative: "It was a day something like right now, dry, hot, and dusty dusty. It might 'a' been July, I'm not too sure, but it was July or August. Burning up, I won't ever forget." Her hot and dusty day, full of the sounds of marching Union and Confederate soldiers, immediately places the scene of her narrative—even for the least traveled and least read of her audience—in the smoldering rural South.

The intense heat James Kelly describes in *Of Love and Dust* is, like Sidney Bonbon, Marcus' nemesis. The sun, "that white hot bitch way there in the sky," works against him when Sidney is riding his horse no more than six inches behind Marcus; as the black stallion's breath pours down "on the back of [Marcus'] neck" "that old sun . . . white, small, and still strong—[shines] down . . . like nothing is happening." The work under that hot Louisiana sun, along with the brutal psychological circumstances Sidney creates, is the first test Marcus must undergo in Sidney's scheme to break him. Of course, in the final analysis Marcus, a newcomer to the quarters, triumphs over the heat, which functions as a character, and over Sidney, whose scheme fails. In his triumph, he proves himself superior to Sidney and the plantation system because Marcus' "act of rebellion," says John Wideman, "is a beacon exposing the evil of one form of life and heralding the possibility of another" (*Callaloo #3*).

Like the intense heat in *Of Love and Dust*, the hot white dust enshrouds the quarters and the people in it. The dust is, in fact, one of the recurring images in the novel. When Marcus first appears with Sidney, they bring with them to the quarters a cloud of dust. In the quarters, the "dust in the road [is] nearly as white as" Aunt Margaret's dress on the evening she goes to tell James Kelly about Marcus' first intimate encounter with Louise, Sidney's wife. Everywhere he goes in his 1941 Ford, Marshall Hebert brings dust. Gaines himself has commented that the dust signifies "the absence of love, the absence of life." The dust following Marshall Hebert symbolizes the death he brings in the end—the death which separates the lovers (Marcus and Louise, Pauline and Sidney) who "cannot love as they would want." "These people," Gaines continues, "wanted to love, but because of the way the system is set up, it was impossible to love. Dust."

Like the slave quarters of the Old South, the Laurent Quarters in "Bloodline," the Hebert Quarters in *Of Love and Dust*, the Sampson Quarters in *Miss Jane Pittman*, the Marshall Quarters in *A Gathering of Old Men* are enclosed communities whose limited space forces each inhabitant into the private lives of others. The unpainted homes or cabins, each with two front doors opening onto a front porch or gallery, are situated close to one another, as each of the cabins faces the dusty road which divides them into rows and which leads directly to the fields. As Thadious Davis puts it, every "house is within sight of every other; every resident known to one another" (*Callaloo #21*). So are some of the intimate details of their private lives. That involuntary intimacy in *Of Love and Dust* proves invaluable for the narrator and reader; James

Kelly gives the reader information a first person narrator-participant could not acquire firsthand. His neighbors, who voluntarily and involuntarily see other neighbors' doings, pass on information about them to James Kelly and other neighbors. How could James Kelly know the details of Marcus' movements in the quarters on his last afternoon on Marshall Hebert's plantation if one of the neighbors did not tell him? James Kelly is working in the field at that time, but Charlie Jordon, who reports the details to him, is at home across the road from James Kelly's cabin:

> He [Charlie Jordon] saw Marcus come out on the gallery and stand with his hands on his hips. After looking up and down the quarter, he went back in again. Charlie could see him pacing the floor just inside the room. Then a few minutes later he was on the gallery again, this time with a bottle of beer. He was still in his shorts. Charlie said he would stand in one place awhile, then he would start pacing the gallery. Then he would go in my room or his room. Everytime he went in my room he came back with a bottle of beer, Charlie said.

Charlie Jordon is not James Kelly's only informant; there are other inhabitants who, from observing others, tell him what they see and hear in the quarters. How else would he know the intimate details of Sidney Bonbon's or Marcus' visits to Pauline's home if Aunt Ca'line and Pa Bully had not listened to the privacies of their neighbors or sat on the gallery those hot summer nights? The quarters as a physical territory is a limited space where intimacies cease to be private as soon as they come into existence. Gaines exploits the reality of this limited space, providing his narrator with "reliable" informants and his readers with a detailed sketch of a geography of the imagination.

IV

> From my gallery I could see that dust coming down the quarter, coming fast, and I thought to myself, "Who in the world would be driving like that?" I got up to go inside until the dust had settled. But I had just stepped inside the room when I heard the truck stopping before the gate. I didn't turn around then because I knew the dust was flying all over the place. A minute or so later, when I figured it had settled, I

went back. The dust was still flying across the yard,
but it wasn't nearly as thick as now. I looked toward
the road and I saw somebody coming in the gate.

—*Of Love and Dust*

A careful examination of some of the images of place in *Catherine
Carmier* will tell us much about Gaines's conception of the quarters as
a social entity. The quarters we see in *Catherine Carmier* is also under
siege; one ever feels the presence of the materialistic Cajuns, who gradually seize the land from the declining white gentry and root out the
black population from the quarters. But the central focus of the novel
is neither the decline of the white gentry nor the Cajun takeover—however much the latter figures into the complication and resolution of the
plot. *Catherine Carmier* deals with a few days in the social life of the
people of the quarters: their relationships to one another, the return and
reception of kin, and their attitudes towards intraracial color codes and
traditional institutions, such as the church, school and marriage. The
main focus of the novel, however, is the nature and the effects of the
"secret" love affair between Jackson Bradley and Catherine Carmier. In
addition to the Jackson-Catherine love story, the novel also examines
familial relationships in Miss Charlotte's household, to which Jackson
returns, and Raoul Carmier's household, to which Lillian returns. In
Catherine Carmier, Gaines, as in "A Long Day in November," presents
his quarters as a social entity, with its inhabitants in private and public
relationships and conflicts.

The conflict in Charlotte's household comes from Jackson's inability to become one again with the place and the people of the quarters. His estrangement is as inevitable as change. Gaines first suggests
Jackson's alienation from his ancestral home as soon as he arrives at his
Aunt Charlotte's home: "Jackson looked toward the house. . . . Everything—his aunt, the house, the trees, the fence—seemed strange, and yet
very familiar." In addition to feeling estranged from his aunt and her
home, Jackson feels distanced from Brother who was his best friend:
"before he [Jackson] left here—they had been inseparable." But now
Jackson "could not make himself feel about Brother as he did before."
Through a series of images of place, Gaines demonstrates to us why his
character, who has just returned from a long stay in California, can
never fit again in the quarters near Bayonne. One of the most directly
pointed moments signaling his alienation occurs when he looks from his
bedroom window into Charlotte's garden:

The half dozen rows of beans that ran beside the house were nearly dry. Everything else in the garden had that half-green, half-yellow color.

I should have told her, he was thinking. I should have told her then that I'm going back. How can anyone stay here? Just look at this place. Everything is drying up; everything is half dead.

Jackson's thoughts on what he sees are not only his reflections on place; he thinks the same of the people with whom he cannot communicate. His failure to understand his Aunt Charlotte and his inability to continue to cherish the institutions, codes, and rituals she and the community hold dear set him apart from the quarters.

His conversations with Madame Bayonne and Catherine Carmier, the only people with whom he has significant relationships, tell us that his life is empty, that he has lost his sense of place and, hence, self. At one point, he tells Madame Bayonne that he is "like a leaf . . . that's broken away from a tree. Drifting." He will not find himself in Bayonne, in California, or in any other place until he affirms archetypal modes through which self-assertion can be made. To assert himself, Jackson has to affirm, for example, the traditions, manners and institutions of a specific community. Because he does not abide the cultural imperatives through which Charlotte and her neighbors define themselves, neither Bayonne nor its quarters can give Jackson refuge. After all, everything there is dying, "drying up."

Jackson's garden is also a reflection of the Carmiers' household, which is often represented by images related to death: we usually see the house in darkness or semidarkness, surrounded by "big oak and pecan trees" which look "like sentinels." When Lillian Carmier first returns home, the decaying "house, big, old, paintless," depresses her; and when Jackson looks at it, usually from afar, the Carmier house, like the Carmiers themselves, suggests an existence apart from—yet ultimately a part of—the quarters:

Jackson looked across the road and farther down the quarters at the big, old unpainted house where the Carmiers lived. He could hardly see the house for the trees in the yard, but the house looked no different from the way he left it ten years ago. Regardless of how bright the sun was shining, the big trees in the yard always kept the yard and the house in semidarkness.

Raoul Carmier's house, a symbol of the dying code by which he lives, is, in its tomb-like image, forbidden territory to members of the quarters and the rest of the world. As Madame Bayonne tells Jackson, Della has been forbidden to talk with people outside the household; members of the Carmier family " 'have put her in this position—behind those trees and nothing, hear me clearly, Jackson, nothing outside those trees is allowed in that yard.' " Later Madame Bayonne warns Jackson directly: " 'A word to the wise—' she started, then stopped. 'Don't go behind those trees, Jackson. It won't come to any good.' " In other words, to go past the trees is to face trouble. When he does, Jackson ultimately confronts Raoul, who obsessively guards his family, especially Catherine who, until his fight with Jackson, is his only "prop."

The images Gaines uses to describe the Carmier house also reflect the nature of the family's relationship to the quarters community, and the family members' relationships to one another. Although they too are descendants of Africans, the Carmiers, who are Creoles, have alienated themselves from the quarters; and as well, their home, which was once the overseer's house for the Grover Plantation, is separated from the rest of the quarters by a fence and a row of tall trees. The origin of the Carmiers' separation dates back to the creation of Creole societies in Louisiana which were built upon intraracial color codes seldom violated in social relationships. Neither black nor white, the Creoles only socialized with and married other Creoles—not blacks or whites. Raoul imposes the same isolation upon his family. He forbids his dark-skinned wife to talk with the people in the quarters, and he kills Mark, Della's son, not because he is born outside their marriage but because, says Alvin Aubert, he is dark in color. Catherine, who becomes Raoul's source of strength after the birth of Mark, is likewise forbidden to socialize with people in the quarters. She must, then, maintain a secret relationship with Jackson, who is not only black but is a threat to Raoul because he plans to take Catherine away.

Once Jackson passes through the gate and goes beyond the trees, he engages, as all the quarters knows, in a doomed relationship. Madame Bayonne's warning is not the only one given him; he knows from his early childhood relationship with Catherine, and from his Aunt Charlotte's words, that an affair with Catherine is forbidden. His ignoring the tradition of Creole-black separation is another violation that alienates him from the quarters. Unlike Jackson, the people in the quarters accept that unspoken intraracial arrangement. But Jackson defies it, tragically entrapping himself in a relationship that only leads to his fight with Raoul Carmier and his loss of Catherine. He learns that the world of the quarters in *Catherine Carmier* has its own social structure which the individual is expected to respect, that the consequence of not doing so is the psychological distancing which places the individual and the community at odds with each other. The result is the position in which Jackson Bradley and Lillian Carmier find themselves: alienated from their families, the community, and its social heritage.

The long-term residents of Gaines's quarters communities do not suffer Jackson's estrangement. In fact, most members of the quarters bond together for their common good. Eddie in "A Long Day in November" never would have solved his domestic problems if, in the quarters, private lives were not communal concerns. The attempted move of Aunt Fe in "Just Like a Tree" becomes the problem of the entire community which, in spite of inclement weather, pays its final respects. The quarters community has evolved traditions and values which its different institutions maintain as sources of support for its members in crises. It is an extended family to which each member owes allegiance, and it is an exacting social entity whose structure evolved from the experiences its residents have undergone since slavery.

V

> This time it was not one or two, it was many. They was not marching, they was not hurrying; it didn't look like they was even talking to each other. They was walking like every last one of them was by himself and any little noise could turn him around. But the longer I stood there looking, the more I saw coming toward me. Men, women, children. . . . No, not everybody in the quarters was headed that way. . . . But the number of people I saw coming toward me was something I never would 'a' dreamed of.
> —*The Autobiography of Miss Jane Pittman*

Within the chronology of plot dating in the Gaines canon, the quarters community first appears as a political entity in *Miss Jane Pittman*, when Uncle Isom asks his ex-slave master to allow him and the other freed-men/women to return to the quarters to decide whether they will remain on his plantation or leave it now that they have been "set free" by the Emancipation Proclamation. The gathering reveals a confused and divided community which, with the weight of a past that did not prepare them for such a sudden "emancipation," fails to speak as one collective voice. When we see the quarters later on the Bone, Dye, and Sampson plantations, we meet a restored community which, in physical and psychological terms, is the same as the one the bonds-men/women knew before the Civil War. "It was slavery again, all right," says Miss Jane. "No such thing as colored troops, colored politicians, or a colored teacher anywhere on the place. The only teacher to come there was white; the only time he came was winter when the weather was so bad the children couldn't go into the fields." It was slavery again, be-cause the White South was resistant—in fact, hostile—to change that would grant political, social, and economic equality to the entire popu-lation of the region.

The inhabitants of Gaines's quarters remain as the "new slaves" for the agricultural South into the mid-twentieth century, when the Mar-shall Heberts, the Robert Sampsons, and the Frank Laurents begin to lose control over the quarters and the rest of their plantations to the Cajuns. When they acquire their new power, their land, and their trac-tors, the Cajuns gradually force most of the black population from the land; the Cajuns become the new oppressors of the members of the quarters. The struggle in Gaines's quarters, then, is a continuous fight against the oppressive elements of the past in the present; the public and collective energy of the quarters is directed toward devising political strategies that will free the inhabitants of the oppressive designs of the White South.

In the opening of Book IV ("The Quarters") of *Miss Jane Pittman*, Miss Jane discusses one of the political strategies common to all human-kind: the selection of a leader. "People always looking for somebody to lead them," she says:

> Go to the Old Testament; go to the New. They did it in slavery; after the war they did it; they did it in the hard times that people want to call Reconstruction. They did it in the Depression—another hard times; and they doing it now. They have always done it—and the Lord has always obliged in some way or another.

These statements sum up the quarters' political quests in Books I-III, in which Uncle Isom, Big Laura, Ned, and Miss Jane herself have all served as leaders in one way or another. These statements also preface what Miss Jane's narrative in Book IV demonstrates: that the quarters on the Sampson plantation, like those on plantations from slavery to the pres-ent, needed a leader; that Jimmy Aaron was sent to Sampson to be their new leader; that Jimmy, with his preparation and his vision, assumes and acts out the role of leader for the quarters; and that, as a result of Jimmy's leadership, the people in Sampson Quarters set into motion the action which will bring about their second emancipation.

Before he can assume the role of leader, however, Jimmy, as Miss Jane shows, must go through certain steps. He must be educated by the community. He must be tested. And, as a result of going away, he must again be "educated"—this time, by Miss Jane, on how to move the people to follow him. Jimmy's first stage of education consists of hearing over and over, from the lips of adults, information about the history of the quarters ("Jimmy sitting right there listening to all we had to say"); seeing changes in the quarters and elsewhere on the plantation ("Jimmy saw this place changing, and he saw all the people moving away"); and performing, even at an early age, good deeds for members of the community—e.g., he wrote letters and read the Bible and the newspaper for people in the quarters. In other words, as a youngster, he had to become knowledgeable and supportive of the quarters he would lead in the future. Because the quarters "made him the One," the deliverer of the oppressed of Sampson, the people there also wanted to make sure he was one of them:

> We watched him every move he made. We made sure he made just the right ones. If he tried to go afoul—and he did at times—we told him what we had heard and what we had seen.

As Jimmy grows older and is formally educated in the schools, and as he travels to other places beyond Sampson, he—visionary, thinker and leader—"outgrows" the quarters. Upon his return, he is tested when the people reject his new ways, especially his public speech-making, and his new ideas. But, still committed to leading the quarters out of its neoslave condition, he heeds Miss Jane's word, his re-education from the community itself:

> "The people here ain't ready for nothing yet, Jimmy," I said. "Something got to get in the air first. Something got to seep all through their bones. But it's not out there yet. Nothing out there now but white hate and nigger fear. And fear they feel is the only way to keep going. One day they must realize fear is worse than any death. When that time come they will be ready to move with you."

When the people again accept Jimmy as their leader, they kill the fear that is within themselves and prepare to march with him into Bayonne to challenge that white hate from which they have long suffered. They are the "multitude" Miss Jane sees. They are prepared as individuals and as a group to fight for their emancipation. And when they hear of the death of their leader (an echo of Ned's death in Book III), and Miss Jane takes her heroic step past plantation owner Robert Sampson, the quarters' new stride toward self-emancipation from the negative elements of the past in the present is intensified.

The second major political turn of events in Gaines's quarters occurs in *A Gathering of Old Men*, where the defense of one's civil and human rights becomes the first and final stand taken by a group of old men in a dying community during the late 1970s. In the past, these old men might have appeared as "faithful retainers" who were prepared to "endure" as William Faulkner would have his "good Negroes" do. Gaines takes his eighteen old black males and makes them self-affirming men with a dignity and self-respect, however belated, that baffle Sheriff Mapes and other whites. These old men, along with their quarters families past and present, have known hurt and violence that was not of their making: through the voice of Joseph Seaberry (a.k.a. Rufe) we get a listing of some of the wrongs committed against black families in Marshall Quarters. These old men's recollections are a choral litany for the quarters; their voices merge as a kind of contemporary chorus recounting physical and psychological violence done them and their immediate families, as the list of wrongs they cite reverberates down the centuries. What they say of the present is essentially an echo of the past; its effects are a continuance of the institution of slavery—against which they finally take a stand.

Their stand, like the political struggle of the quarters since the nineteenth century in *Miss Jane Pittman*, is against the "creations" which Copper, in "Bloodline," says are Frank Laurent's and those of white men before him:

> . . . the chains and sticks. You created them four hundred years ago, and you're still using them up to this day. You created them. But they were only a fraction of your barbarity—Uncle. You used the rope and the tree to hang him. You used the knife to castrate him while he struggled with the rope to catch his breath. You used fire to make him squirm even more, because the hanging and the castration still wasn't enough amusement for you. Then you used something else—another creation of yours—that thing *you* called law. It was written by you for you and your kind, and any man who was not of your kind had to break it sooner or later. . . .

The old men's stand in *A Gathering of Old Men* is against the whites' violation of the land, which the blacks need for emotional and ancestral attachment as well as a source of survival. The field and the graveyard, for Grant Bello, evoke memories as private history and kinship. The field reminds him of his people who worked the land long before Beau Boutan and his clan began leasing it. The collective stand the black men take in *A Gathering of Old Men* is the response of a community under perpetual siege; it is the culmination of four hundred years of political struggle, part of whose beginnings Gaines captures in *The Autobiography of Miss Jane Pittman.*

Gaines's quarters community is a political entity which spends a great portion of its energy developing strategies its inhabitants hope will free them of oppression. Its members slowly acquire a leverage to force political change, and the concept of the quarters as a confined place to control black laborers gradually dies, but not without elderly black men —Mathu, Rufe, Cherry, Big Charlie and others—reclaiming their dignity. And as the Cajuns take more and more land, the quarters, in the words of Robert Hemenway, becomes

> more decrepit than ever: weed choked, weather beaten, mostly abandoned; the flowers once near the garry—four o'clocks and palms of christians—are now only a memory. Here Gaines's old men gather together in strange reunion, drawn to the quarters of their youth by the first killing of white by black in the history of St. Raphael Parish.

By the 1970s, Gaines's quarters community is—physically, socially, and politically—an entity almost dead.

VI

> Marshall Quarters was a narrow little country road, all white with dust, and weeds on both sides. The one or two old clapboard houses seem deserted, causing the place to look like a Western ghost town. All you needed was a couple of tumbleweeds to come bouncing down the road.
>
> —*A Gathering of Old Men*

As the central focus of Gaines's symbolic geography, the quarters proves to be "a plausible abode," to use Eudora Welty's words, for his rural black characters and, hence, the stage on which he has built a set to act out in fiction the "Louisiana thing that drives" him. Not only is the quarters a phenomenon in southern history; the quarters, as an actual community, constitutes a ready-made world for the fiction writer. At the beginning of his writing career, Gaines recognized the quarters as such, and he exploited its aesthetic possibilities by building a great portion of his fictional world upon it. He made the quarters the nucleus of his sense of place; for he realized that, as a center of meaning, the quarters has its own inhabitants and, therefore, its own history, its own cultural and political imperatives, its own social structure, its own world view. He knew too, that its very presence in his fiction would evoke in his readers certain emotional responses that would validate his characters as well as their world.

Historically, the world of the quarters and those similar to it are the crucible from which evolved the bases of Afro-American culture and life. The quarters, then, evokes, among other things, country blues of the kind Marcus in *Of Love and Dust* might have sung in order to stay the rage that is part of the struggle in which the community, from the period of slavery to the twentieth century, has been engaged. In fact, some blues lyrics of Lightnin' Hopkins and actual cases of black men on plantations murdering other blacks occasioned the writing of the novel *Of Love and Dust* (*Callaloo #3*). The quarters also evokes the tradition of storytelling (factual and fictional) that sustains the words of all Gaines's narrators, especially those of Miss Jane Pittman. These narrators record the political struggle of their communities: the individual and collective efforts to fight against the very oppressive forces that created and perpetuate the quarters. In all of Gaines's work, the quarters embody the historical circumstances through which the two Souths, Black and White, are wedded, and out of which Afro-American expressive culture has developed.

As a symbolic space, the quarters, in the hands of Ernest Gaines, takes on epic dimension; like William Faulkner's Yoknapatawpha, it is a microcosm in which humankind, undaunted in its Sisyphus-like struggle, wills to prevail. Through the quarters as a center of meaning, Gaines, on the one hand, explores facets of a particular southern experience which, on the other hand, becomes symbolic of modern human experience in its questions about the individual, the family, the community, and the past. Gaines's quarters and the rest of his St. Raphael Parish are also unlike Faulkner's north Mississippi county; Gaines's quarters, as I have pointed out, is not fixed geography with characters who appear in more than one narrative. Instead, Gaines's quarters, like the rest of his St. Raphael Parish, is a fluid concept which he shapes and reshapes as he creates each narrative. Together the narratives do not recount the doings of a single community; rather they record the spiritual, social, economic, political strivings of a people in the act of becoming. Although it is a dying physical entity in historical reality, the quarters in Gaines's fiction is a ritual ground of communion and community to which Gaines, the man and the artist, returns again and again for perception and sustenance.

ROBERT G. O'MEALLY

The Rules of Magic: Hemingway as Ellison's "Ancestor"

We get changes of identity, often symbolized—in strict obedi-
ence to the rules of magic—by the changing of one's name, as
the new synthetic character is felt to require a corresponding
verbal change; or there is a formal choice of "ancestors," as
one in meeting the exigencies of his *present*, proposes to coerce
the *future* by a quasi-mystical revising of the *past*.
                                                    —*Kenneth Burke*

... true jazz is an art of individual assertion within and against
the group. Each true jazz moment (as distinct from the un-
inspired commercial performance) springs from a contest in
which each artist challenges all the rest; each solo flight, or
improvisation, represents (like the successive canvases of a
painter) a definition of his identity: as individual, as member
of the collectivity and as a link in the chain of tradition.
                                                    —*Ralph Ellison*

THERE HAS BEEN MUCH ADO about Ralph Ellison's complex
debt to Richard Wright. Ellison himself shifts back and forth. Perhaps
he comes closest to explaining his own uneasiness in the face of any
simplistic formulation of his literary paternity when he reminds his
readers of his own father's untimely death and of his ambivalent feelings
about his stepfathers. When he met Wright the last thing Ellison wanted
was another father. But then again it's Ellison who calls the name of
father when invoking the images of certain favorite "ancestors," notably
William Faulkner and Ernest Hemingway. In some ways, the Faulkner
example is as easy to see as the Wright: in Ellison's fiction one hears a
voice as deeply southern as Faulkner's—a voice as rich and as quick with

164

exalted southern lies, told with conversational jam-session style as well as with poetic eloquence. In both writers, too, one finds the shared impulse for technical experimentation along with a shared vision of the human plight, and of man's capacity to overcome.

Yet it is Ernest Hemingway whom Ellison most emphatically chooses as his own, even pitting him against Wright. Why was Wright "family" and Hemingway a chosen "ancestor"? In 1964 Ellison wrote:

> Not because he [Hemingway] was white or "accepted." But because he appreciated the things of this earth which I love and which Wright was too driven or deprived or inexperienced to know: weather, guns, dogs, horses, love *and* hate and impossible circumstances which to the courageous and dedicated could be turned into benefits and victories. Because he wrote with such precision about the processes and techniques of daily living that I could keep myself and my brother alive during the 1937 Recession by following his descriptions of wing-shooting; because he knew the difference between politics and art and something of their true relationship for the writer. Because all that he wrote—and this is very important— was imbued with a spirit beyond the tragic with which I could feel at home, for it was very close to the feeling of the blues, which are, perhaps, as close as Americans can come to expressing the spirit of tragedy. . . . But most important, because Hemingway was a greater artist than Wright, who although a Negro like myself, and perhaps a great man, understood little if anything of these, at least to me, important things. Because Hemingway loved the American language and the joy of writing, making the flight of birds, the loping of lions across an African plain, the mysteries of drink and moonlight, the unique styles of diverse peoples and individuals come alive on the page. Because he was in many ways the true father-as-artist of so many of us who came to writing during the late thirties.

The essay from which this excerpt comes tries to refute the "segregated" idea that black artists must depend on other black artists as prime models and teachers. Ellison brings home his rhetorical point by preferring Hemingway, in whose work one finds no admirable Afro-American characters: instead one finds wisecracks about background "niggers" with flashing smiles. But Ellison's point is not "merely" rhetorical. His essays and fiction show that Ellison has changed his mind about Hemingway, and then changed it again. Throughout his career Ellison has played Hemingway riffs, somewhat like a jazz player improvising on blues chords—or playing with and then against a jam session "gladiator." Sometimes the Hemingway influence on Ellison is obvious, sometimes not. But for Ellison, Papa Hemingway never completely disappears.

In part to point out some of the ironies of segregation, Ellison says that as a youngster he read Hemingway while waiting his turn in Negro barbershops in Oklahoma City. Probably what he first saw were the feature stories and "letters" Hemingway wrote for *Esquire* during the thirties: dispatches from Europe, Africa and the West Indies concerning, for the most part, war, bullfights, hunting, boxing, fishing and, inevitably, the struggle to create good art. But by 1933, when Ellison left Oklahoma to study music at Tuskegee, Hemingway also had published his greatest stories and novels as well as *Death in the Afternoon*. In Hemingway's writing, Ellison would easily recognize the frontierlike Michigan, not so unlike the territory just beyond the limits of Oklahoma City. Both places had Indians, vast open spaces and good areas to fish and hunt. And like Hemingway, Ellison played high school football; he could readily identify with the undefeated sportsmen of *Men Without Women* (1927) and *Winner Take Nothing* (1933).

In the beginning, Ellison, a fledgling trumpet player, was claimed by the music of Hemingway's sentences. When the literal meaning escaped him, Ellison could get a sense of what Hemingway was up to by the sheer pitch and rhythm of his writing. And later he related Hemingway's understated but allusive style to jazz:

> Jazz was eclectic . . . at its best. . . . It made the whole world of music, of sound, its own. And it took what it needed from those areas. You hear references to opera, to church music, to anything, in something by Louis Armstrong or any other jazz man of the thirties, forties, or fifties. So this acquaintance with jazz made me quite aware that allusions to ideas and to other works of art were always turning up in Hemingway.

Ellison found that Hemingway's style, especially "the what-was-not-stated in the understatement, required study." Like the blues, Hemingway's style implied a great deal more than was expressed outright.

In Hemingway's fiction what was implied was a heroic attitude toward life's troubles and changes, a resiliency and steadfastness. He would not spell it out, but Hemingway could make his reader feel "that some great crisis of courage had occurred and just was not said," notes Ellison, "and I related this to jazz." In 1945, Ellison wrote of the blues: "Their attraction lies in this, that they at once express both the agony of life and the possibility of conquering it through sheer toughness of spirit. They fall short of tragedy only in that they provide no scapegoat but the self." In this spirit, Hemingway's heroes endure with stoicism so much unmeaning agony and terror that Albert Murray calls Hemingway not just a blues-writer but "an honorary Negro," a title Hemingway once chose for himself. Indeed, what Ellison has written about the blues is also true of certain heroes in Hemingway: "The blues voice . . . mocks the despair stated explicitly in its lyric, and it expresses the great human joke directed against the universe, that joke which is the secret of all folklore and myth: that though we be dismembered daily we shall always rise up again." Ellison describes Jake Barnes, the wounded survivor and narrator of *The Sun Also Rises* (a novel Murray says could just as well be called "Jake's Empty Bed Blues," "Blues for Lady Brett," or even "Rocks in My Bed"), in terms that express an extreme version of the blues-hero's plight and challenge: "Ball-less, humiliated, malicious, even masochistic, he still has a steady eye upon it all and has the most eloquent ability to convey the texture of his experience."

In the late thirties, Ellison continued to choose Hemingway as a model. Hemingway was simply a "greater writer than the participants in the Negro Renaissance," said Ellison in 1967. Hemingway had spotted the "so-called 'Jazz Age' [as] a phony, while most Negro writers jumped on that illusory bandwagon when they, of all people, should have known better." Ellison perceived the Hemingway hero's feeling of being at odds with American society to be quite similar to the feeling of blacks and the influence of Carl Van Vechten's fictionalized Negroes to be moribund. The Hemingway heroes held "an attitude springing from an awareness that they lived outside the values of the larger society, and *I* feel that their attitudes came closer to the way Negroes felt about the way the Constitution and the Bill of Rights were applied to us." In this context Hemingway again evokes for Ellison the world of jazz:

> I believe that Hemingway in depicting the attitudes of athletes, expatriates, bullfighters, traumatized soldiers, and impotent idealists, told us quite a lot about what was happening to that most representative group of Negro Americans, the jazz musicians—who also lived by an extreme code of withdrawal, technical and artistic excellence, rejection of the values of respectable society. They replaced the abstract and much betrayed ideals of that society with the more physical values of eating, copulating, loyalty to friends, and dedication to the discipline and values of their art.

In the sixties Ellison was quoted as overstating the case by saying that Hemingway "tells us more about how Negroes feel than all the writings done by those people mixed up in the Negro Renaissance."

In the mid-thirties, when he first put his trumpet aside and began writing "in earnest," he chose Hemingway (along with Wright) as a principal guide. He went about the task of learning to write with Hemingway-like intensity and singleness of purpose, and refused for a time even to attend musical performances for fear of being sidetracked. In 1937, Ellison started trying to learn Hemingway's sentence structure and his means of organizing a story. Like a young musician practicing *études* (or like an apprentice photographer learning to compose a picture by looking at a master's photographs through a camera lens), Ellison would copy certain Hemingway stories in longhand: "in an effort to study their rhythms, so as not just to know them but to possess them."

In his work on the Federal Writers Project (1936–1939), Ellison would listen to his Harlem informants' talk and "very often," he recalls, "I was able to get it on paper by using a kind of Hemingway typography, by using the repetitions. I couldn't quite get the tone of the sounds in, but I could get some of the patterns and get an idea of what it was like." Thus he could avoid "falling into the transcription of dialect," which he had found unsatisfactory in Wright's fiction. Quite unlike Wright, who, in a typical piece of dialogue in *Uncle Tom's Children* (1938) has Aunt Sue say, "Ahma old woman n Ah wants yuh t tell me the truth," Project Worker Ellison records the words of a Harlem yarn spinner in this way:

> I hope to God to kill me if this aint the truth. All you got to do is to go down to Florence, South Carolina and ask most anybody you meet and they'll tell you it's the truth . . .
>
> It was this way: Sweet could make hisself invisible. You don't believe it? Well here's how he done it. Sweet-the-monkey cut open a black cat and took out its heart. Climbed a tree backwards and cursed God. After that he could do anything. The white folks would wake up in the morning and find their stuff gone. He cleaned out the stores. He cleaned up the houses. Hell, he even cleaned out the dam bank! He was the boldest *black* sonofabitch ever been down that way. And couldn't nobody do nothing to him. . . .

Here Ellison was practicing how to capture the sounds of vernacular without distracting the reader with misspellings and apostrophes.

Impressed by the Oklahoman's ability to talk about Hemingway,

Wright invited Ellison to contribute to *New Challenge* magazine in 1937. Ellison's first review, which pinpointed the need for "greater development in technique," and his short story, "Heine's Bull" (which did not appear because the magazine folded), were both stamped in the Hemingway mold. And in a feature story entitled "A Congress Jim Crow Didn't Attend" (1939), Ellison's report for *New Masses* on the National Negro Congress, one overhears Hemingway's cadences and deadpan tone in the face of dramatic action which is deliberately detailed. Ellison writes:

> Outside of Baltimore we began passing troups of cavalry. They were stretched along the highway for a mile. Young fellows in khaki with campaign hats strapped beneath their chins, jogging stiffly in their saddles. I asked one of my companions where they were going and was told that there was an army camp near by. Someone said that I would find out "soon enough" and I laughed and said I was a black Yank and was not coming.

Later in the same piece, Ellison describes the conference hall in Hemingway terms:

> The auditorium had that overwhelming air usually associated with huge churches, and I remembered what André Malraux once said about the factory becoming for the workers what the cathedral was, and that they must come to see in it not ideal gods, but human power struggling against the earth.

In 1932 Hemingway wrote: "If a writer of prose knows enough about what he is writing about he may omit things that he knows and the reader if the writer is writing truly enough, will have a feeling of those things as strongly as though the writer had stated them." Hemingway's understatement intrigued Ellison, but he had serious doubts that it was a style he wanted to adopt wholesale. In his 1940 review for *New Masses* of Langston Hughes's first autobiography, *The Big Sea*, Ellison makes not just political but artistic objections to Hughes's understatement:

> In the style of *The Big Sea* too much attention is apt to be given to the esthetic aspects of experience at the expense of its deeper meanings. Nor—this being a world in which few assumptions may be taken for granted—can the writer who depends upon understate-

ment to convey these meanings be certain that they do not escape the reader. To be effective the Negro writer must be explicit; thus realistic; thus dramatic.

But in 1940 Ellison declared that although the "hardboiled" Hemingway style was successful for conveying American violence ("a quality as common to Negro life as to the lives of Hemingway characters"), it nonetheless had a "negative philosophical basis." Even after he had begun *Invisible Man*, Ellison's dissatisfaction with Hemingway seemed to center on the unstated or understated elements of Hemingway's prose. In the mid-forties Ellison expressed concern about the fact that no fully drawn blacks appeared in Hemingway's work; how did he feel then about black freedom, and about the black American's tragic quest for equality? Ellison had begun to feel that the concern for the Negro and for the values which his presence connoted in American fiction were not just *unspoken* by Hemingway; they were *nonexistent*. "It is not accidental," wrote Ellison in 1946, "that the disappearance of the human Negro from our fiction coincides with the disappearance of deep-probing doubt and a sense of evil." Perhaps Hemingway was not so much the spokesman for the 1920s Lost Generation as he was "a product of a tradition which arose even before the Civil War—that tradition of intellectual evasion for which Thoreau criticized Emerson in regard to the Fugitive Slave Law and which has been growing swiftly since the failure of the ideals in whose name the Civil War was fought." Rather than probing "the roots of American culture," Hemingway "restricted himself to elaborating his personal style." This narrow naturalist explored neither society nor morality, but instead indulged in "working out a personal problem through the evocative, emotion-charged images and ritual-therapy available through the manipulation of art forms." If freedom was still at issue, it was solely *personal* freedom; and if the writing involved rituals, they were cynical rituals of defeat. "Beneath the deadpan prose," wrote Ellison in 1946, "the cadences of understatement, the anti-intellectualism [lies] the concern with every 'fundamental' of man except that which distinguishes him from the animal." This writing, like the literary stereotype, conditions the reader to complacent inaction, said Ellison. "And when I read the early Hemingway," wrote Ellison, "I seem to be in the presence of a Huckleberry Finn who ... chose to write the letter which sent Jim back into slavery."

Ellison's own fiction since 1944 shows that he has remained dissatisfied with understatement in his own writing. In addition to its other problems, the clipped phrases of understatement do not compare with "the rich babel of idiomatic expression" which he heard in New York, and which he had known in the South. Robert Penn Warren has written that Hemingway's "short, simple rhythms, the succession of coordinate clauses, the general lack of subordination—all suggest a dislocated and ununified world. The figures who live in this world live a sort of hand-to-mouth existence perceptually, and conceptually. Subordination implies some exercise of discrimination—the sifting of reality through the intellect. But in Hemingway we see a Romantic anti-intellectualism."

The author of *Invisible Man* sifts through reality in sentences which, in their driving complexity, often echo Faulkner or Wright more than they do Hemingway. The reality Ellison wished to project in fiction was so "mysterious and uncertain and . . . exciting," he said, that it would "burst . . . the neatly understated forms of the novel asunder." In 1955, Ellison told a symposium of writers that his former mentor's laconic characters may have expressed the disillusionment of the postwar era, but when the depression hit and "reality was ripping along," Hemingway's images no longer were adequate as a guide for confronting experience. Hemingway had produced fiction that was ultimately too provincial to escape its particular setting and time. Yet in the same discussion Ellison said that Hemingway "links up pretty close to Twain."

This linkage with Twain, which, for Ellison, spells adherence to the American novel's greatest themes and most characteristic forms—this sense of belonging to the national literary canon joining nineteenth-century prose masters to contemporary stylists—is the theme of most of Ellison's literary essays after 1950. Ellison had begun again to change his mind about what was implied "beneath the dead-pan cadences" of Hemingway's prose. He was now back squarely in Hemingway's corner. "Neither the American fiction of the twenties nor of the fifties," wrote Ellison, "can be understood outside the perspective provided by the nineteenth century" (1957). For it was in the nineteenth century that Emerson, Thoreau, Whitman, Melville, Twain, James and Crane wrote explicitly about American democracy and the lingering problem of freedom and unfreedom as it centered on the man beneath the social hierarchy, the Negro. With the great nineteenth-century themes in mind, Ellison now read *A Farewell To Arms* as an ironic comment upon, and ultimately an affirmation of, the "sacred assumptions" of American life:

> For as I read Hemingway today [1957] I find that he affirms the old American values by the eloquence of his denial; makes his moral point by stating explicitly that he does not believe in morality;

achieves his eloquence through denying eloquence; and is most moral when he denies the validity of a national morality which the nation has not bothered to live up to since the Civil War.

The confusion about Hemingway's motives—about what went unsaid in his fiction—stemmed not from Hemingway's failure, but from that of his readers and his less skilled and less moral imitators. "For although it is seldom mentioned," wrote Ellison, "Hemingway is as obsessed with the Civil War and its aftermath as any Southern writer." When Hemingway's Nick or Jake took to the woods for a round of fishing or hunting (or when Frederic declared his separate peace), they turned their backs on a society whose ideals had become so tarnished that they preferred to set up frontier outposts (like Huck's and Jim's raft) where the values of freedom and friendship could be upheld, if only in a small space and time.

Ellison's new view of Hemingway's content was linked with a changed view of his style. What in the forties Ellison had begun to put down as Hemingway's decadent "morality of craftsmanship," he now described as Hemingway's fineness of technique. But the writer's technique itself, said Ellison in 1957, has moral implications. Even when "the question of the Sphinx was lost in the conundrums" of perfectly turned phrases, the Hemingway-inspired emphasis on the value of technique reminded readers that "literature, to the extent that it is art, is *artificial*." This reminder that literature is man-made is a moral reminder insofar as it helps the reader recall that language can be seductive, therapeutic, even magical. But it can express falsehood as well as truth. This is a warning for all readers to be on their guard as critics, aware that the most alluring fictions are skillful acts of word-magic, brightly inviting castles of language.

By the sixties and seventies, Ellison would extend this metaphor of "morality of craftsmanship." Now an encomium, "craft under the pressure of inspiration" is the writer's essential formula:

It's one thing to have a feeling, an insight, to hear in your mind's ear a rhythm, or to conceive an image. It is the *craft*, the knowledge of what other people have done, of what has been achieved by those great creators of the novel which gives you some idea of the possibility of that image, that nuance, that rhythm, that dramatic situation. It's not dry technique or craft that I'm talking about; it's craft which makes it possible for you to be more or less conscious of what you are doing and of the tools that you have to work with.

Repeatedly, Ellison uses the example of the physician to discuss the writer's responsibility. A doctor misdiagnosed his own mother's illness and caused her untimely death. A surgeon's slip killed Bennie Moten, then at the top of his career as a jazz bandleader, and his fans wanted to lynch his careless doctor. Writers, in Ellison's view, also have lives in their hands and thus bear a social (at times Ellison used the word *sacred*) responsibility to know what they are doing. In 1942, Hemingway had compared the writer's calling to that of the priest:

> . . . a writer should be of as great probity and honesty as a priest of God. . . . A writer's job is to tell the truth. His standard of fidelity to the truth should be so high that his invention, out of his experience, should produce a truer account than anything factual can be. For facts can be observed badly; but when a good writer is creating something, he has time and scope to make of it an absolute truth.

Ellison elaborates on this insight, observing that not only must the moral writer always do the best work he can, but when "you [writers] describe a more viable and ethical way of living and denounce the world or a great part of society for the way it conducts its affairs and then write in a sloppy way or present issues in a simplistic or banal way, then you're being amoral as an artist." Since writers provide "disastrously explicit" images which influence readers in their search for the meanings of their lives, then false images, or images faultily projected by inadequate craft, can cause confusion, dismay, and even death.

The writer's task, Ellison has said, is to do nothing less than to help create reality. "While fiction is but a form of symbolic action," he wrote in 1981, "a mere game of 'as if,' therein lies its true function and its potential for effecting change. For at its most serious . . . it is thrust toward a human ideal. And it approaches that ideal by a subtle process of negating the world of things as given in favor of a complex of man-made positives." Isn't that just wishful thinking, though? Aren't you "expressing your own hopes and aspirations for Negroes, rather than reporting historical reality?" he was asked in an interview in 1967. "But hope and aspiration are indeed important aspects of the reality of Negro American life, no less than that of others," he replied. "Literature teaches us that mankind has always defined itself *against* the negatives thrown it by society and the universe. . . . Let's not forget that the great tragedies not only treat of negative matters, of violence, brutalities, defeats, but they treat them within a context of man's will to act, to challenge reality and to snatch triumph from the teeth of destruction." The writer imbued with the proper sense of his craft's "sacredness" knows that his job is to provide readers with strategies for confronting the chaos of the contemporary world or, in Kenneth Burke's phrase often quoted by Ellison, to provide the reader with necessary "equipment for living."

Which brings us to *Invisible Man*—Ellison's most comprehensive piece of "equipment for living." How does Hemingway figure there? Invisible Man, like most of the heroes of Ellison's short stories, is an intelligent and sensitive youngster, a brownskin cousin of Nick Adams, straining toward manhood in a world full of the blues. And certain of *Invisible Man*'s controlling metaphors mirror the images and actions in Hemingway's work: metaphors of life as a war, a game or a fight (or a prizefight, or even a bullfight)—life as an encounter between the individual and the forces set against him. Like the old waiter of "A Clean, Well-lighted Place," Invisible has been through a lot, and needs plenty of light (in the case of Ellison's character, 1,369 filament bulbs) to feel secure in the threatening world. Furthermore, *Invisible Man* itself comprises a classic defense of art that brings to mind Hemingway's descriptions of fighters, sportsmen and writers as artists who assert their values and skills against encroachments by fakers, fools and unfeeling power-brokers, and sometimes by killers. Invisible Man, like Hemingway's apprentice heroes, learns at last to confront his experience directly, and he earns the perspective that it takes to do what Jake Barnes can do—to tell his troubling tale with the force and eloquence of an artist. Ellison informs his reader that almost as soon as he first heard, in his mind's ear, the words "I am an invisible man," the voice sounded "with a familiar timbre of voice": unmistakably black American, ringing with blues-toned irony. *The Sun Also Rises* makes us wonder how Jake achieves his ironic voice, his truce with his grim reality, and this novel traces Invisible Man's achievement of a voice with which to overcome the trouble he has seen.

In one of the novel's key passages, Invisible Man hears his grandfather's deathbed words, spoken to Invisible's father:

> "Son" [the old man said], "after I'm gone I want you to keep up the good fight. I never told you, but our life is a war and I have been a traitor all my born days, a spy in the enemy's country ever since I give up my gun back in the Reconstruction. Live with your head in the lion's mouth. I want you to overcome 'em with grins, agree 'em to death and destruction, let 'em swoller you till they vomit or bust wide open. . . . Learn it to the younguns," he whispered fiercely; then he died.

To unlock the full meaning of these magic words, the puzzled grandson must journey through hundreds of pages of hard and contradictory living. What he finally discovers is that life *is* a war, and it is a war wherein to be a good soldier, snapping to attention and obeying all orders, is to work against one's people and oneself. In this cosmic war the first step toward victory involves more than learning the techniques of warfare; it involves getting oriented by realizing that things "ain't what they used to be," and that they are not even what they seem now. It involves having a mature perspective on oneself, on one's ideals and on one's enemies, in whose very camp one must dwell. In short, the key is to become *conscious* in a profound sense: resigned like a bluesman to a life of war.

The war the grandfather refers to in his dying speech is linked with the American Civil War. He tells his son to "learn it to the younguns," the grandchildren a generation removed from the War Between the States. The point is that the Civil War continues in America. The issues of property versus human rights; individual, state and section autonomy versus the power of the union; and a sheaf of other American political and economic issues centering on the abiding problem of Negro freedom—remain unresolved. American life is a civil war in which the black man (and everyone) must fight, over and over again, to be free. Part of becoming conscious involves seeing, as Invisible eventually does, that his problem is not unique: "it goes a long way back, some twenty years." And it goes back still further, to the Civil War and especially to Reconstruction, when many Americans tried, in vain, to face the tragic challenges of living in a democracy. "The writer is forged in injustice as a sword is forged," wrote Hemingway. And a war, especially a civil war, can make or break a writer, he said. His own code heroes are often soldiers at war who must test themselves not just in theory but in the real world of intense, dangerous action. The Civil War in the background of *Invisible Man* (surfacing especially in allusions to Douglass and to other nineteenth-century figures and erupting in the riot at the novel's climax) helps to forge Invisible's consciousness as a man of eloquence who is able "to make a judgment about our culture."

Conditioning by the mass media blinds today's readers to the extraordinary violence of *Invisible Man*, so violent that Ellison wondered if antiviolence commentators would snipe at the book. Fights occur in scene after scene—hand-to-hand battles which rehearse the background struggle of the continuing Civil War. Invisible's fight with the "blind" white man in the Prologue, the yokel's fight with the prizefighter of scientific method, the battle royal free-for-all, the Golden Day fisticuffs, Invisible against Lucius Brockway, Tod and Invisible versus Ras, and Tod versus the cops are just some of the novel's main fights. Several allusions are made to the Johnson and Jeffries fight—that symbolic encounter between the races. At one point Bledsoe promises to help Invisible because the young man shows ire and "the race needs smart, disillusioned fighters."

> "Therefore [Bledsoe goes on] I'm going to give you a hand—maybe you'll feel that I'm giving you my left hand after I've struck you with my right—if you think I'm the kind of man who'd lead with his right, which I'm most certainly not."

Up North, the Brotherhood meetings were generally as noisy and smoky as smokers or prizefights, the reader is told; in fact, Invisible's first speech is made in the very auditorium where, significantly enough, a popular fighter had lost his vision in the ring. Each of these physical fights, brawls and prizefights, has its own symbolic meanings in context. But one can say that in the world of *Invisible Man* the struggle for meaning and endurance is not only metaphysical but *physical*. The would-be hero must put his own body on the line, and only if he has the resiliency, the strength and the technical skill can he avoid a whipping—or, if he cannot avoid a whipping, he can at least know what it's for. Lacking science and quickness, the Prologue yokel prevails through sheer strength and inspired timing:

> The fighter was swift and amazingly scientific. His body was one violent flow of rapid rhythmic action. He hit the yokel a hundred times while the yokel held up his arms in stunned surprise. But suddenly the yokel, rolling about in a gale of boxing gloves, struck one blow and knocked science, speed and footwork as cold as a well-digger's posterior. The smart money hit the canvas. The long shot got the nod. The yokel had simply stepped inside of his opponent's sense of time.

The Invisible Man, the comic yokel for most of the novel, is battered by swift and scientific battlers in scene after scene. In time, of course, he learns he must have science *and* power—and an alert sense of what time it is; he must be both *hare* and *bear*. Either way, of course, life will give him a thrashing.

What he learns too is the Hemingway lesson: that he is caught up in a violent game which attains a certain grace when played well. The banished Golden Day inmate (one of the crazy war veterans) gives some advice on how life's game is played:

". . . For God's sake, learn to look beneath the surface," he said. "Come out of the fog, young man. And remember you don't have to be a complete fool in order to succeed. Play the game, but don't believe in it—that much you owe yourself. Even if it lands you in a strait jacket or a padded cell. Play the game, but play it your own way—part of the time at least. Play the game, but raise the ante, my boy. Learn how it operates, learn how you operate. . . . You might even beat the game. . . . Down here they've forgotten to take care of the books and that's your opportunity . . ."

Here Ellison defines the "they" against which Invisible's most strenuous fight must be waged: "They?" says the vet. "Why the same *they* we always mean, the white folks, authority, the gods, fate, circumstances—the force that pulls your strings until you refuse to be pulled any more. The big man who's never there, where you think he is." To an extent it is the *"nada y pues nada"* that Hemingway's heroes struggle against; the sense of dissolution and meaninglessness and the excruciating pain threatening the prizefighter Jack in Hemingway's "Fifty Grand," the ever-ready opponent that threatens to sock you blind. Then, too, more than for Hemingway, Ellison's "big man who's never there" is Clio; he is *History*.

Ellison's "they" is nonetheless comparable to the bull which Hemingway's matadors must confront, and which, in the symbolic language of *Invisible Man*, the "youngun" from the South must learn to bring down. For Hemingway the bullfight is not so much game (or fair contest between equals) as it is tragedy and ritual in which the bull, that embodiment of power and aggression, meets "death in the afternoon." And it is art. Indeed, Hemingway claims to "know no modern sculpture, except Brancusi's, that is in any way the equal of the sculpture of modern bullfighting." Furthermore, "it is impossible to believe the emotional and spiritual intensity and pure, classic beauty that can be produced by a man, an animal and a piece of scarlet serge draped over a stick."

Bulls and bullfighting turn up in *Invisible Man*. Metaphors that bring to mind the tragedy of the bull, as Hemingway glosses it, are, in fact, central to the novel's meanings. "Bledsoed" from the college campus, Invisible recalls the place in terms that included "the big seed bull":

Did its bellow still awaken the coeds on spring mornings? Of course our man could not comprehend the irony of his rosy recollection of "the big seed bull" bellowing in the wasteland. Nor could he connect his vision of bull and "hard dry crust" of a campus with the world of *The Sun Also Rises* where the wastelanders wander aimlessly from scene to scene, unregenerated by the ceremony at the novel's heart, the fiesta of the bull.

Certain characters in *Invisible Man* resemble bulls. Ras fights Tod "like a drunken bull." The "short, heavy figure" "butts" and "bulls" his opponent, and pulls his blade "panting, bull angry." And Jack reminds Invisible of a dog named Master who "barked the same low note when angry or when being brought his dinner, when lazily snapping flies, or when tearing an intruder to shreds." Note that this fellow with the telling name (one which Invisible would apply to "Marse Jack" later in the novel) is a *bull*dog. Like him, Jack is unpredictable and violent. And like Ras he is Invisible's antagonist with the bull-like power to turn and kill. Jack is not only some sort of a bull of a dog, he is one-eyed—and Hemingway specifies that one-eyed bulls are too wildly violent to be fair opponents even for the best of matadors. Still, Invisible's task in each case is to learn how to confront the tough killer with style and effectiveness enough to bring him down.

The Hemingway-style metaphors reach a crescendo in *Invisible Man* when Jack takes Invisible to a place in Spanish Harlem "where the neon-lighted sign of a bull's head announced the El Toro Bar." Suddenly Invisible finds himself in a bar from the world of Hemingway. But this is not quite a "clean, well-lighted place" or a muffled "Killers" lunchroom; Ellison fills the room with loaded talk and symbols—even the music is significantly titled. Four beer drinkers argued here in Spanish while "a juke box, lit up green and red, played 'Media Luz.'" As Invisible wonders about the purpose of Jack's bringing him to El Toro, he considers the picture behind the bar. Invisible thinks:

> Before me, in the panel where a mirror is usually placed, I could see a scene from a bullfight, a bull charging close to the man and the man swinging a red cape in sculptured folds so close to his body that man and bull seemed to blend in one swirl of calm, pure motion. Pure grace, I thought, looking above the bar to where, larger than life, the pink and white image of a girl smiled down from a summery beer ad on which a calendar said April One. . . .
>
> "Here, come back," he said, nudging me playfully. "She's only a cardboard image of a cold steel civilization."

I laughed, glad to hear him joking. "And that?" I said pointing to the bullfight scene.

"Sheer barbarism," he said, watching the bartender and lowering his voice to a whisper.

A moment later, as Jack and Invisible discuss the ideological training session, Invisible sees another bullfight scene further down the bar. In this one "the matador was being swept skyward on the black bull's horns."

"The aficionado, or lover of the bullfight," writes Hemingway, "has this sense of the tragedy and ritual of the fight so that the minor aspects are not important except as they relate to the whole. Either you have this or you have not, just as, without implying any comparison, you have or have not an ear for music." Invisible is by no means an *aficionado*. But his instincts seem right. He sees the sculptural beauty of the work of the matador close to the bull—so close they "seemed to blend in one swirl of calm, pure motion." And he uses one of Hemingway's key words, "grace," to describe the climaxed moment of artistic perfection, the moment which Hemingway has said brings spiritual and emotional "ecstasy," and when man's immortality seems, for an instant, achieved. If these flashes of insight place Invisible on the side of tragic ritual and art, his sighting without comment of the other image, that of the upended matador, shows he still has more naiveté than *afición*. Presumably he doesn't know what to make of this other side of the bullfighter's art. Hemingway tells us that all bullfighters get gored—it is part of their initiation as seasoned fighters; how one comes back from the injury (tempered and tested or defensive and cowardly) determines one's true mettle as a matador. Seeing the goring scene as a *separate* frame—not part of the continuum in the life of a bullfighter—marks Invisible as a novice: he praises one aspect of the scene but does not see that aspect in relation to the whole bullfight. Nor does he see that this Hemingway bar, with its coded messages against the wall ("where a mirror is usually placed"), is another warning to him. Art and grace are achievable, yes, but there is no way to avoid the slashing test of the horns.

Another twist is that One-Eyed Bull Jack, utterly blind to the art and ritual of the bullfight, terms it "sheer barbarism." He's more perceptive in interpreting the picture of the white girl on the beer ad as "a cardboard image of a cold steel civilization." In fact, his suddenly cleared mood ("as though in an instant he had settled whatever had been bothering him and felt suddenly free") and his laughter suggest that he perceives in the scene a joke richer than Invisible Man does, a joke reflected by the juxtaposition of the images and the April Fool's Day calendar. In this setting of the El Toro, Jack names Invisible chief spokesman of the Harlem district. And, as the reader finds out at the novel's end, he's about to set up the Invisible Man as a betrayer of his people, as a chief sacrificial victim, number one dupe. In a sense, this bull is trying to turn the tables on the would-be matador, making him a comic butt for the bull's secret horns. As the hero discovers, it's a "comic strip world" he's been put in, and Jack, faintly smiling and blind though he may be to tragedy and rituals, manipulates Invisible, using lures, fakery and force. It's a world where Jack seems to turn gracefully with Invisible one moment but shifts as quickly as a bull to "sweep him skyward" in the next.

"Western culture," wrote Ellison about the challenge of Wright's Black Boy, "must be won, confronted like the animal in a Spanish bull-fight, dominated by the red shawl of codified experience and brought heaving to its knees." This confrontation with all of Western culture comprises Invisible's great challenge; and it is directly connected to his quest for identity. He fights off a series of imposed misconceptions of what he has been, and thus of who he is. In so doing he rejects not only misstatements of the "facts of the case," but of theoretical schemes in which the facts assume meaning. While theories of "history" abound in *Invisible Man*, Jack and the Brotherhood present the most complete and seductive idea of the way the world turns—the idea whose rejection by Invisible paves the way for his own freedom. "Beware of those who speak of the *spiral* of history," Invisible finally learns. "They are preparing a boomerang. Keep a steel helmet handy. I have been boomeranged across my head so much that I now can see the darkness of lightness." History repeats, he affirms, but not in a neat geometric circle, and if history moves forward or upward, the meaning of the sweep is nonetheless contradictory. "Contradiction," says Invisible, "that . . . is how the world moves: Not like an arrow, but a boomerang." Symbolically, Invisible Man duels not just with Jack (or the others that try to bull and bully him); in a profound sense he also must confront and master history.

Invisible sees, for example, that while the Brotherhood has written off Tod as a sellout and a traitor, he can assert his own version of Tod's life and death: his own sense of Tod's history. "All right," Invisible thinks, "so we'll use his funeral to put his integrity back together." The funeral oration (not just Invisible's words themselves but "the pattern of my voice upon the air") along with the spontaneous outburst of

"Many Thousand Gone" assert that Tod's death was not a meaningless loss but a tragic one. "Such," says Invisible Man, echoing Hemingway, "was the short bitter life of Brother Tod Clifton."

With this lesson of Tod and then of Rinehart in mind, Invisible sees the Brotherhood historians writing a history that ignored the real experiences of blacks, among others. Not taking into account the essential ambiguity (the Rinehartness) of experience—that, for instance, the ones lowest down in the social hierarchy might be snide tricksters or even "the bearers of something precious"—Brotherhood's formulas were too spare and simple for Harlem. Nor did they take into account that even painful experiences can be interpreted in a positive light: "And now," Invisible finally sees, "all past humiliations became precious parts of my experience, and for the first time, leaning against that stone wall in the sweltering night, I began to accept my past and, as I accepted it, I felt memories welling up in me. It was as though I'd learned suddenly to see around corners."

"To see around corners," says Kenneth Burke, "is to gain perspective on one's self and one's situation, to grasp enough of the true pattern of events to have a handle on the future." Incongruous as it seems, Invisible Man sees the truth of his predicament only when he sees that, "highly visible" as he is, he is *unseen* by the official historians—if he is seen at all by anyone. Hence the ironic laughter in his first report to Ellison: "I am an invisible man." Much "boomeranging" of his expectations taught him the comic nature of things; his laughter is earned by his encounters with bull-necked experience.

At the novel's end, the hero also has earned the heroic title, even if he is more a comic than a tragic hero. In his memoirs he looks back on his experience and sees it in ritual terms which recall the rites of initiation, purification and rebirth one encounters in *The Sun Also Rises*, *Men Without Women*, *In Our Time* and Hemingway's essays about hunting and bullfighting. Like many Hemingway characters, Invisible is transformed by witnessing and suffering great violence and caprice. Like the audience at a good bullfight (as reported by Hemingway), readers of *Invisible Man* feel "changed" by Invisible's dances with death. Like a Hemingway bullfighter, Invisible has come close to the bull's horns, he has been upended; and despite his scars, he has come back battling. The novel itself is his act of supreme "grace under pressure," the ultimate Hemingway laurel. By the Epilogue he has confronted his tormentors, figured out the magic words and symbols (his grandfather's and those in his suitcase) and he has endured the wounds of his tragic knowledge. Finally he is freed of his illusions—freed of his imposed names and the imposed schemes of how the world moves. In time, he has stared down fake versions of history. Having learned that history is no more than a fiction, a "lie," he pieces together his own history, his own "exalted lie."

To Ellison, Hemingway was a guide and a "father-as-artist" in part because he was a worthy sparring partner, a "cooperative antagonist." (Like Hemingway, Ellison has said that he must go toe to toe with the best writers of his time and—to keep the stakes high—with the best writers of all time.) But Ellison also chose Hemingway as his true "ancestor" because he insisted on telling his "lies" as he himself saw them, despite all precedents and influences, political and otherwise, to tell them any other way. Over and over again his heroes make their forthright stands as artists whose integrity and talent and craft were all they either had or needed to clear a place where they could feel at home in an embattled world. One of his most gifted sons, Ellison, creates in *Invisible Man* a novel as distinct from the Dreiser-Howells-Wright naturalists' and realists' work as is *The Sun Also Rises*. In Ellison's book, signs and symbols are presented and meditated upon, but they are never explained away, as Wright's images sometimes are. In this sense Ellison "understates" his case, *à la* Hemingway; the metaphor of invisibility, for instance, retains its rich mystery. But more like Wright and Faulkner than like Hemingway he is also careful not to be misunderstood, and adds his essay-like Epilogue to drive his fictional point home. Invisible Man is not a laconic Hemingway tough guy; he is a talker who says his piece in language more extroverted and southern than Hemingway's characters use. Ellison, in other words, took what he needed from Hemingway without merely copying his style. Still Invisible Man, much more like Hemingway's Jake and Nick than like Bigger Thomas, takes on the world, body and soul. And at the novel's end, he only wants to last, as Hemingway put it, and to get his work done: to tell his story truer than the facts.

ANTHONY BARTHELEMY

Mother, Sister, Wife:
A Dramatic Perspective

> I would like very much to live in a world where some of the
> more monumental problems would at least be solved; I'm
> thinking, of course, of peace. That is, we don't fight. Nobody
> fights. We get rid of all the little bombs—and the big bombs.
> —Lorraine Hansberry,
> *To Be Young, Gifted and Black*

PERHAPS NO SINGLE WORK by a black American playwright
has reached so vast an audience as Lorraine Hansberry's *A Raisin in the
Sun.* A success on Broadway in 1959, the play enjoys frequent revivals
by professional and amateur theater groups alike. It remains in print
twenty-five years later, and the 1960 movie version appears regularly on
our televisions. Unknown to this immense audience is the fact that *A
Raisin in the Sun* responds to an earlier play by black playwright Theo-
dore Ward and constitutes the middle third of a larger literary debate—
a debate that began in 1938 when Ward's play *Big White Fog* opened
in Chicago under the auspices of the Federal Theater Project. Playwright Joseph Walker contributed the final third in 1973 when he wrote
his Obie winning play *The River Niger.* As the first of the three, Ward's
play is innocent of any attempts "to correct" or to displace a precursor
text. *Big White Fog* quite simply dramatizes the story of a long-suffering
black family from Chicago's Southside during the ten years between
1922 and 1932. Hansberry in *A Raisin in the Sun* seeks to correct Ward's
representation of black women and to place black political aspirations
firmly within the traditional American bourgeois context by counter-
ing the revolutionary Marxist politics of *Big White Fog.* Although *The
River Niger* equivocally endorses/condemns sixties militancy, Walker

really sets for himself a conservative, traditionally male political and social agenda. Stated quite simply, *The River Niger* valorizes male dominance and female submission. Together the three plays provide an interesting study of the influence black playwrights have on each other and reveal the power that dramatic representation possesses. The plays also demonstrate the influence of a playwright's personal political agenda in shaping character and theme.

The central male character of *Big White Fog*, Victor Mason, holds a college degree, but because he is black he can only find work as a laborer. He places his hopes for the future in Garveyism, and throughout the play, even after serious reversals, Victor maintains the dignity and race pride symbolized by his dedication to the United Negro Improvement Association and its causes. However, not so fortunate are the play's female characters. Each of the four principal female characters represents a version of flawed black womanhood, and each in some very important way assists the larger racist society in crushing Victor's hopes for himself and his family. Significantly, the playwright describes each of these women as mulatto; Victor and his sons, in contrast, are all darker, Victor himself being described as "black." Victor's physical blackness helps to isolate him from the women in his own family, and when acrimony arises, he becomes the victim of intrafamilial, intraracial and intersexual color prejudice.

No member of the family spews this poison more frequently than Martha Brooks, Victor's vicious mother-in-law. Financially dependent on the generosity of her son-in-law, Brooks repays Victor with contempt and insults. Although she has the good sense not to articulate the depths of her contempt and bigotry to Victor, she never forgoes an opportunity to humiliate her daughter and her grandchildren. Victor's dream of going back to Africa she mocks, claiming not to be an African herself. Boastfully she reminds her daughters of her white and superior "Dupree" blood and taunts Victor's wife for having married a man with a dark complexion: "She ain't got mah blood in her veins—No Dupree would-er thought 'bout marryin' sich a black crank in the first place." Brooks even demonstrates her bigotry while playing with her "copper-colored" granddaughter, Caroline. When the woman tires of playing with the youngster, she returns to the child her black doll and remarks bitterly: "Here, you take this black thing! I don't want no more to do with it!" The child, no older than thirteen, understands all too well her grandmother's bigotry and attempts to soothe her doll's wounded pride with sympathetic words: "Poor lil black Judy. Grandma treats that honey-child like an orphan, don't she?" Ward, to be sure, makes clear his distaste for Brooks, and at times she seems no more than a malicious fool. Nonetheless, Brooks serves as a poor example of a generation of black women. She brings nothing of worth to the family and the household, neither money, nor love, nor pride, nor dignity. Brooks remains prouder of her bigotry than her blackness.

Although Victor's wife, Ella, rejects her mother's prejudice, in the end Ella proves to be an unreliable and unsupportive wife. In times of trouble, she humiliates her husband with relish and vigor equal to her mother's. When Victor and Ella discover that their eldest daughter has prostituted herself in order to save the family from eviction, Ella torments Victor: "It was fate all right. Fate from the day she was born—with something less than a black fool for a father she was booked for the gutter!" As Victor lies dying, the victim of a policeman's bullet, Ella refuses to go to her husband and comfort him. She appears cruel beyond belief, sulking and nursing her own imaginary wounds as her husband dies from real wounds. As she stands looking out the window, we see all too well that she does in fact have Dupree blood in her veins.

Ella's sister Juanita represents a more vicious kind of woman. A true American capitalist, Juanita will stop at nothing to make money and to acquire more comfort and goods. She and her husband, Daniel, prey on other blacks as landlords of a building of "kitchenettes." Financially more successful than Victor, this couple possesses none of the race pride that gives Victor so much dignity. When the depression hits, Juanita in her desperate search for money allows her building to become a brothel. In an act that symbolizes how greed ultimately smothers human decency, Juanita attempts to lure her niece, Victor's and Ella's younger daughter, into prostitution. Luckily, the girl does not fall victim to her aunt. Juanita, like the other Dupree women, proves herself to be heartless and selfish. She knows neither race pride and solidarity nor the meaning of family.

If Victor has any success in transmitting his values, he has it with his two oldest children, Les and Wanda. But like the other female characters in the play, Wanda in the end raises questions about Ward's portrayal of women. In an act of desperation and remarkable, albeit misguided, selflessness, Wanda does surrender to the readily available money of prostitution. With her family facing eviction, she acts to get the money the family needs in the only way she knows how. Although Wanda enters into prostitution, she does so only to allay the desperate circumstances of her family. On several earlier occasions she refuses the advances of the white man to whom she finally surrenders. It is important to note that Wanda becomes the victim of a white man; Ward clearly intends to show how racist, capitalist America victimizes blacks, even the young and innocent, when it ought to protect them. But this notwithstanding, Wanda's sacrifice is neither unambiguous nor uncomplicated, and in the context of *Big White Fog* her actions are more ominous. No woman in this play can be construed as a positive representation of black women. The sole woman who acts unselfishly does so by becoming a prostitute. One might have sympathy for Wanda, respect her motives and recognize the good in her, but to seek redemption in prostitution is not an unequivocal good. Whether Ward realized or intended what he had wrought does not alter the reality of the play; the images of black women we take away from this play are overwhelmingly negative, and it is no wonder that Lorraine Hansberry set out to correct those negative images in *A Raisin in the Sun.*

The domestic situation of the Younger family of *A Raisin in the Sun* is similar to that of the Mason family. Black men struggle for success in a racist America that denies them the opportunity to achieve their goals and to realize their potential. Specific plot similarities also exist. Both families live in Chicago's Southside; three generations share the same living space; an elderly widow is the oldest member of each household. The men make bad investments and lose the families' savings (Victor invests in Garvey's Black Star lines; Walter Lee is swindled). Black America's relationship with Africa is probed in *Big White Fog* through Victor's Garveyism; in *A Raisin in the Sun*, Beneatha Younger becomes romantically involved with a Nigerian student who awakens her interest in her African heritage. These similarities and more Helen Keyssar notes in her book *The Curtain and the Veil: Strategies in Black Drama.* But the similarities in plot make the dissimilarities in female representation all the more striking and meaningful. In fact, we must finally recognize that Hansberry wrote *A Raisin in the Sun* with a feminist commitment and her portrayal of black women is politically charged.

Just two days before the first performance of *A Raisin in the Sun* in New Haven, Hansberry wrote her mother:

> Mama, it is a play that tells the truth about people, Negroes and life and I think it will help a lot of people to understand how we are just as complicated as they are—and just as mixed up—but above all, that we have among our miserable and downtrodden ranks—people who are the very essence of human dignity. That is what, after all the laughter and tears, the play is supposed to say. I hope it will make you very proud.

That Hansberry sought to affirm the dignity of black people and to make her mother proud—she dedicates the play "To Mama: in gratitude for the dream"—goes far to explain Lena Younger, Mama of *A Raisin in the Sun*. In her mother, Hansberry found a real life example of the strong black woman who fights and endures for her family. In a letter to the New York *Times* in April 1964, Hansberry recalls a remarkable episode concerning her mother, an episode that surely helped to shape Lena and the action of *A Raisin in the Sun*. After the Hansberrys moved into their home in a "hellishly hostile white neighborhood," her mother literally armed herself to protect her family from "howling mobs." "And I also remember," she writes, "my desperate and courageous mother, patrolling our house all night with a loaded German luger, doggedly guarding her four children, while my father fought the respectable part of the battle in the Washington Court."

Proud, strong and brave, Lena is all that Martha Brooks is not. Lena demands of her children respect and dignity, and in return she gives them love and understanding. Although Brooks may represent a version of the black mother who is obsessed with the color of her children's faces and the texture of their hair, Hansberry and other black women see her more as an aberration. Hansberry's Lena represents the proud norm, the woman who takes in ironing, cleans white folks' houses and who never ceases to boast: "I come from five generations of people who was slaves and sharecroppers—but ain't nobody in my family never let nobody pay 'em no money that was a way of telling us we wasn't fit to walk the earth. We ain't never been that poor. We ain't never been that dead inside."

In the 1920 essay "The Damnation of Women," W.E.B. Du Bois wrote:

> So some few women are born free, and some amid insult and scarlet letters achieve freedom; but our women in black had freedom thrust contemptuously upon them. With that freedom they are buying an untrammeled independence and dear as is the price they pay for it, it will in the end be worth every taunt and groan. Today the dreams of the mothers are coming true. We have still our poverty and degradation, our lewdness and our cruel toil; but we have, too, a vast group of women of Negro blood who for strength of character, cleanness of soul, and unselfish devotion of purpose, is today easily the peer of any group of women in the civilized world.

It is this woman who is missing from Ward's play and whom Hansberry felt compelled to restore, to place before both white and black America as the true representative of black women. Ward's Brooks knows only self-hatred and self-deprecation; Lena Younger displays "the very essence of human dignity."

Hansberry draws the other female characters with the same feminist intent. Ruth, the wife/mother of *A Raisin in the Sun*, is a firm but loving mother. She takes in ironing so that she can contribute to the family income. And unlike Ella of *Big White Fog*, Ruth never wavers in her support of or devotion to her husband. She takes his part against his mother on the subject of opening a liquor store:

Mama: We ain't no business people, Ruth. We just plain working folks.

Ruth: Ain't nobody business people till they go into business. Walter Lee say colored people ain't never going to start getting ahead till they start gambling on some different kinds of things in the world—investments and things.

After it is learned that Walter Lee has lost the money, even Mama loses for a moment her determination and thinks it best to remain in their old, cramped and dismal apartment, but not Ruth. She knows that to save her marriage and her family they must move into the new house. She demands that the family rise to the circumstances and meet them with renewed resolve and strength:

Mama: [I] Just aimed too high all the time—

Ruth: Lena—I'll work . . . I'll work twenty hours a day in all the kitchens in Chicago . . . I'll strap my baby on my back if I have to and scrub all the floors in America and wash all the sheets in America if I have to—but we got to move . . . we got to get out of here. . . .

Ruth's response, so unlike Ella's, reflects the "truth" about black people and black women Hansberry sought to bring to the stage. "Black women could hardly strive for weakness," Angela Davis writes in *Women, Race and Class*: "they had to become strong for their families and their communities needed their strength to survive. Evidence of the accumulated strengths Black women have forged through work, work and more work can be discovered in the contributions of the many outstanding female leaders who have emerged within the Black community. Harriet Tubman, Sojourner Truth, Ida Wells and Rosa Parks are not exceptional Black women as much as they are epitomes of Black womanhood." Broadway had seen many black housekeepers and chorewomen, but Hansberry animated for Broadway and America the black women who struggle against the odds for husband, family and community. She created female characters in the image of Ida Wells and Harriet Tubman. After all, Hansberry knew in the most personal way one of these "epitomes of black womanhood."

As Ruth embodies the strength and determination of these epitomes, her sister-in-law, Beneatha, possesses their pioneering spirit. Beneatha, unlike Juanita and Wanda, the daughters in *Big White Fog*, does not seek salvation through prostitution. She wants to be a doctor, and although she receives abuse from her brother and her American suitor, George Murchison, for her ambition, her mother and her Nigerian suitor, Joseph Asagai, support and encourage her. Like Wanda, Beneatha is motivated by generosity and selflessness, but how different are their paths. She wants to be a doctor because ". . . [t]hat was the most marvelous thing in the world. . . . I always thought it was the one concrete thing in the world that a human being could do. Fix up the sick, you know—and make them whole again. . . ."

To be sure, Beneatha is her brother's most harsh critic and she comes to despise him after he loses the money, including the three thousand dollars that were to be set aside for her medical education. But her mother, who knows too well the bitterness of defeat, tells her why she must love her brother even more when he is down:

> Have you cried for that boy [Walter Lee] today? I don't mean for yourself and for the family 'cause we lost the money. I mean for him; what he been through and what it done to him. Child, when do you think is the time to love somebody the most; when they done good and made things easy for everybody? Well then, you ain't through learning—because that ain't the time at all. It's when he's at his lowest and can't believe in hisself 'cause the world done whipped him so. When you starts measuring somebody, measure him right, child, measure him right. Make sure you done taken into account what hills and valleys he come through before he got to wherever he is.

Ruth already knows this; that is why she cannot allow the family to relinquish its new home, its new life and its hopes. Perhaps Lena speaks here not just to Beneatha but to Ella Mason as well, for Ella receives no such lesson from her mother, Martha Brooks.

As we see in Beneatha, Hansberry's women are not plaster saints. They confess their errors, and they learn from each other. But they are women in whom Hansberry could take pride. Lena may waver in her determination, but she does not attack her son, nor does she evidence any bigotry. Ruth may argue with her husband, but never does she turn on him. Beneatha, critic that she is, remains a fiercely proud black woman who has some growing up to do but needs no apology. From her parents, Hansberry has said, she learned that "above all, there were two things which were never to be betrayed: the family and the race." The Younger women live this ideal.

As I noted above, Hansberry had a secondary political agenda in writing *A Raisin in the Sun*. In the last scene of *Big White Fog*, the Masons are being evicted from their Chicago home. It is 1932, and they like many other families are unable to pay their rent. Victor's son Les, a committed socialist, persuades his father to resist the eviction. Bailiffs arrive and begin removing the furniture; moments later Les's comrades arrive singing "The Battle Hymn of the Republic." Victor joins his son and the other socialists and they begin carrying the furniture back into the house. Victor is fatally wounded by a bailiff for resisting the eviction. In the last scene of *A Raisin in the Sun*, moving men arrive to carry the Youngers' furniture out of their rented apartment and into their newly purchased home. The movement of the furniture is an important symbol for Hansberry. As the furniture is moved out, it signifies the family's move out of the ghetto and into bourgeois America. They have taken possession of their share of the American dream. Progress is being made. Surely Hansberry wants us to see this as an improvement over the socialist solution in *Big White Fog*. In *Big White Fog* the furniture is being moved back into a run-down, rented house. The Masons seem to be reclaiming only the past. Though there was real trauma when Hansberry's family took possession of their new home, there was also real triumph and progress for the race. Hansberry transfers that triumph onto the stage, and by so doing, she sets as a goal for black America not the Marxist revolution proposed by *Big White Fog* but the attainment of equality in bourgeois America.

The triumph of the Younger family is indisputably engineered by Lena. She goes out alone, finds the home and makes the down payment from her ten thousand dollar insurance check. Her son Walter Lee initially opposes her decision, and for a moment he considers accepting the bribe from the white neighborhood association not to move into the house and their all-white neighborhood. He does a chilling Uncle Tom routine to show the family how he will humiliate himself to get the money from the neighborhood association. Earlier he demonstrates questionable judgment by giving sixty-five hundred dollars to someone who swindles him. And he proves to be somewhat untrustworthy by actually stealing the three thousand dollars Lena wants set aside for Beneatha's medical education. Walter Lee's actions raise questions about Hansberry's portrayal of black men. Does she see them as weak? foolish? childish? Does Lena in her strength perform the castration of her son that William Grier and Price Cobbs attribute to black mothers in their book *Black Rage*: "The black mother shares a burden with her soul sisters of three centuries ago. She must produce and shape and mold a unique type of man. She must intuitively cut off and blunt his masculine assertiveness and aggression lest these put the boy's life in jeopardy."

While it is difficult to dismiss Walter's accumulated errors, it is also difficult to suggest that Hansberry's play leaves uncorrected the denigration of black manhood. Walter Lee is surely no Victor Mason. However the play ends celebrating not just the Youngers taking possession of their new home but also Walter Lee's coming finally "into his manhood." Throughout the play there is a lament for the absence of black manhood, manhood lost when Big Walter, Lena's husband and Walter Lee's father, died. The play does not suggest that true black manhood does not exist; it is just not present in the Youngers' house. And nothing is an adequate substitute for that absence, least of all the ten thousand dollar insurance check Lena gets after Big Walter's death. "Ten thousand dollars they give you. Ten thousand dollars," Lena says as she examines the newly arrived check. Hansberry's stage directions to the actress speaking these words are significant here: "She [Lena] does not look at RUTH; her eyes seem to be seeing something somewhere very far off." It is clear that Lena would give up the ten thousand dollars for the return of her husband. It is equally clear that Big Walter presided over his family as a traditional patriarch. Although Lena confides to Ruth, ". . . there was plenty wrong with Walter Younger—hardheaded, mean, kind of wild with women," she overlooks his flaws and loves his strengths. It is the strength of his father that Lena demands from her son: "I am waiting to hear how you be your father's son." The ideal of black manhood is there; unfortunately, it goes unemulated until the last scene.

In the end, Lena commands Walter to act like the *pater familias*, and although there is a certain amount of irony, probably unintended, in her demand, rather than "intuitively cut off and blunt [Walter Lee's] masculine assertiveness," Lena pushes for just the opposite. When Walter finally becomes his father's son, he hands down a legacy of pride and dignity to his young son, Travis. He tells the representative of the white neighborhood association: ". . . we called you over here to tell you that we are very proud and that this is—this is my son, who makes the sixth generation of our family in this country, and that we have all thought about your offer and we have decided to move into our house because my father—my father—he earned it." When the representative looks to Lena to overrule her son—something the audience knows she would not hesitate to do if she thought him wrong—she replies: "I am afraid you don't understand. My son said we was going to move and there ain't nothing left for me to say." When Walter truly fills the role of *pater familias*, Lena abdicates with joy; she willingly retires to her garden. Now that her son has grown into a man, she can tend her "feeble little plant."

It may seem strange to say Hansberry's intentions were feminist, if at the play's end Lena seems to surrender and lovingly endorses the idea of patriarchy. But the play endorses patriarchy not at the expense of female strength or female governance. Manhood in *A Raisin in the Sun* is wholly compatible with feminism. Lena does not surrender judgment to Walter simply because he is a man; she acquiesces because Walter is right. Manhood cannot be achieved until Walter demonstrates the pride and dignity that the women already possess. Hansberry would agree with Du Bois who wrote in "The Damnation of Women": "What is today the message of these black women to America and to the world? The uplift of women is, next to the problem of the color line and the peace movement, our greatest modern cause. When, now, two of these movements—women and color—combine in one, the combination has deep meaning."

The feminist revision of *Big White Fog* by Hansberry served as a catalyst to playwright Joseph Walker who in his play *The River Niger* challenges and faults Hansberry's representation of black men and women. In his play, Walker places before us another image of black men and women, one that is as politically charged as Hansberry's. Like her, he identifies his agenda in the play's dedication: "This play is dedicated to my mother and father and to highly underrated black daddies everywhere." The question that the dedication raises is this: Will Walker in rehabilitating "highly underrated black daddies" adopt an antifeminist agenda? However, before we turn to the play to seek the answer to this question, it would be useful to look at Walker's personal reminiscences of his father and mother. As Hansberry's recollections of her mother inform her portrayal of women in *A Raisin in the Sun,* so too do Walker's. In a page-long sentence entitled "Joe Walker's Autobiography" that appears just after the dedication page in the text of the play, Walker writes:

> . . . [daddy] was a bad-loud-talking dude of five feet eight inches tall, whom I once saw beat up a man six foot five because he insulted my seven-year-old dignity by beating the daylights out of me on account of I and my buddies were on a hate-little-girls campaign, throwing bottle tops at the cutest little brown oak girl . . . whom I don't think I really hated in retrospect because of her almond-shaped eyes—anyway, my pop was some dude . . . my ma, man, was a scornful bittersweet lovable crazy lady who was not quite as sweet as Mattie in *The River Niger* but who was pretty goddamn sweet and giving anyway.

Of course, Walker's play is not wholly autobiographical; however, he publicly acknowledges a correspondence between his mother and Mattie, the principal female character, and no doubt intends for there to be an equally strong correspondence between his father and the play's hero, John Williams.

Personal correspondence notwithstanding, *The River Niger* presents to us a family that obviously and purposely resembles the ones—or one—that we have seen in the two previous plays. There are three generations in the same household, the oldest person being a widow. There is a couple with children. The family struggles to survive financially. There is the question of Africa, and in this play a Jamaican cynic, a sort of anti-Garvey. And, of course, the play's denouement results from American racism and the efforts of this black family to resist and overcome this pervasive fact of life. A closer look at the family and the action of the play will reveal its important and self-conscious dissimilarities to *A Raisin in the Sun.*

The River Niger opens with the Brooks/Lena analogue, Wilhemina Brown, creeping into the kitchen to sneak herself a drink. After pouring herself a cup of coffee, she "stealthily" locates her hidden bottle of Bourbon from which she pours into her coffee "an extremely generous portion." This comic scene indicates the kind of treatment the elderly black woman will receive in the play and, of course, instructs us how to view her. But everything about her is not humorous. Like Brooks in *Big White Fog,* Wilhemina, "a fair skinned black woman," takes pride in her light complexion and never hesitates to boast of her bigotry. Although she describes her late husband as "black as a night what ain't got no Moon," she happily disparages others who are black. To her daughter Mattie and son-in-law John, whom the playwright describes as "brown," Wilhemina brags of her children: "And ain't none of 'em black either. . . . Mattie's the only black child I ever spawned—my first and last, thank Jesus."

Wilhemina continues to drink and meddle and pontificate throughout the play, and she is the source of much comedy. However, Walker does allow her to redeem herself; she achieves this redemption as she acknowledges that she has played an important role in hampering and ultimately ruining her son-in-law's chances for success. Warning her grandson of the dangers of an early marriage, she confesses: "Look at your father. He wanted to be a lawyer, didn't he? Then I jumped on his back, then those two no good daughters of mine, then their two empty-headed husbands—then you. The load was so heavy till he couldn't move no more. He just had to stand there, holding it up." Conventionally in the drama, self-knowledge no matter how harsh, if honest, is never unwelcomed nor condemned. Yet when Wilhemina indulges in self-evaluation, the results go beyond individual follies and insensitivity. She warns Jeff because she believes that her behavior is typical of female behavior; she cautions her grandson against marriage and women. In the larger political debate on the image of black women Wilhemina's self-assessment produces even worse fruit; women become the real and present danger. Men must be cautious. The conventions of drama only increase the ambiguity of Wilhemina's self-revelation/self-deprecation.

Perhaps ambiguity describes best the nature of Walker's representation of female characters. As the play's hero proclaims: "So we're contradictions—so what else is new?" The principal female character, Mattie, described as "an embittered but happy woman" in the list of characters, is one such contradiction. Mattie always knows her place as a woman. In the midst of a heated family debate, her husband declares: "I'm the head of this house." She quickly responds, "Ain't nobody disputing that." Like her mother, Mattie too understands her part in ruining her husband's chances for success. In a history of her married life given to her son's soon-to-be fiancée, Ann Vanderguild, Mattie tells of all the burdens she placed on John's back and of his failed potential. Finally she says: "I got nobody to blame but myself." Mattie's sense of self is defined by her relationship to John and her unshakable belief that she, his loving black wife, with the help of her mother and sisters and their selfish husbands, turned John into a failure and an alcoholic. Because of this she is willing to accept anything that John does, including his playfully obscene and derisive behavior. But Mattie counts all of this as a part of her "treasure" and offers a panegyric to John and presumably to the rest of the "highly underrated black daddies" in the world:

> A good man is a treasure. White folks proclaim that our men are no good and we go 'round like fools trying to prove them wrong. And I fell right into the same old trap myself. That's why I can't get angry with that man no more. Oh, I pretend to be, but I'm not. Johnny ran a powerful race with a jockey on his back who weighed a ton. So now he's tired. Do you hear me? Tired—and he's put himself out to pasture—with his fifth a day, and I say good for Johnny. I knew he was a smart man. Good for Johnny. If our men are no good, then why are all these little white girls trying to gobble 'em up faster than they can pee straight?

While one assumes that the referent of "them" in the sentence "White folks proclaim that our men are no good . . ." is "White folks," it could also be "our men." Consequently the meaning of this sentence is somewhat ambiguous. Whom are black women trying to prove wrong, white folks or their men? While it is clear that "white folks" are wrong, black women are fools because they do not ignore the mendacity of whites; instead they give heed to it. Note that the praise of black men seems to require self-deprecation from black women. Racism alone does not destroy black men according to Mattie and the play; racism aided by black women proves to be the real culprit.

Mattie's devotion to her husband receives its final test at the play's conclusion, a conclusion that is in many ways a reprise of the last scene of *Big White Fog*. Through a series of blunders, a group of black militants arrive seeking refuge at the Williams' house. John, who has searched for a battlefield on which he could fight for his people, finally finds one, but he receives a mortal wound in an exchange of gunfire with a police informant whom he kills. Dying, John contrives a plot in which he will be thought guilty of an earlier shooting. After John dies, Mattie, so unlike Ella, takes control of the situation, proclaiming: "Shut up! And tell it like Johnny told you. He ain't gonna die for nothing, 'cause you ain't gonna let him! Jeff—open the door, son! Tell 'em to come on in here! And you better not fuck up!" These are the last words of the play, and they are Mattie's. She, not her adult son, assumes control at her husband's death. Interestingly enough the play's end focuses attention on its own ambiguous treatment of black women. Mattie's strength is real and also a real asset at this time. For her to be less than strong would mock her husband's sacrifice. Yet the fact that she, rather than her son, assumes control promotes female dominance and matriarchy. Surely Walker intends us to view Mattie's powerful and unwavering response as good, but the situation that he sets up valorizes female strength. However, neither her son nor her husband, were he able, would object to this situation.

The ideological justification for Mattie's ascendancy can be found at least in part in the comments of Ann Vanderguild, the third female principal. Immediately after Ann arrives on the scene, she requests assistance in finding a job as a nurse from Dudley, the Jamaican doctor. He replies: "Oh, these strong black women!" "I'm only strong," Ann responds, "if my man needs me to be, sir." John enters the discussion with the proud observation: "You hear that, Dudley, a warrior's woman! A fighter. . . ." Clearly the play endorses this concept of womanhood, and Ann lives by her motto. She allows Jeff to protect her and to make decisions for her. Never does she exert her will. When she asks to participate in the plot to discover the police informant, Jeff adamantly refuses to grant her permission; he agrees only after another man assures him that it will be safe: "It's safe, Jeff, I swear. You know I wouldn't have my woman doing anything that would put her in a trick. No jeopardy, man, I promise." The "fighting lady Ann," like Mattie, knows when to make meat loaf and when to fight; decisions, however, are always made within the boundaries established by the head of the household.

It is impossible to ignore in the characterization of Ann a certain amount of correction of Beneatha. First and foremost, Ann is a nurse, a traditionally female profession, and nurses, we all know, take their orders from (male) doctors. Nursing actually serves as an interesting metaphor for the role of women espoused by *The River Niger*. Women should be strong, but that strength should be circumscribed by male dominance. Beneatha accepts the authority of no one. Only when her brother demonstrates pride and dignity does she respect him as a man, but she never surrenders her ambition or assertiveness. Also, both Beneatha and Ann are central to their plays' discussion of black America's relationship to Africa. Beneatha longs to know her African past. From her African suitor she receives a proposal of marriage and an invitation to return to Africa to practice medicine. Beneatha is offered a future in Africa, a romantic, cultural and professional future: "Three hundred years later the African Prince rose up out of the seas and swept the maiden back across the middle passage over which her ancestors had come . . ." (*A Raisin in the Sun*). Ann, on the other hand, has come from South Africa; she comes to North America to escape the oppression in

Africa. Her brothers have also had to flee South Africa for political reasons. Her father remains in jail nine years later because he, in a move that foreshadows John's, sacrifices himself for his sons' freedom and safety. There is neither romance nor a future in the Africa of *The River Niger*. The romance is in America and most significantly in the African-American male. The paradigm of *A Raisin in the Sun* is totally reversed in *The River Niger*. African-American men are the desired, the free and, as we shall later see, the new African.

What do we learn in *The River Niger* of this African-American man? The play's hero is a "bad-loud-talking dude," the long-suffering John, the alcoholic poet who seeks a battlefield and finally dies for his people. He had the promise of a great future but because of American racism and four black women, he fails and puts himself out to pasture with a fifth a day. But all of this notwithstanding, he loves his wife Mattie, his mother-in-law Wilhemina, and his son Jeff. When he returns from a binge, having been gone six days, he explains to his wife: "I wanted to write a love poem—to you, Mattie. Words are like precious jewels, did you know that? But I couldn't find any jewels precious enough to match you, Mattie." John's profession of love supposedly compensates for his disappearance and absence at a moment of great personal crisis for Mattie who earlier learns that she has inoperable breast cancer. But the play, like Mattie, truly loves John and indulges his every act.

While on his binge John writes a poem that he offers to Mattie as a token of his love. The poem, "The River Niger," as John admits, "ain't a love poem." It is, however, a panegyric to black manhood, and in it, the poet translates himself into Africa, transplanted to America, but Africa nonetheless.

> I am the River Niger!
> I came to the cloudy Mississippi
> Over heels of incomprehensible woe.
> I ran 'way to the Henry Hudson
> Under the sails of ragged hope.
> I am the River Niger,
> Transplanted to Harlem
> From the Harlem River Drive.

In this redaction of Langston Hughes's "The Negro Speaks of Rivers," John claims for himself and his black compatriots the heroic past as well as an exclusive right to the African future. The trope that he employs incorporates and transcends the African past. Black American men, as Ann recognizes, possess the power to engender a pan-African world:

> Hold hands, my children, and I will flow to the ends of the earth
> And the whole world will hear my waters.
> I am the River Niger! Don't deny me!
> Do you hear me? Don't deny me!

Africa's glorious future will come when Africa in its manifestation as the American male is no longer denied.

But as ambiguity defines the nature of female representation, so does it define male representation. John's disappearance (desertion?) at Mattie's moment of crisis clearly raises questions about his reliability. He may be tormented by Mattie's illness and impending death, but his response is not unproblematic. Similarly, **John's death at the end of the** play prompts questions; foremost among these is this: Is his death really meaningful? Does it achieve anything for blacks? John earlier tells Dudley that he seeks a battlefield on which to fight for his race. But John dies in a battle which produces a Pyrrhic victory at best and which wins only symbolic results. In fact, John falls victim to incompetent black revolutionaries as much as he does to white racism. After these revolutionaries fail to locate the police informant and to complete successfully a guerrilla action they arrive at the Williams' home in desperate need of assistance from competent black men. Finally the informant is discovered to be "the closet homosexual" Al. John attempts to subdue Al, but Al fires and mortally wounds John. In the meantime, the police close in. In the end, John and Al are dead; the revolutionaries have accomplished nothing meaningful, and some impotent, entirely useless and, ironically, wasteful macho bravado has been displayed. John's death wins nothing. John believes that he will die for the cause he holds to be worth his life: "I found it, Dudley—I found it . . . my battlefield—my battlefield, man! I was a bitch too. . . ." Like so many other battlefields, this one too bears a waste of men. Painfully absent from this is any unequivocal, authorial comment on the waste of John's death. John himself proclaims it to be poetry and dies boasting of his prowess.

As in the earlier two plays the son learns something valuable from the father; machismo is the virtue John passes to his son Jeff. Walter Lee's son Travis learns from his father and grandmother a lesson in pride and dignity. Victor's son Les who converts his father to Marxist revolutionary politics also learns to be proud of his black heritage from his Garveyite father. Of course, Jeff learns things in addition to machismo from his father; foremost among these is a real sense of race pride. Like his father he seeks a battlefield, but Jeff intends to become a lawyer and to fight in the courts. He distrusts the revolution that the incompetent militants seek and presages the play's conclusion when he says: "The revolution ain't nothing but talk, talk, talk, and I ain't gonna waste my life on talk." He will marry the "fighting lady Ann" and presumably enjoy the status of *pater familias*. Jeff offers to assist his former gang in finding the informant, but wants no part of their urban guerrilla tactics. He wants to be his own man, free of the claustrophobic restrictions placed on him by others who have less than his best interest at heart. For *The River Niger*, Jeff is the future. He is black American manhood at its finest, self-assured, self-possessed. He is the heir of the River Niger.

As is often the case, in *The River Niger* machismo is accompanied by its near-cousin, misogyny; of course, the antifeminist agenda of the play does facilitate its descent into misogyny. We have noted earlier that there is some ambiguity in the representation of female characters, but that ambiguity is resolved when one considers the accumulated language of the play. Hostility, sometimes aggressive, sometimes subtle, characterizes the language of males about females in this play. One obviously must consider the play's idiom, a kind of street-wise, bad dude style; but coupled with the ideological goal of the play, this language cannot be dismissed as unintentionally hostile or as harmless. Examples abound, but none better than the clearly pornographic words of Dr. Dudley Stanton. Dudley, who earlier jokes of how his mother supported him through college and medical school by prostitution, tells of his medical examinations of women: "I distribute sugar pills and run my fingers up the itchy vaginas of sex-starved old bitches. Women who're dried up, past menopause—but groping for life. They pretend to be unmoved, but I feel their wrigglings on my fingers. I see 'em swoon with ecstasy the deeper I probe." Although there is nothing else quite as excessive as this, the play finds ample opportunity to identify women as "bitches" and "superbitches." Were this language restricted to a few individuals, it would be easier to see it as language that partakes in characterization and mimesis. But the language is used uncritically and in fact is a constituent part of the male behavior that the play valorizes. When John dedicates "The River Niger" to his "superbitch," the play's pervasive hostility towards women, whether it is active or passive, becomes impossible to deny or overlook.

Although the misogyny articulated in *The River Niger* does have its unique roots in black American culture, this misogyny is no worse than that which permeates Western culture. What differentiates the manifestations of misogyny in black culture from its manifestations in the majority culture are the permutations that result from racism. The systematic sexual abuse that black women suffered in America during slavery and well into the twentieth century is widely documented. To consider this abuse to be only the libidinous excesses and license of white men is to misunderstand the political nature of that abuse. Black women had no real political control over their bodies, and their husbands, brothers, fathers and lovers were raped of their power to protect their women from the unsolicited sexual aggression of white males. Indeed, white males used their sexual power over black women as an emblem of the political power that as white men they held over black men. "Sexually as well as in every other way," Winthrop Jordan writes in *White Over Black*, "Negroes were utterly subordinated. White men extended their dominion over their Negroes to the bed, where the sex act itself served as ritualistic re-enactment of the daily pattern of social dominance." In effect, the bodies of black women became the battlefield on and over which men, black and white, fought to establish actual and symbolic political dominance and to demonstrate masculine prowess. Truly black men had more than wounded machismo at stake here: the lives and safety of their female relatives and friends were in real danger. Yet the passive role thrust upon black women by this struggle in a very real way served to minimize their individuality and humanity and to objectify them as possessions and symbols. Also because the victimization of black women was intended to humiliate, to emasculate black men, female oppression paradoxically became a version of male oppression and consequently could be construed to be less significant than male oppression. The oppression of black women by white men when viewed only in its racist context allows for the continuation of that oppression by black men. Nor should we forget that there was an obvious political reason for black men to establish their dominance over black women. Of course, black men would neither desire nor establish a system of oppression against their mothers, sisters, wives and lovers as ruthless and brutal as the one white men instituted against black women, but because the oppression of black women by white men was so politically charged and in part aimed directly at black men, the relationship between black men and black women necessarily reflects these facts. Additionally there exists the belief that the black mother in preparing her son to survive in a racist America "must intuitively cut off and blunt [her son's] masculine assertiveness and aggression lest these put the boy's life in danger." Accordingly, Grier and Cobbs hypothesize in *Black Rage*: ". . . black men develop considerable hostility toward black women as the inhibiting instruments of an oppressive system. The woman has more power, more accessibility into the system, and therefore she is more feared, while at the same time envied. And it is her lot in life to suppress masculine assertiveness in her sons." Grier's and Cobbs' failure to distinguish here between female lovers and mothers should not go unnoticed. The assertion made here is that all black women partake in this emasculating activity and that all black men respond with a general hostility toward women. Calvin C. Hernton in his book *Sex and Racism in America* offers yet other and somewhat contradictory reasons for alleged male hostility towards females: ". . . there arose in me an incipient resentment . . . towards all black women—because I could not help but compare them with white women, and in all phases of public life it was the Negro female who bowed her head and tucked her tail between her legs like a little black puppy." The important common denominator here is racism, but its release becomes misogyny. Whether or not we agree with Grier's and Cobbs' assessment or Hernton's is irrelevant. These ideas, expressed as they are, go a long way to explain how racism informs sexism in black America. And it is from this that *The River Niger* takes shape. No matter what Hansberry's intentions, to those who subscribe to this image of black women, Lena, Ruth and Beneatha all seem to participate in that emasculating tradition identified by Grier and Cobbs.

Related to the problem of misogyny and machismo in *The River Niger* is the question of sexual identity. Who among the characters is trustworthy and a true heir of the River Niger? The women who know their role in a male dominant society become the play's "superbitches." Men who demand and exercise male prerogative over women and win for themselves hierarchical power over their male colleagues are the play's real revolutionaries. Its counterrevolutionaries are those who do not align themselves with this paradigm, most notably Al, the "closet homosexual," police informant. However, Al's sexuality is really overdetermined in this play. His sexual passivity—and the play makes it clear that he is passive—symbolizes his separation from real black manhood and hence real blackness. Al does not understand his blackness: he denies Africa and the play's definition of manhood. By not being true to his manhood, Al cannot be true to his blackness. Perversely, he defends the majority culture that oppresses black people, that dams the River Niger. Al proves to be untrustworthy and the "real men," Jeff, John and Dudley, must ferret the Als out and destroy them.

It is, finally, the intraracial intersexual struggle that seems to consume *The River Niger*. At the end of *Big White Fog*, the Marxists are moving the Masons' furniture back into the house. The hoped for revolution—were it to come—would protect the dispossessed. In *A Raisin in the Sun*, the furniture is being moved out and the dispossessed move to take possession of their dream deferred. At the end of *The River Niger* there is no movement. Everything including the furniture remains in place; the movables are fixed. John dies not for a cause but to demonstrate a point: black men, black fathers are heroic and heroically macho. The play calls on black women to learn this lesson before it is too late, before they are bereft of their men. Yet the real irony of this conclusion is its unintended feminist correction of *Big White Fog*; Mattie does exactly what Ella ought to do. But Mattie is left to protect the past, to insure that John's sacrifice does not turn into an egregious waste. Nothing else stands to be won. We move nowhere, out of nothing, towards nothing.

Perhaps it is for these reasons more than any other that Hansberry still has the last word in this debate. After her play was seen by one of the nine young students who integrated Central High in Little Rock, Hansberry received this fan letter:

> Dear Miss Hansberry,
>
> I'm one of the nine students that attended Little Rock Central High School. . . . I wish all the students could have seen the play before entering Central in '57. It would have made us prouder to enter Central because we knew we were not the only Walter Lee Youngers.

These nine students—three males and six females—entered Central High in defiance of Arkansas Governor Orval Faubus' vow that "blood would run in the streets" if black pupils attempted to enter Central High School. The six teenage girls were as vulnerable and as valorous as their male peers. The young man's observation that they were all Walter Lee Youngers is apt, but then again they were all Lena Youngers too. Together they threw out some of America's most hated furniture and brought in some bright new pieces.

CLYDE TAYLOR

Black Writing as Immanent Humanism

"New ideas can only come from new social forms."
—Sergei Eisenstein

FROM TIME TO TIME, brash temperaments examine black writing beside some shining model of their abstract imagining and end up raging at the recalcitrance of their contemporaries. In "The Myth of Negro Literature" LeRoi Jones was disgusted with black writers because they were bourgeois and did not write like Melville. My own spasm of this sort came a few years back when I lamented the seventies as a comatose decade for black writing. Checking back, things were usually not as bad as the ranters thought they were.

When he was twenty-eight, Richard Wright took a backward glance at his predecessors and saw only a bunch of literary clowns who went as ambassadors "a-begging to white America. They entered the Court of American Public Opinion dressed in kneepants of servility, curtsying to show that the Negro was not inferior, that he was human. . . ." He was dropping the slab on the past to leverage his hoped future for black literature.

"Blueprint for Negro Writing," his 1937 essay, has double fascination today. The first is the general intelligence, overriding a few stumbles, of his insightful prognostications of what was needed to make a healthy black literature. They are prophetic because many of the goals he set would get an amen from today's writers. Even more striking, they are prophetic because—and this is where a backward glance at his forward view is encouraging—the dreams Wright had for black writing in the thirties are nearly all realities or work decidedly in progress.

What he wanted was writing independently *for* black people, addressed to their hearing, intimate with their daily realities, and expressive of the socioeconomic backgrounds needed to elucidate their experiences. Wright saw two ideologies—black nationalism and Marxism —contending as channels for the productive release of creative literary energy. But he cannily pictured neither as ready-to-wear dogmas. "Yet for the Negro writer, Marxism is but the starting point." Wright already demonstrates the independence that would later throw him out of the United States Communist Party. As critical principle, his next sentence sounds more African than Euro-American. "No theory of life can take the place of life." He likewise saw nationalism as a persuasion that must be accepted, possessed, and understood by black writers as part of the ideological make-up of the black community, but only to be transcended.

Important as these ideological coordinates remain, the contemporary force of Wright's prophetic reflections lies in their timely vision of black writing as a revolutionary power for human liberation. Since this essentially spiritual goal remains unreached (looking for the fulfillment of such goals is how we often end up ranting), we can recognize the health of black writing per Wright's "Blueprint" in the growing conviction among writers and readers that black literature has matured into a confident, irrepressible, consolidated energy for liberating people.

How this came about, if we can understand it, will demonstrate that it *has* come about, will make clearer what black literature presently is.

Black writing has transformed itself in an era when creative black people were responding to major changes in the world after World War II. In other words, the dynamics of liberation at work in black literature is part of an accelerated global movement of peoples and societies to get free of former repressions. "Perspective for Negro writers will come," Wright accurately predicted, "when they have looked and brooded so hard and long upon the harsh lot of their race and compared it with the hopes and struggles of minority people everywhere that the cold facts have begun to tell them something."

The two world developments that bookend the maturation of black writing are the proliferation of claims of the United States as superpower and the emergence of the concept of the Third World. All along black writers had insisted that theirs was a literature squarely based on the human condition and not parochial forays into protest literature. The struggles of minority peoples did break out everywhere after World War II, including the United States, and the comparisons black people made did tell them something. China, Vietnam, Cuba, the Congo, Algeria, Angola, Chile, South Africa, Lebanon, Grenada, El Salvador—not everyone could miss the relationship between the domination blacks had endured in America and the far-spread applications of power where the

United States and its white or imitation European allies were busy protecting their interests. Slave-guilt, insecurity, inferiority started falling away with isolated self-perception and as blacks became more aggressive in the push for human rights. History has been kinder to writers who share Wright's liberationist goals (not necessarily his opinions and attitues) than to begging ambassadors.

The centrality to human experience of black writing becomes more plausible with advances in world liberation efforts. The blighted circumstances under which Africans in America have had to flesh out their lives has been *the* human condition for all but a few privileged exploiters. Peoples' history reverses the precepts of mainstream Western literary criticism which pushes literature into spaces for those who are privileged and therefore "free," those who are not but accept the example of those who are, and the rest of us, who write mere protest literature. If black writing, raging for freedom, expresses the human condition, in what condition does that leave white writers, readers, and their concerns?

Obviously, two views of the condition of humanity are at odds here. Less obvious is the contention between two humanisms. One counts *human* in the distance of the break with nature, the dominion over nature, and by extended practice, over those who have made less of a break with nature. The other situates *human* in balance with nature, and balance within society.

Cultural historians naturally seize on moments and movements like the sixties in black literature, but a black-oriented humanism has been accelerating during the last half-century. The legacies of the 1960s are important, even when festooned with false consciousness. The pugnacity of militant black poetry voiced a determination to fight and die for the right to be oneself—brutal in phrasing, but necessary, according to Hegel's lord-bondservant relation, for the dominated to claim the honor that is an adjunct to self-consciousness, to humanhood. Black writing in the sixties reflected the violence of self-reclamation in the face of hostility. It made a violent and therefore decisive break with inert literary traditions. It sharply redirected literary norms towards popular black speech and thought, as already illustrated in folklore and popular culture. It shaped a new dominant voice for black literature, closer to "the collective sense of Negro life in America," that Wright sought.

Another lasting significance of that cultural revolution was the reidentification with Africa. It surprises to look back and find Wright— who along with Ellison and the early Baldwin insisted on identifying American blacks with Western man—understanding clairvoyantly the need of coming black writers to heal the wound that severed blacks from their ancestral homeland. Wright saw that "Negro writers must have in their consciousness the foreshortened picture of the *whole*, nourishing culture from which they were torn in Africa, and of the long, complex (and for the most part, unconscious) struggle to regain in some form and under alien conditions of life a *whole* culture again."

Recovery of Africa has been significant in ending what Orlando Patterson calls the "natal alienation" of all slave existence, the enforced arrest of all vital relations with any of one's kin, contemporaries or ancestors, past or to come. With all its limits, Haley's *Roots* succeeded as popular, myth-making literature in helping to end the Topsy situation in black imagination, the self-concept of having just grown out of a plantation owner's greedy thoughts.

Of many manifestations, the narratives of Ishmael Reed, especially the masterpiece *Mumbo Jumbo*, demonstrate the security of the new African identification by possessing it so thoroughly as to play among its historical spaces while completely at home with his literary persona. "Theme for Negro writers will emerge," Wright prophesied, "when they have begun to feel the meaning of the history of their race as though they in one life time had lived it themselves throughout all the long centuries." A celebratory, carefree wit has entered black writing, the alacrity of family reunion, the intoxicating light of new day after the long night of solitary confinement.

Explicitly, Africa has been introduced into black American writing as spiritual speech, not merely the cabaret images of the so-called Harlem Renaissance, nor yet as naturalistic possession, based in familiar experience. The repossession has so far been lyrical, metaphorical, hallucinatory, mythical, as one grasps the personality of a parent one meets for the first time as an adult. Aside from Haley's researched synthesis, Alice Walker's *The Color Purple* is singular in episoding Africa and Africans as lived experiences. More frequently, Africa is exalted epiphany in some of the best poems of Henry Dumas, Baraka, Jayne Cortez, Etheridge Knight. Africa is invoked in recent novels to lift the narrative to expanded vision: the ancestor who flew home in Toni Morrison's *Song of Solomon*; the African captives who walked home across the seas in Paule Marshall's *Praise Song for the Widow*; the African women who bare their breasts in Jadine's dreams in Morrison's *Tar Baby*, who inspire unaided flight again in Richard Perry's *Montgomery's Children*, who are still captive slaves in the hold of modern cruise ships in William Melvin Kelley's *Dunsfords Travels Everywheres*, who sail a skeletal ghostship along the Mississippi collecting the bones of black victims in Dumas' "Ark of Bones," or who survive in family tradition in Lucille Clifton's *Generations.*

The recovery of Africa sprang from the energies of black nationalism. The Third World concept challenges the chauvinist elements of that nationalism. Through this concept and its applications in world politics, black consciousness has sifted the clarifying perceptions of Marx and other socialist theory. The example of Fanon was notable: black psychiatrist of Martinique, Parisianized, serving the French in Algeria by treating the victims of French torture, who then abruptly joined the Algerian revolution and became its chief ideologist. The example of Nkrumah, Che, Patrice Lumumba, Amil Cabral, Samor Machel. The black opposition to the war in Vietnam.

Part of the process of realizing that they were not alone, not some isolated herd of victims who had earned their pariahdom through some freaky subhuman constitution, as many white American intellectuals still want to argue, was the appreciation by African-Americans of the nationalistic source of world resistance against domination; but the persistent role of socialism has been noted as well. These history lessons were pointed enough to demand an about-face from Amiri Baraka, from cultural nationalism to revolutionary socialism. More generally, the nationalism of black contemporaries has been modified, partly by Third World history, to one, in Wright's forecast, "that knows its ultimate aims are unrealizable within the framework of capitalist America; a nationalism whose reason for being lies in the simple fact of self-possession and in the consciousness of the interdependence of people in modern society." One also encounters some skepticism about the viability of democratic socialism in today's international politics.

The Third World is being absorbed into black writing imaginatively, metaphorically, culturally. It figures as the Mutafikah in *Mumbo Jumbo,* a cell of hip secret agents burglarizing museums to repatriate cultural treasures. It figures in the sensitive portrayal of Paule Marshall's splendid "Brazil." In the liberationist poems of June Jordan, Baraka, Audre Lorde and Jayne Cortez. In the appreciations of Latin culture in Ntosake Shange and Quincy Troupe. In the publication and promotion of Third World American writers by Ishmael Reed, whose Before Columbus Foundation sponsors a nonaggressive America of civilizations that came to this continent from Africa, Asia and Ireland before the colonizing, exploitative European system arrived.

If Africa deepens the self-concept of black writing, the Third World gives it fuller dimension. It takes from Africa a reinforcement of the value already placed on oral culture, the organizing energies of ritual, sources of sacred symbology, nonlinear organization of time and space, magic. Third world cultures have fed these impulses. Fantasy, psychokinesis, astrology, spirits, legends, myth, dreams, premonitions figure in contemporary black writing as acknowledged presences in the lives of its characters, checking a naturalism that too easily ends in *victimage*, but also evidencing the flow of vast transrational consciousnesses undisturbed by Western cognition. Under the impress of these sources, fresh formalistic possibilities are opening out, but particularly in black narrative.

The most powerful present energy in post-Wright black writing, the womanist perspective, was unguessed by him. ("Womanist" distinguishes an orientation among black women from white feminism, per Alice Walker's *In Search of Our Mother's Garden*.) Paradoxically, it may be decisive in restructuring the humanism his blueprint aimed for. Building on the male-directed initiatives of the sixties, black women writers posed a dialectical challenge to the false male consciousness in that movement. They exposed the manhood militance in black writing as convenient self-service.

More robust conceptions of life become unavoidable once the equally honorable prizes of female consciousness, of the interior life of children, of the inescapable circumstance (though black male writers had mostly tried to escape it) of family came into the picture. This rounder perspective arrived when a longer view of history was needed, after shortfall leaps toward instant social change. Where black consciousness focuses on the goal of sociopolitical freedom, that freedom becomes one among many pursued in black humanist thought. (By black humanism I mean a humanism oriented by black people, not confined to them.) The post-sixties mood has been to regard white racism as a snowstorm, to borrow a figure from Wright's fiction—a hostile element of climate that, if perennial, must be permanently contested, not only to vanquish it but also in order to reach the warmer goals of living. And since every life has storms, the stormy weather in black writing is no less planted in the essential condition of humanity because it has the totally gratuitous inclemency of Western sociopathy to deal with. Where the endings of narratives by black men were often flawed and self-conflicted, unable to declare a "victory" mocked by historical reality, black women writers restored the place of love, growth, and healing as satisfactory resolutions in both life and literature.

One courageous representation of the higher levels of womanist consciousness is June Jordan's *Civil Wars*. In producing, to my reckoning, the first major collection of essays by a black woman, Jordan has variegated the role of shaping literary and social perception held by the essay collections of Jones, Baldwin, Ellison and Wright. In a "Declaration of an Independence I Would Just as Soon Not Have," she searches for balance among the claims made on her by black consciousness, feminism and the Third World, symptomizing the intricacy of themes and issues of the broadening humanism.

This respect for complexity is held high in the novels of Toni Morrison, possibly the keenest literary influence among current black novelists. Her fiction cherishes the awareness of surprise, the slippery variousness of human being, its wild, freaky undersides, its asymmetrical balances, estranged from coded ideologies, feminist or otherwise. Black women writers, Morrison included, underscore the priority of life over theories of life—but this does not mean that theories of life are banished. They may reject literary ball-hugging, but less often noticed, they have replaced it with a committed, humanist attitude toward society.

White readers sometimes too quickly feel themselves let off the hook by the ascendancy of black women writers and their attention to black male chauvinism. "It's not a protest novel" has become the obligatory code of recommendation between white critic and reader. The insanity of the social order, the deterioration of contemporary values under the onslaught of consumerism, evergreen racism—all gifts of white civilization—are often signified by corner-mouth allusions in some recent novels, as well-known givens. Wright would probably lament this premature sophistication, as I do, in taking too much needed sociopolitical examination for granted.

Southern novelist Reynolds Price reviewed Morrison's *Song of Solomon* with one reservation to his praise: it didn't include white people. The generous interpretation is that he didn't want to be let off the hook. (Imagine white novelists complaining that their white colleagues don't include black characters.) Morrison fulfilled Price's wish in her next novel, *Tar Baby*, a wonderful expression of the new humanism, not only in its effortless integration of politics and story. The white family sympathetically but scathingly pictured in the novel, whose presence drew resentment from reactionary reaches of black nationalism, is integral to Morrison's post-plantation island microcosm of the West and the rest of us. Her narrative possesses the *perspective* on social reality Wright hoped black writers would achieve. A parable on the economics of unequal exchange is implied in the response to a few stolen apples. Similarly sutured among the minutest observations of social manners are shrewd, original commentaries on class domination, Vietnam, me-ism, capitalism, consumerism and of course racism. *Tar Baby* lives at the height of its time.

The ultimate political revelation of the womanist position, the needed illumination that revises Marx, is the recognition that the central, meaningful principle of life is the struggle towards self-realization, not just against economic or racial injustice—which means that neither Marxism nor black nationalism are final answers, as Wright had noted—but against all forms of domination, by anybody. Womanist expression exhibits occasional lapses into self-righteousness and jingoistic particularism, hostages to future confoundments of its best principles. Carrying this inevitable deadweight, black women have nevertheless mediated the fusion between co-evolving black consciousness and black humanism.

Black women writers have touched different points of emphasis within this broad, almost religious world view, from the intricate observation of individuals slogging on towards selfhood to the militantly ideological promotion of womanist ideas. Alice Walker has done both with genius in *The Color Purple*. The notion of the "great work" is suspect as a patriarchal, canon-hardening manipulation of cultural imperialism. Knowing this, *The Color Purple* is still a great novel. If the Nobel prize committee is ever going to redeem itself as something more than a white, male book-of-the-year club, *The Color Purple* should be one of the first books it reads. The novel's wiliness lies among the almost inexhaustible number of ways it provokes us to feel and think beyond the complacently defined levels of our personal realities.

One secret of its majesty lies in its tapping the emotional and formal strengths of the ex-slave narrative. Black humanism is refreshed by this genre's favored trajectories from social death (Orlando Patterson's characterization of slavery) to selfhood and personal freedom. Male obtuseness has obscured the patterning of the ex-slave narrative in Janie's development in *Their Eyes Were Watching God* because we don't want to recognize the near-slavery in which some black men have held their women. This familiar, metonymic trajectory, from nothing to something, makes Celie's triumphant coming-through a paradigm of immanent humanity finding itself.

Walker's novel fulfills the need that Wright foresaw, in view of the incapacities he then perceived in the black church and the black middle class, for the black writer "to do no less than create the values by which his race is to struggle, live and die." The utopianism of *The Color Purple* adds handsomely to the formation of a black humanist dream, most unlike the American dream in neither fulfilling itself at others' expense nor excluding anyone from its hopefulness.

The difference black women writers have made is easily missed if confined too narrowly to print. They play a singular, preeminent role as intellectual and spiritual leaders in womanist thought and in American feminist thought as well. They are a political force. The Rainbow political concept needed the preparation of their creative initiatives. They are powerful advocates for ideas apart from their creative work. In Maya Angelou an exalted presence interprets the new humanism to the times in a way that recalls the personal greatness of Paul Robeson.

Instead of creating a separate chamber in African-American literature, black women's writing has flowered in the heart of it. They have recouped the rejected or misunderstood womanist visions of earlier writers like Zora Neale Hurston. And through their energizing of the new humanism, they have helped us see that it is not new at all, was richly seeded there all the time, breaking through in courageous isolation in Sterling Brown, Langston Hughes, Robert Hayden, Margaret Walker, Gwendolyn Brooks and others—some whose attempts to articulate it were swamped in degrees of victimhood and repression. So black writing is revitalizing earlier work in much the same way that jazz has become historically eclectic. The sense has never been stronger of black writing as a sustaining tradition.

The notable situation in black writing today is the flexible sharing of progressive, liberating values. Wright was working from the drawing board, not life, when he looked to the future for "the ideological unity of Negro writers and the alliance of that unity with all the progressive ideas of our day." Yet the cultural unity that does exist, reflected in Claudia Tate's *Black Women Writers at Work*, is about as close to Wright's star-filled gaze as black writing has come since slavery. It is there not only in the casual expressions of independence: Ntosake Shange saying "We do not have to refer continually to European art as the standard," or Nikki Giovanni declaring that "Very few Black women are writing out of respect for what White people think." It is also there in the sense of communion. Toni Cade finds her greatest influence in "the community of writers . . . writers have gotten their wagons in a circle, which gives us each something to lean against, to push off against." This cultural unity shows up in the intense intertextuality of current work, so that it is easier than ever to envision characters and their backgrounds turning up in the works of other writers.

Benjamin DeMott recently assessed contemporary American fiction as damaged by a post-sixties emotional deadening, "diseased response," "feelinglessness," "inner deadness"—compared to writers of earlier decades. Remarkably, he fails to look at black, particularly black women's, fiction of the times. No matter the constricting walls of the academic humanities and the national endowment reorganized to defend those battlements, black writing is finding lively, unauthorized reception around the world. Its health and vigor is one of the better kept secrets of the American literary nepotarchy frozen in its cultural narcissism.

A wry historical turnabout has taken place. White critics used to disparage black writing for being parochial, insufficiently absorbed in the human condition, lacking universality. The way the world turns today, it is white writing that suffers these deficiencies and black writing that embodies their contrary strengths.

But neither the aims Wright imagined nor the humanist direction in black writing could be satisfied by achieving a social awareness comparatively saner than in majority American literature that might have been there all along. Without the chance to evolve with recent transformations in the literature, the Richard Wright of 1937 might in fact have been as contemptuous about it as he was wrong about *Their Eyes Were Watching God*. Such was his critical and ideological arrogance that both Wright and his blueprint might be dismissed by many contemporary black writers (along with my retroactive interpretation).

But from the realism and clarity of Wright's position, some disturbing shadows hover over black writing. A large, supportive black audience has yet to be won. Many educated, even brilliant blacks don't read literature at all, and the print literacy of millions is being squandered. Maturity in black writing *as literature* is waxing beside the incipient horror of the declining quality of African-American life—rising poverty, the plague of unemployment, the collapse of family structure, the self-destruction and disappearance of black men, the secularization and weakening of black values in the polluted environment of the American mainstream.

Only the most naive interpretation of historical process could lay such crises on the shoulders of literature. A sensible Marxist precept urges proportion in estimating the impact superstructure can have on base. Common sense should further restrain our estimation of the impact of black writing on the American superstructure. The wider impact of black writing would have to be gauged in its multiple exchanges with other powerful energies: the media, education, the total spread of black communications, i.e., popular thought, music, press, political dialogue, etc. The advancing confidence, self-knowledge, and sense of direction of black writing within these contexts offer sources of hope and inspiration for the battles to be fought against old and new terrors, and that should be enough to ask of it.

Yet it says something about recent black literature and challenges still facing it that the most direct, analytical understanding of the massive social disorientation at the core of black society that we witness today is to be found in *Native Son* (1940) and other Wright fictions. If this is unacceptable, allow an alternative question: where is the intelligence in black writing that would now frame a blueprint or formulation of needs for the next four to five decades as perceptive and on target as Wright's was? And what kind of writing or creative work will have to be produced so that black ancestors in the twenty-first century can look back at these formulations with measured satisfaction, as we can today look back on Wright's?

AMIRI BARAKA

WHY'S/WISE

WHY'S/WISE IS A LONG POEM *in the tradition of the* Griots*
—but this is about African American (American) History. It is also like
Tolson's Liberia, *WCW's* Paterson, *Olson's* Maximus *in that it tries to*
tell the history/life like an ongoing-offcoming Tale.

I've been working on the piece now for almost two years; there are
some 25–30 parts, which are just now beginning to appear.

Also each part of the poem carries music with it.—AB

What about Literature? W-15

(Mr. Jelly Lord)

Fred D., my
main man
had tolt all
up there
How he scaped
& got to out
side, straight up
slavery
days

---

*The African Singers-Poets-Historians who carried word from bird, mouth to
ear, and who are the root of our African-Amer Oral Tradition.

My man
Fred, was
trying
to move
us
too

"Go on,

            Go on"

This trans lation

            speaking
            in
            tongues
                        p66–67 SNarratives
& there were others
both sisters
    & brothers
                    List
                        Names

                            Equiano
                            Roper
                            Brent
                            Brown
                            Pennington
                            The Crafts
                            Bibb
                            Rahahman
                            Montejo
                            etc.[1000]

"You are loosed from your moorings, and are free; I am fast in my
chains, and am a slave! You move merrily before the gentle gale, and I
sadly before the bloody whip! You are freedom's swift-winged angels,

that fly round the world; I am confined in bands of iron! O that I were free! O, that I were on one of your gallant decks, and under your protecting wing! Alas! betwixt me and you, the turbid waters roll. Go on, go on. O that I could also go! Could I but swim! If I could fly! O, why was I born a man, of whom to make a brute! The glad ship is gone; she hides in the dim distance. I am left in the hottest hell of unending slavery. O God, save me! God, deliver me! Let me be free! Is there any God? Why am I a slave? I will run away. I will not stand it. Get caught, or get clear, I'll try it. I had as well die with ague as the fever. I have only one life to lose. I had as well be killed running as die standing. Only think of it; one hundred miles straight north, and I am free! Try it? Yes! God helping me, I will. It cannot be that I shall live and die a slave. I will take to the water. This very bay shall yet bear me into freedom. The steamboats steered in a north-east course from North Point. I will do the same; and when I get to the head of the bay, I will turn my canoe adrift, and walk straight through Delaware into Pennsylvania. When I get there, I shall not be required to have a pass; I can travel without being disturbed. Let but the first opportunity offer, and, come what will, I am off. Meanwhile, I will try to bear up under the yoke. I am not the only slave in the world. Why should I fret? I can bear as much as any of them. Besides, I am but a boy, and all boys are bound to some one. It may be that my misery in slavery will only increase my happiness when I get free. There is a better day coming."

    Till the explosion came
        they sang toward

We never go back
    (for long)
    Only
    forward

This is the stage of
    our DuBois
& his the bulwark
    of us
    our saying & thinking
        articulator

of our
insides

true
measurer
of these
outsides

link from Fred
& he now dead

And under the sun
my boy
there is the thread
of track
where we runners
spin
fast faster
than
light

Can you see
the baton? (Well
Feel
It!)

From Fred to E.B.
to   Langston
to (Zora to Richard &Ted &
Jimmy &)
Margaret

to
WE!

A NOTE TO
PRESIDENT PASADOEKEEOH!
& His Wise Ass Reply W-16

[Ornette]

For this
for nothing
it dont swing
it cant sing
 ahrgh !
  hell w/ numbers
   & Barons
   & sun spanked lip
    of
    corn
  Oh Say
  we can
MURDER them
 can you
 See
  Oh
Say
we can
you
 See
MURDER

 porter
 reekin'

VAYA CON DIOS
contraption

constructed
of
pomade sculpture
shoulder
pads
horsies
whore sees

              (A RAY GUN)

Ho Ho!
Hum
  Ho
    Hum

  (it was america
  that patch
  unner
  the desert

  the parchment
  red
  upside
  down
  sd
'!Nigger"

            (He Replies)

        stop dancin
        in the wind
        feet aint touchin
        the ground

I've beat
you
&
hung
you
&
sent yr
picture
round

Stop dancin
Stop wigglin

I am Elvis Nightingale
Jim Crow Señor
President Wilkie's ghost
Lincoln's bullet hole

Rachel Sumner, a "wide girl"
Mason & Dixon
August Cream
Don Lee

& Maulana bug out

Pressure Dude of these
Uncreated
Vacancies!
& I spit

power
yr toes light up
to salute spookarabian
bandito

So quiet
 its silence
murders best in the
 no sound
  dark

No we aint givin up La Isla
 Encantada
 nor
E.116th St. either

the shorties are coming
the interesting crazy people
murderers name
    Boutique Buddy
    Expensive Earl
    Stiff Siff
    Underwater Turncoat
   Left Friend Ball-No

    Up under stairs shivering-Johnny
    Joey with the "dumb" wife
     & other
     flags of our
Holy light

  I wan to splain
   you in
  yr lank witch
   Ham
  & Cheese
that I is everybody's
 Daddy

 Every booties
  Pirate

& the No for every
  Yes!

Now are there
  questions?
                (transmission
                    weakening)

You, in the back
  row

  OPEN FIRE!

Courageousness

In the 60's, there was emotion to go round
barreling explosions, at and against, waves
of running, the world itself was feeling, all
feeling. I felt that.
Those shadows haunt us now in various ways.
Women's mouths at odd angles like laughing.
People we know can reappear carrying shadows
which seem to fall from their hands, but musically.
If we wanted to we could locate boxes packed tight
with skulls and odors, murmurs of some distant
hysteria.
There *was* a rush of us. Some of us wondrous lovely
gorgeous people. That feeling and talking. Such moving
about away and toward. We pointed our fingers alot. We
roared like something out of nature. Like chained beasts
climbing through windows, sometimes we was strange.
The taste of us was acquired and hypnotic, glass crackers
& onions, some dark beer to wash it down. And here these
    maniac
street lamps are still batting off and on, surely they've had to
change whats inside them making them do that. It cant be the
    very same

ones. Like these workmen opening our heads
to fix the wires, or put in new batteries,
change a cracked globe or yank the old bulb.
In the 60's there was enough feeling enough emotion
to go round. There was no reason to be square, that's what
we felt. We could do anything, be anything, even free. That's
how young we were. That's now long ago, that was.

I Investigate the Sun

I investigate
the sun. Let it do me
when it come. I am commissioned
by not only charcoal people with brilliant
hues, but laborers in the woods pausing for a moment
to sing while young master dies of that stuff where your blood
too thin to clot. I investigate the sun—and for my trouble, get music
abstract designs I figure out. I fancy myself Pythagoras sometimes, some
times Langston Hughes. You see, I investigate the sun, for people with hard
dirty hands. I find out what its fire and brightness means. For the old lady
polishing floors up on the hill for the permanently smiling, I support her
music, as it trembles against that dazzling flo' I give her Ra or if she want
BB King, I bring that back as well, do tell, I investigate the sun. Call me
agent proxy paid representative, a lobbyist for those without lobbies, think
of me as surrogate for those who sing under impossible weights or resist bald
head guys with pointed teeth and white collars pulled outside they coats
suppose to be powerful. My rejoinder and answer, my constant line they all
grow hard against, where are you in the sun's shine, what you know of its
fire? Have you checked your vain insistence against life's life, yellow & red
& atomic before atomic. How does your projection list against Ra's ra ra?
No, for real, I investigate the sun. I am paid for this vocation, it's not
above my station, sun checker for a nation, magnifying glass for a class,
I investigate the sun. Bring back its dance and music, it's design and
hip rime. Sun poet Sun singer Sun warrior Sun why you what you who you **how you**
those my questions as I rise into its hot glamour. I investigate the sun.
Doubt it if you will, what does a shadow know anyway? I investigate
the sun

Aug 29, 1982
NYC Comm Corr. Fac.

MICHAEL S. HARPER

Polls

Some bloods can't count and won't vote;
imagine Desmond ahead of Trane
on the wrong instrument.
—I'm not saying Desmond can't play—
but *Playboy* was embarrassed,
sounding like swing all over again:
whuhfolks creating jazz—best records in the world
being sold under the counter;
Mile's soundtrack for a movie
only ten inches wide.

Trane created a freak show;
everybody scared he wouldn't salute
the old musicians,
the women of salutation,
his mother, cousin, wife,
the best connections
from the kitchen to the best restaurants.

Some knew such playing
is possible
only when you're ready to die.

Most whites always keeping score,
making it too easy to find the way,
guaranteeing you'll never feel loss,
black and white on paper,
in the ground.

Obscurity

When he lost his leg
above the knee
he wasn't drunk;
cold sober
and sweet in the cheeks,
his compositions
on *fm* radio
right next to his mouthpiece,
woodshedding, leading the war.

Then there was the year of bad
phrasing; another, content,
with short interludes
of playing too loud.

Most women couldn't stand it;
not *his* woman,
who thought Lester Young
was an excuse
for Coleman Hawkins,
two family names
on the same instrument.

Disc jockeys were favorable
after the leg was gone;
blind with diabetes,
still drinking *rooster red*,
he could come alive
in jam sessions
with another's mouthpiece—
his own in the woodshed
housing the wooden leg.

Engagements

To work steady you play the easy
tempos; drinks, on the starched
tab, are free; a flask hidden
from the cleaning lady.

Engraved by a club owner,
short on grit and sentiment,
he went sweet and lost his teeth
while still in his teens;
the roll of the bhang,
on Arabian paper,
couldn't save him,
stockingcap pulled down
on each player's ears.

Alive, on the tab,
and no credit for his song,
he was forced to mingle in the crowd,
some of the best-dressed
losers in the world.

There was smack:
oh the distances you could make up
in a hurry
with the proper bloodstream,
payback,
the cost of the song.

Rage at the hottest tempos,
or play slow.

Sugarloaf

Untempo ruined his style;
Trane would come in,
ruining the fabric
of swing, of bebop.

At the bridge Chambers would stop
humming in the high registers,
Philly Joe in the outhouse
kicking his traps,
one last exit blocked for Garland,
out of doors in block chords,
trying to double-clutch and catch up,
giving the finger to the engineers.

We are always our best audience,
resting on the breastbone
of each performance,
refusing, in greasepaint,
and monkey suits,
to entertain, the mask
on blonde fables at midnight,
without candlelight.

In Newport, (Sweden was over)
there was only Japan,
the taste of Blue Note,
the only sheet music
you could read.

When you pay the heavy dues of practice
play through the pain;

the easy chops are for playing after the break,
nowhere to go but the ruint swoops
of the counterpuncher,
unwinding to cycles of Lester
leaping in waterfalls of addiction:
paychecks for the bills long past due.

Bandstand

Monk's dissonant hat
willing every change of direction;
all those influences in your head
touching the wrong target—
none of this recorded,
the ears of the kitchen painted black,
all the musicians in common clothes,
dressing for the ancestors.

You learned to appreciate the pews,
the cooling iron,
the cooling board where the bodies,
guns in the recording studios,
became the tuning forks,
meals eaten while running in place
for Mother and Dad
who could dance.

My Book on Trane

—for McCoy Tyner

Waiting in lineups
in the rain you hear cosmic
conversations, "how many feet
above sea level,"
as though you could sign up
to play with Trane in the back room.

"What's the point waiting
for the last set if you can't see,"
and you smiling, underage,
protected from the blonde waitresses,
your new wife chilled to the bone
adrift in the fog of this music.

Every fool thought Trane should be taller,
an oak standing in water in his alligator
shoes, nobody able to hear Jimmy above the deafening
timber of Elvin, always able to hear.

Sonny, 'just out of retirement,'
traveling with barbells,
had to have somewhere to play;
Clifford's dead; Miles won't play
facing crowds, addicted to playing 'live.'
One night I thought I'd have to squash
my hero, a dime-sized table, him
with his cuffs in my drink, peering
into the blue-green waters of Hawaii,
off Broadway, the Black Hawk, in North Beach.

Aiisha's always prettier in the rain,
the music loudest outside
coming into the brake—
the smoke coming off Elvin
as he strides across the street
to a working phone,
just like jetlag:
you can't believe the arc of light
in plain sight:
waiting for the drum major
from Pontiac with his brothers,
the steam coming off his wet clothes
in droves.

CYRUS CASSELLS

Atlantic Window

—for Stanley Kunitz

Abundance begins here—at the sea lip:
On the Cape I have come to God and Proteus, come to rest in
    the wild places:
The bold, supernal dunes, the whisker-still galaxies of
    marshlands,
The beaches where I pause and study
The Atlantic, teal and taciturn, the Atlantic, glittering and
    fluent,
As on blonde days the fishermen stagger
And the bluefish wake to the breathless dream of land.

Having combed the autumn dunes,
I have been on desolate moons, wind-worked to pure
    scrimshaw,
And found deer, cranberries, a plum dusk,
Pools of sweet water cached in the sand.

The streets stink of fish, after the dark
Gimcrack shawls of squalls and rain.
I amble through rumors of shipwrecks, ghosts,
Sense the red broom-sweep of the beacon even in my sleep—

I have my tremendous window.
The moon-jacklit boat comes to it, shimmering,
And the bride-sweet cirrus cloud,

And sometimes the streak of a squirrel, like the deft, sudden
Stroke of the watercolorist, whose sentient brush distills the
    bay.

And now, clear and fugitive, in jack-in-the-box splendor,
The baby whale blooms into view:
Wild world; wild messenger—you are the moment's crown,
    sea-loved:
When providence brims to the outermost land,
No lack, no lack, but in my human mind.

MARILYN NELSON WANIEK

Mama's Promise

I have no answer to the blank inequity
of a four-year-old dying of cancer.
I saw her on t.v. and wept
with my mouth full of meatloaf.

I constantly flash on disasters now;
red lights shout *Warning. Danger.*
everywhere I look.
I buckle him in, but what if a car
with a grille like a sharkbite
roared up out of the road?
I feed him square meals,
but what if the fist of his heart
should simply fall open?
I carried him safely
as long as I could,
but now he's a runaway
on the dangerous highway.
Warning. Danger.
I've started to pray.

But the dangerous highway
curves through blue evenings
when I hold his yielding hand
and snip his miniscule nails
with my vicious-looking scissors.
I carry him around

234

like an egg in a spoon,
and I remember a porcelain fawn,
a best friend's trust,
my broken faith in myself.
It's not my grace that keeps me erect
as the sidewalk clatters downhill
under my rollerskate wheels.

Sometimes I lie awake
troubled by this thought:
It's not so simple to give a child birth;
you also have to give it death,
the jealous fairy's christening gift.

I've always pictured my own death
as a closed door,
a black room,
a breathless leap from the mountain top
with time to throw out my arms, lift my head,
and see, in the instant my heart stops,
a whole galaxy of blue.
I imagined I'd forget,
in the cessation of feeling,
while the guilt of my lifetime floated away
like a nylon nightgown,
and that I'd fall into clean, fresh forgiveness.

Ah, but the death I've given away
is more mine than the one I've kept:
from my hand the poisoned apple,
from my bow the mistletoe dart.

Then I think of Mama,
her bountiful breasts.
When I was a child, I really swear,

Mama's kisses could heal.
I remember her promise,
and whisper it over my sweet son's sleep:

> *When you float to the bottom, child,*
> *like a mote down a sunbeam,*
> *you'll see me from a trillion miles away:*
> *my eyes looking up to you,*
> *my arms outstretched for you like night.*

I Send Mama Home

I send you down the road from Paden
scaring bobwhites and pheasants
back into the weeds;
a jackrabbit keeps pace
in front of your headlights
if you drive there at night.
I send you to Boley
past a stand of post oaks
and the rolling blackjack hills.

On Pecan Street
a brown rectangle outlines the spot
where King's Ice House used to be.
The Farmer's and Merchant's Bank
is closed, grizzled boards
blind its windows.
The ghosts of Mister Turner,
the murdered banker,
and Floyd Birdwell,
the right hand of Pretty Boy Floyd,

spill like shadows
over the splintering floor.

This was the city of promise,
the town where no white man
showed his face after dark.
The *Progress* extolled it
in twice weekly headlines
as "Boley, the Negro's Dream."

Mama, I give you this poem
so you can drive past
Hazel's Department Store,
Bragg's Barber Shop,
the Truelove Cafe,
the Antioch Baptist Church,
the C.M.E. church and school,
the Creek-Seminole college.

I deliver you again
to your parents' bedroom
where the piano gleamed
like a black pegasus,
to the three-room farmhouse,
to the Oklahoma plains.
I give you the horses, Prince and Lady,
and the mules. I give you your father's car,
a Whippet, which you learned to drive
at a slow bounce through the pasture.
I give you the cows and calves
you and your brother played rodeo on,
the full smoke house, the garden,
the fields of peanuts and cotton.

I send you back
to the black town you missed
when you were at college
and on the great white way.
I let you see
behind the mask you've worn
since the fifty year ago morning
when you waved goodbye from the train.

The Century Quilt

—for Sarah Mary Taylor, Quilter

My sister and I were in love
with Meema's Indian blanket.
We fell asleep under army green
issued to Daddy by Supply.
When Meema came to live with us
she brought her medicines, her cane,
and the blanket I found on my sister's bed
the last time I visited her.
I remembered how I'd planned to inherit
that blanket, how we used to wrap ourselves
at play in its folds and be chieftains
and princesses.

Now I've found a quilt
I'd like to die under:
Six Van Dyke brown squares,
two white ones, and one square
the yellowbrown of Mama's cheeks.

Each square holds a sweet gum leaf
whose fingers I imagine
would caress me into the silence.

I think I'd have good dreams
for a hundred years under this quilt,
as Meema must have, under her blanket,
dreamed she was a girl again in Kentucky
among her yellow sisters,
their grandfather's white family
nodding at them when they met.
When their father came home from his store
they cranked up the pianola
and all of the beautiful sisters
giggled and danced.
She must have dreamed about Mama
when the dancing was over:
a lanky girl trailing after her father
through his Oklahoma field.

Perhaps under this quilt
I'd dream of myself,
of my childhood of miracles,
of my father's burnt umber pride,
my mother's ochre gentleness.
Within the dream of myself
perhaps I'd meet my son
or my other child, as yet unconceived.
I'd call it The Century Quilt,
after its pattern of leaves.

MARGARET WALKER

My Mississippi Spring

My heart warms under snow;
flowers with forsythia,
japonica blooms, flowering quince,
bridal wreath, blood root and violet;
yellow running jasmine vine,
cape jessamine and saucer magnolias:
tulip shaped, scenting lemon musk upon the air.
My Mississippi Spring—
my warm loving heart a-fire
with early greening leaves,
dogwood branches laced against the sky;
wild forest nature paths
heralding Resurrection
over and over again
Easter morning of our living
every Mississippi Spring!

Black Paramour

I am the woman of kings;
the love supreme of emperors;
of ancient nubian conquerers,
and men of destiny.
I couched with the Borgias and the Caesars,
with Claudius and Antony,
and I knew Rimini.
I was with the Bourbons
and I colored the pages of all the tedious stages
in History. Poets and composers
worshipped at my shrine.
I nourished them with nectar and with wine,
ambrosia of the gods.
Lust for power, wealth, and fame
pulsed through their sensual veins,
while music, art, and poetry, and sculptured stone
thrived round my purple throne.
I was the fate of Empires lost
when kingdoms crumbled into dust.
My hate drew dire revenge and vengeance from on high;
your late Olympus heard my cry
and Eros, Bacchus, Venus all enraged
Black Isis, Astoreth, Astarte, all upstaged
invoked their Ares-Mars for war.
Cupidity and their vulgarity
brought evil to my side
and in those days of danger made me ride
far from the death of love and dreams
to find another light-of-love
and still a regal queen
today, I quickly leave the scene

before they know the deadly role I play:
the asp upon my bosom, the poison on my tongue;
how much my sexual royalty has wrung
and what by politic I mean;
what storms my slaves of passion stirred,
how much because of me occurred,
nor let them now forget they knew my dust
forgetting all their vampire lust
while I remain eternally the same—
Black paramour, eternal vestal flame.

Birmingham 1963

Out of my heart's long yearning from the
    fullness and futility of an overbearing
    patience and a suffering long waiting;
Out of the deepest long denial of sacrifice and
    slowly germinating complaint;
Through the streets of Birmingham the ghosts
    of bitter memories are waking and walking
    close with pain.
Hate is beseiged and beseeched in the streets
    of Birmingham. O my God, the naked pain
    in the streets and jails and alleys and
    the overlooking hills of Birmingham.

BRENDA MARIE OSBEY

"In These Houses of Swift Easy Women"

In the room the women come and go talking of Michelangelo.
          —T. S. Eliot, *"The Love Song of J. Alfred Prufrock"*

in these houses
of swift easy women
drapes and the thin panels between them
hug to the walls—
some promise of remembering,
litanies of minor
pleasures and comforts.

these women know subtlety
sleight of hand
cane liquor
island songs
the poetry of soundlessness.

a man could get lost
in such a house as this
could lose his way
his grasp of the world
between the front room
and the crepe myrtle trees out back.

The Bone Step-Women

i do not hear the words
the women speak on touro street
i only see them moving
in vertical lines
their hands angled out
from their hips and thighs

i know they are singing
but i do not know the song.

they separate my bones
into neat white stacks
moving them in the dust
like bits of stone
one finds something of interest
in the way they are cast
ramshackle
on the side of the road
stirs them into dustclouds
sends up a slipshod rain
her own aging joints
toil toward motion

she is dancing in the dust
between the alleys of my bones.

The Wastrel-Woman Poem

she goes out in the night again
wastreling about
her thin-woman blues
slung over one shoulder
an empty satchel
one carries out of habit.

the first time you see her
you think her body
opens some new forbidden zone
you think she has something to do with you
she never does.
at least not the way you mean.
not here.
not any more.
lives ago perhaps
she would have been
your second cousin
a lover who murdered you
a woman who passed you on market-day
but never spoke
threw bones to the ground
or stepped over you
as though you were dust or air
some spirit she knew of
but did not counsel.

the first time you see her
a story begins
that has nothing to do with you:

a woman uncle feather knew
and never told you of
you were so young
and one day he lost the connection
between your question
and her name

her name could have been anything
but you never would know
she would pass
and look into your eyes
directly
as if you were not there
as if she knew it
and would not tell.

tak-o-me-la
tak-o-me-la

something you hear when she passes
sounds from another living
but there she is
wastreling about you

someone calls to you
you watch your thin-woman move
between baskets of fish
and date-wine bottles

you turn to answer

heart like a brick
down between your knees.

Devices of Icons

*(to Charles H. Rowell, after hearing Audre
Lorde read on 10 April 1980, a preliminary)*

1.
i don't quite recall
the name or scheme of the poem
but i know it had to do
with young black men dying early
eating themselves
blood and intestines
hands and feet and eyes

i suppose it
had to do with eulogy

it had to do with your echo.

2.
how you have prided yourself
in these tales i spin
but in the spinning i saw
how the ones that spoke of pain
you held somewhat longer
fingering the edges
of a page holding someone else's pain
and called it
aesthetic

and i need to let you know
that each of us is a character
in his own pain.

3.
but, father
maker of icons
feeler of cults
i have seen you drinking in sorrow
when your own had run dry
and i have seen you dancing a solo
against the bodies of people
who crowded you
away from yourself
into a corner
meant to be a kingdom

and did you love there?
did you ever love there?

4.
i want to hear you speak a word
that is not sorrow
i want to hear you bring forth
as you do with no one present
stripped bare in the evening's broken sun
holding your thighs
knees bent like a granny-woman
head tilted back
moaning
moaning
in the valley

moaning beyond your own
bent-kneed
fear.

5.
i had meant to tell you
years from now
what i knew you saw and felt
beneath that magnolia tree
just off gentilly boulevard
when i met you
but you look at me
secret
and name me daughter

and i can not pretend i do not see you
and you can not pretend
you are not seen.

CHARLES H. ROWELL

Grandpa Paul

You used to hold
my left hand.
Yours was wet and
sticky
and smelled of cigar.
When I would leave
and go with daddy or mamma
sometimes
I would put my hand
to my nose
and dream of manhood
all the way home.

You knew the directions.
From your own land
into town,
where white men—
black, too, sometimes—
glared at you—and me.
Perhaps,
it was how you held
your head
in that upturned way,
so familiar to this family,

how you spoke
without chewing the edges
of your words,
or how you walked
so imperial
my rehearsal
cannot repeat.

Down to the creek
brought you bass, cat,
or perch.
You taught me
blackberry vines,
water oaks, beavers. . . .
I have not forgotten
your cane
splitting the head
of that moccasin.
Or your gnarled fingers
nesting those robins
back into the tree—
the young
squawking their stringy necks
back at you.

Thirty years later
five hundred miles away
my back holds tight and tall,
and the lifelines
inch from my palm
to travel up
my closing hand.

Window

—for Brenda Marie Osbey

1. I stand
   before
   the dining room window
   fronting
   my summer garden,
   declaring itself
   at the final reaches
   of the yard.

   Among the year's chorus
   of voices—
   friends' and enemies'—
   was Andrew saying,
   "This window
   is no place
   to see the world.
   You have to go out
   among the people."

2. Much bigger than mine,
   daddy's garden
   had the expanse
   of a universe,
   where I held battles
   with armies in early corn.
   They never confronted me,
   but ambushed from behind—
   what with my plywood gun
   like big brother's rifle
   from Pork Chop Hill.

I hunted them—
Saturdays mostly.
Got two or three
before mamma
would call me for lunch.

Usually
the language
of Alabama loam
was friendly and precise:
telling me
the ways of melons
and tomatoes.
The heads of cabbages
and lettuce
perfected the aim
of my slingshot bazooka.
And when I'd turn my back
for chow
they'd rise up
in planned attack.
I always remembered
the security
of okra and collards
and the gate
by the chinaberry tree
as old as daddy.

That tree was a watchtower.
Sometimes Elvin
and I climbed it.
And if he saw a car
on the road out front
he'd ask,

"Who that?
Who . . . who . . . ?"
And I'd say,
"Old owl,
the featherass bird.
Can your feet
fit a limb?"
And he'd rush down
from the tree
and I after him.
And we'd wrestle,
play old gray horse,
knife,
or some other game:
"Old gray horse."
"I'll ride."
"How many times . . . ."
Two or four or one.
And we'd exchange our loot
of chinaberries
from each other's hands.

3. This window
   orders a lost life,
   but I believe
   I am
   among the people
   here,
   where I know
   I must come
   to keep watch.

MICHAEL S. WEAVER

Paradise Revisited

in the south now,
they work in factories,
leaving the wooden houses
and fields of corn
to put eight hours in pulp mills,
farms are too small
to bring in the big money,
all day on a tractor
on seventy-five acres
is nothing except close to God,
the poverty of clothes
worn smooth and dull;
shelling peas and canning
is done in leisure time now,
some fields go unweeded,
hogs are down to one sow,
all but three sucklings are sold;
men and women come home
to stand motionless
in the silence for a while,
to forget the noise, the clutter,
in the evening old farmers
relax the way they always have,
on their porches lying down,
barefooted, stray cats watching,
dry flies singing in the trees,

chickens clucking and strutting,
while the air turns and tumbles,
sucking pine needles
along a velvet tongue.

A New Nephilim

after the Lord
laid the world out,
kissed it full with water,
angels made the first life,
coming on the young women
at night singing, rushing
breezes stirring across naked
skin, giant men were born who
knew all that God knew, becoming
gods themselves, the populated
myths of Greece and Rome. it was
too much, God killed them all
in surging oceans, their memories—
Ovid's dreams. now in a
single hundred years the rape
of night breezes has seeded
the planet with industry,
the thunder the giants made
when they leaped for stars—
God's anger around us,
seething, swollen with hot breath,
yellow eyes on our disobedience
like bloody fires in the night,
or the eyes of the cats.

A Tin Roof Song

the music is a tap dancer's sliding soft shoe,
a regimen of holy roller churches where pastors hold
the pulpit swinging the other hand freely, receiving
the Holy Ghost descending, in the house the music
settles frazzled black farmers, in Africa under
the stupor, the glaze of hunger—in America under
a driving will to be. harder the rain falls,
darker the night rolls beneath a moon singed
with nights rolling and forgotten with memories
of ancestors. music from rain incites us to dance,
clay-stained, black toes wiggle in sleep to thunder,
a steady slurping of rain falling in sand,
a slow clap of wooden screen doors as dogs retreat.
lightning cracks on far sides of fields
splitting edges of forests, lighting tree tops,
an unfamiliar ritual has begun, a past is incarnate,
a West African mask with eyes like black lips
mounted on a sleek, doll body for its divination,
it is the soul of our fathers and mothers.

MELVIN DIXON

After Prayers at Twilight

Pirogues in silhouettes on the sea,
fishermen hauling their gleaming smelly catch
up the hub of beach brick, harmattan dust
in their hair and everywhere. Night sips
this drought crest of the continent.
I, too, came from the sky. You can't see
my footprints anymore. Look there,
quickly, the spilled calabash of sunset.
Burnt air clinging to my congested clothes.
Now can you see them?
Crescent toes, brown stars.

Dakar, Senegal

Winter Gardens

In the garden of the Tuileries
men move stiffly through the cold,

their eyes freeze on one another's
until the grating screech of lens

on lens, irregular sparks
of gravel against gravel,

skin to skin.

Their feet chart the ground
in the different language I read.

The signs repeat in Central Park,
Golden Gate, or Lake Shore Drive,

and I'm the New World hunter
circling, circling back.

All our footprints lead the same.

Mother's Tour

At the Louvre you find Mona Lisa
gone secretly to Japan, Egyptian mummies
closed, Greek statues so arresting
and erect that you stumble. I catch you
falling, but not the pain rising inside.
Hours later you can't walk. I translate
in Emergency broken foot? sprained ankle?

As the swelling eases you limp
to where my friend and I have slept.
Sightseeing us naked and embraced and chiseled
in surprise breaks what your pills and gauze
held tight, sends us packing separate souvenirs:
his razor, my guidebooks, your figurines
cracked from travels that swell our distance.

Altitudes

—for Richard: centripetal, earth sign.

1.

It was memory that had me. Memory
with a smile and two feet, olive skin
and Gauloise on the breath saying
"bonjour" and asking my name and
waiting for the quick free fall.

I wanted the live vowels of that tongue
opening like legs and lips in love
back in 1973. So I stalked the old
neighborhood in this City of Lights
where I come from any place dark: Martinique,
Guadeloupe, Haiti, and yes Harlem, sometimes.

"Pourquoi tu parles si bien le francais?"

His names were different, but the ache
the same. Next time I won't go empty
or drain myself too soon. How could I have known
the old taste of his mouth would be a thirst
in mine, or come up in my sleep
whispering, *Remember? Remember?*

2.

Seven-hour night from New York and up
into the whoosh of jet propulsion, layer
after layer of clouds. Miles below:
the Atlantic. Hours ahead: me.

You ask about my road weary feet, tobacco breath,
and thighs brown and turbulent as the Seine.
Your grey eyes pull me up for air and promise:
"These are my last words on Paris and lost love,
my last journey back."

First sky, then altitude. Suspension
and the angle of descent to home.
We're made different by it, but never safe.

Cutting mountain fog in Massachusetts to the red
ground in Mali, the chattering sunset in Lagos
or combing traffic below Brooklyn Bridge,
up cobblestones to the teasing moon above Cannes,
we claw out landmarks etched into our skins:
your Africa, my Europe, our America.

Believe me. These things happen:

Years from now in a sudden lift
from the runway, one great letting go
of metal and earth, one piercing whirr
of engines to the applause of clouds,
those bits of gravel in the throat
can churn up saying, *You will remember, remember
me.*

La Chapelle. 92nd Division. Ted.

This lonely beautiful word
                          means church
and it is quiet here; the stone
walls curve
          like slow water.
When we arrived the people were already gone,
green shutters latched and stoops swept clean.
A cow lowed through the village,
pushing into our gloves her huge
sodden jaw.

It's Sunday and I'm standing
on the bitter ridge of France, overlooking the war.
La Guerre is asleep. This morning early
on patrol we slipped down through
the mist and scent of burning woodchips
(somewhere someone was warm)
                          into Moyenmoutier,
cloister of flushed brick and a little river
braiding its dark hair.

Back home in Louisiana the earth is red,
but it suckles you until you can sing
yourself grown.
                Here, even the wind has edges.

Drizzle splintered around us; we stood
on the arched bridge and thought
for a moment of the dead we had left
behind, in the valley, in the terrible noise.

But I'm not sad—on the way back
through the twigs I glimpsed
in a broken windowbox by the roadside
mums:
stunned lavenders and pinks
dusted with soot.
                    I am a little like them,
heavy-headed,
rough curls open to the rain.

                              (September, 1918)

The Gorge

I.

Little Cuyahoga's done up left town.
No one saw it leaving.
No one saw it leaving

Though it left a twig or two,
And a snaky line of rotting
Fish, a dead man's shoes,

Gnats, scarred pocket-
Books, a rusted garden nozzle,
Rats and crows. April

In bone and marrow. Soaked
With sugary dogwood, the gorge floats
In the season's morass,

Remembering its walnut, its hickory,
Its oak, its elm,
Its sassafras. Ah,

II.

April's arthritic magnitude!
Little Joe ran away
From the swollen man

On the porch, ran across
The muck to the railroad track.
Lost his penny and sat

Right down by the rail,
There where his father
Couldn't see him crying.

That's why the express
Stayed on the track.
That's why a man

On a porch shouted out
Because his son forgot
His glass of iced water. That's

Why they carried Little Joe
Home and why his toe
Ain't never coming back. Oh

III.

This town reeks mercy.
This gorge leaves a trail
Of anecdotes,

The poor man's history.

Fifth Grade Autobiography

I was four in this photograph fishing
with my grandparents at a lake in Michigan.
My brother squats in poison ivy.
His Davy Crockett cap
sits squared on his head so the raccoon tail
flounces down the back of his sailor suit.

My grandfather sits to the far right
in a folding chair,
and I know his left hand is on
the tobacco in his pants pocket
because I used to wrap it for him
every Christmas. Grandmother's hips
bulge from the brush, she's leaning
into the ice chest, sun through the trees
printing her dress with soft
luminous paws.

I am staring jealously at my brother;
the day before he rode his first horse, alone.
I was strapped in a basket
behind my grandfather.

He smelled of lemons. He's died—

but I remember his hands.

Dog Days, Jerusalem

Exactly at six every evening I walk
into the garden to wait for the rain.
I'd been told it would come at six
if at all. Following the lizard's
woven escape, I turn on the sprinklers and
watch water fall through itself
like pity, or love.

How silent this tiny, broken applause.
In the library, beneath the fluted lamp,
I have laid out black tea and square orange cakes—
carefully, since no one will see me.
Night comes in on the clear
register of the *shofar*,
poor relative blowing its children home.

HOUSTON A. BAKER, JR.

My Mother's Mother's House

Arriving at midnight,
The pitch street makes no sound,
Squat houses are lightless,
A patchwork of stars hangs low.
My mother gently taps and calls: "Mother."
A sleepy sound, muffled inside, responds,
Takes form at the opened door as my "cousin" Raymond
(Boy adopted when his Mother "went wild.")
"Well, well, y'all managed to get here after all."
My Grandmother pushes through a curtain between rooms,
And hugs us all.
The voices overlap in rushes of affection.
The stove's final embers pop.
Tomorrow, we shall tolerate an old radio's crackling,
Listen in harmony to entertainment from afar.
Already, I taste bittersweet cobbler,
Already know, with boy's sleepy intuition,
That good times are with ancestors;
Their memories are blues voices
Moving through an infinity of years.

Socializing: Roots: Or When My Wife Surprised the Dinner Party with Talk of Her Youth

I see you in North Carolina dawns,
Your knees rattling against the morning chill,
Yellow pump water in six-years hands.
Your city-born Mom has launched you South with toothpaste,
Toilet tissue—warning off dirt and the country.
You return from the field with foaming mouth,
Butt of rural jokes, with flattened toilet rolls in
Your possession—no Sears Catalogue for your tender bottom.
Undaunted, you meet the sun with your own etchings in dust,
Shell dried corn for your Grandfather's *biddies*.
Tough birds all . . .
Your words return southern accents,
Sources of your excellence hidden
Until now.

Carolina, Coltrane, and Love

Grey, autumn squirrel scoots
Across a distant branch,
Sunlight slashes trees,
Revealing textures in Saturday light
Rare as earth itself.

(*In my living room John Coltrane plays* Naima.)

The old gold and stubborn green of Carolina are
Flavored by a neighbor's smoke.

(There is a shaman chanting—torturous—older than earth.)

As my son awakens with a boisterous yawn.

*(A horn invoking chaos, creating comfort—ordering African
    spirit.)*

Today we will complete his African project.
Working together at rituals ancient as the seasons old.

*(Chordal progressions blast barriers! Shaman
gives birth to the world.)*

The squirrel is at our deck.
Dry leaves and sheets of sound,
We discuss forests and rivers
Older than the signs of man.

(On my disc, Naima *gives way to* Om, *a single hand—clapping.)*

Charlotte awakens, stretches toward the sun:

She is motion and energy, embodiment of spirits called.
The ending is Black.
The ending is Love.
The ending of African genius is (always) love.

$\overline{\frac{Sr^*}{Sd}}$: for an African Chronicle

Here, below the line,
Is our ancestral yard,
Replete with codicils and broken-necked guitars;
Pine-needle bed of history.

Above the bar,
An endless play of signifiers,
Harmonica bridges,
Gut-bucket connectives that
Span black time,
All blue.

Double South Spring

Oak tassels descend
Covering earth with green goofer dust;
Pollen-bearing bees divebomb the shadow's silence,
And these are the makings of Faulknerian voices,
Caldwellian harmonies and Walker Percy gentles;
Beside spring roads wisteria weeps its scent
And masters and their descendants are a ghostly
Chorus, a white May dream.

*A Standard designation in semiotics (the science of signs) for signifier (sr) or word, and signified (sd) or meaning.

Down back roads,
In cinder hovels, unweeded plots of paint-peeling shanties,
Nothing is happening.
No new-season resonance moves a progeny of harrowing rows.
Black folk survive by sound alone,
Are in-mates of a single season,
A timeless ritual of
Black and battered guitars.

Prodigal

November rain liberates last gold,
Succulent copper,
Searing red of Carolina trees,
Beating earth in afternoon fury.
His cap dripping under deluge,
The son makes his way through unfurrowed fields,
Pushes aside branches,
Steps through ankle-deep underbrush . . . damp.

(*A single bird takes flight,*
Describes slow circles above the clearing.)

His gaze is fixed by ancestral stones,
Washed in autumn rain,
Guarded by spirits
Whose incantation and percussion have taught him
Blue-steel-and-train-whistle rites of southern life.
Kneeling, knees soaked in earth,
He touches his Father's mark,

Hums gratitude for ancient energies
Transfiguring earth.
He accosts the life above:

"You, Ole African! Reckon you ain't de only one's
Glad I'm home."

Rain.
A circling bird settles toward earth.
Liberated gold.
Succulent copper.
Searing red of Carolina fall.

PINKIE GORDON LANE

Two Poems for Gordon

i. Gordon

       Gordon, now
a man/his jazz
a flight to magic
soaring with a down beat
progressive, cool, funky
His appearance conservative
This boy four generations away
from slaves of the dormant
fields

       His drums
beat a vocal message
He "gigs" his way into
his own world and circles
angels, devils, with African
telecommunications in this
modern idiom

Gordon, my manchild,
grown to mid-proportions/
his silences tracking the
dawn

ii. Rite of Passage

*(for Gordon who is moving away from home into
his own apartment)*

Moving up, out, into
your own orbit
You tell me about Steinbeck's
Flight—and you quote
"rite of passage"
What is that? I ask

You say it is the "right"
to move into your own,
to define your own space,
to grow into the sunlight
of your own cranial sphere,
the shadow of your
walk through time
and music
Your own sadness—
to measure that distance—
your own dance
articulated with the drumbeat
of your heart

Rite of passage—we
each have as a legacy
of growing up and daring
to challenge the terrible
beauty of our own alienation
our own walk in space
our own weightlessness
in a world of spiraling
centrifugal force—a race
to the unknown—

a rite of passage

Old Photo from a Family Album: 1915

*—for Inez West Gordon
and for Ocydee Williams*

This lovely young woman
with the elegant hat,
dress of flowing gauze
sits in a chair—a rocker,
contemplating a feather
poised between two fingers
of her right hand

What photographer arranged
this photo in a studio
with the tapestried background
draped like a mural? See
how he catches
the pensive gaze,
face soft, unsmiling,
full of innocence and hope

She sends the picture
to her lover:

> *Dear William, again*
> *I make another attempt*
> *—Please send me*
> *one of yours . . . or*
> *else you can come*
> *and make one*
> *at our house*

Her body curved, relaxed, slender—
the eyes returning into themselves
She is contained in her
assurance that leads
into the future

     Nothing in this photo
resembles the gross figure
the angry defiance
the abused spirit
of the woman I knew

     The enlarged hand,
fingers swollen from years of work,
would no longer hold a bird's feather
but a torch to light
her way back to corridors

of love expected
of fury diffused to a spiral
of smoke, and a gown
that (shroud of her life)
she might have placed
upon her unmarked
grave

JAY WRIGHT

The Adoration of Fire*

CHARACTERS
Hattie
Bubba
John Hicks
TIME
The present
PLACE
A country spot, near a marsh

(*A brightly lit stage. The dominant colors should be brown and white,
with occasional touches of green and blue. On one side, there should be
a small clear space; on the other, the marks of a buggy marsh. [An ideal
for the play would be to have the audience sitting in or surrounded by
marsh.] No one appears on stage for a few moments. A cow can be heard
lowing and thrashing about, in difficulty, in the marsh. Silence. A woman,
out of sight, sings wordlessly. Silence. A flutelike whistle sounds. Silence.
Footsteps in grass. Hattie, a young black woman in a shapeless, white
cotton dress, wearing a light brown cowhide hat with a red feather in the
band, enters. She has a rough brown cloth bag hanging from her shoulder and a brass bracelet on her right wrist. She occasionally blows the
whistle. She seems to be looking for something, stopping now and then
to listen, moving slowly and turning from side to side. She stops, stands
still and calls softly.*)

HATTIE: Beauty.
(*Pause.*)
HATTIE: Beauty.
(*She moves further toward the deeper marsh.*)
HATTIE: Beauty.
(*Bubba comes behind her, from the same direction from which she came.*

He is a young, strong-looking yet paunchy, black man. He wears an open-necked, short-sleeved, blue wool shirt and khaki pants. He wears a short string of black beads around his neck. One of his back pockets and one of his front pockets bulge. He hurries on, as though he had been trying to catch Hattie, slows and stops.)

BUBBA: Better not step in that mud, lady.

(She withdraws a little.)

BUBBA: I mean, that's a pretty dress. And out here by yourself, you might get mired down and can't get out.

HATTIE: Well, I ain't by myself.

BUBBA: No.

HATTIE: I heard you following me.

BUBBA: I was just scoutin'. I heard you whistlin' and carryin' on. I thought maybe you needed some help.

HATTIE: Scouting?

BUBBA: You know. Just tryin' to scare up somethin'.

HATTIE: In the marsh?

(He pops his fingers and shakes himself once.)

BUBBA: Take it where you find it.

HATTIE: What did you expect to find?

BUBBA: What I've got.

(Hattie's hand goes nervously to her hair.)

HATTIE: Me?

(He takes one step toward her, as though to assure her.)

BUBBA: Hey, no, don't get me wrong. This ain't no strong arm business. I mean, I get a power from the marsh. Get stuffed up in the village. Some Monday mornings, first thing I do when I *wake* up is head for the marsh. Get all that contamination out my system. People look up and say, there go the Hawk, goin' for a cup of mud. 'Course, some of the motherfuckers think I distill the weeds.

(She quickly turns her head away. He notices.)

BUBBA: Oh oh, there I go. I'm a pistol mouth when it comes to callin' the devil. I see too much to be decoratin' everything with berries.

(He takes another step toward her.)

BUBBA: I don't want you to get the wrong impression.

(She turns on him.)

HATTIE: Well, now what impression should I get, Mister . . . ?

BUBBA: Bubba.

HATTIE: Mister Bubba. You "found" me. You keep easin' forward. You got your qualities up on your shoulders and shakin' 'em like a duck. You say you're familiar, but I don't know you. Who are you?

BUBBA: You mean you really don't know The Hawk? Chief firebringer and catch-'em-up down at J.B. Tankersley's Authentic Cotton Mills? Son of John Butler Hicks, the high sheriff, known as The Dipper?

HATTIE: So you're the deputy's son?

BUBBA: I don't blame you for the razor in your voice. I don't like him either.

HATTIE: You got a way of turnin' heat, haven't you?

BUBBA: (*In mock surprise.*) Hey. You got a charm. You the only person ever seen clearly that I'm just play. No harm.

HATTIE: Hardly. Well, I don't have time for this. I'm lookin' for my heifer.

BUBBA: Out here in the marsh?

HATTIE: What you expect? She be sittin' in somebody's kitchen, havin' tea?

BUBBA: Touché.

(*Pause.*)

BUBBA: Well, least I can do is help you look for her.

HATTIE: (*Matter of factly.*) Would you?

(*He nods. She turns toward the deeper marsh, whistles, stops, sings, stops.*)

HATTIE: Beauty?

(*Pause.*)

HATTIE: I guess I'm gon have go down there and get her.

BUBBA: I'll do it, Hattie.

HATTIE: How do you know my name?

BUBBA: Know your old man, too.

HATTIE: How's that?

BUBBA: Listen, a cow ain't all I got on my mind. I tell you I see too much.

HATTIE: Enough to keep quiet, I hope. What I need is to get back my property. I'm sick of the insinuations, how I can't keep anything in hand, not even myself. You'd think I had it in mind to drown Beauty in the swamp. Some folk do take away your pride.

BUBBA: Forget it.

(*He pulls a brown paper bag with a bottle of whiskey in it from his back pocket.*)

BUBBA: Every time I hear a rumor, I crown it with another rouser.

(*He quickly unscrews the top, takes a large wet drink and thrusts the bottle at her.*)

BUBBA: Come on.

(*She shakes her head.*)

BUBBA: Well, if I'm gon scare up this heifer, I got to put a light in my eye. (*He drinks again.*)

HATTIE: You don't know what it's like to be the subject of everybody's bile. When time gets to takin' away your qualities, some people hide behind resentment.

(*Short burst of anger.*)

HATTIE: I can't be my daddy's mama. I can't hold together what wind and rain and old age are breakin' down. I thought I could. But all that I thought was with me and fond of my hand has turned out to be wild and jealous, and happy to see me fall.

(*She looks at him as though she would elicit some encouragement.*)

HATTIE: Do I look like one who would throw away what sustains her?

BUBBA: No.

HATTIE: (*Confidently.*) No. And when I bury my father, I'll have everything he left me and more.

BUBBA: I'm sure you will.

(*He drinks. Pause.*)

BUBBA: Well. Do we chase the heifer, or . . . ?

HATTIE: I didn't mean for you to be encouraged.

BUBBA: Surely. But takin' it light on a blue Monday has a lot to recommend it.

(*She softens.*)

HATTIE: So?

BUBBA: I know who you are now, and you know me. And we've got a couple of mummies for fathers, who may even be the same man for all I know.

HATTIE: That's a thought.

(*He puts his bottle away.*)

BUBBA: Mmh. I suddenly got hungry.

HATTIE: Here.

(*She takes a bean pie from her bag.*)

HATTIE: Take this.

BUBBA: I'll split it with you.

(*He takes out a knife and flicks it open. She holds the pie out to him.*)

BUBBA: You hold it. I'll cut.

HATTIE: Don't cut me now.

BUBBA: No. I'm just sharpenin' the blade for your old man.

(*She withdraws the pie.*)

BUBBA: Hey. Ain't you used to me yet? 'Sides, I'm savin' this for my old man.

(He holds the knife before him and turns it absentmindedly while he speaks.)

BUBBA: He's as crooked as they come. Ask anybody. Any vice, anything underhanded that goes on, if he ain't got a hand in it, I'm Saint Jesus. You don't know how I hate him. I want to see him get it. I could do it myself. Sometimes I dream about it, and I have to stop myself before I hunt him down. Some nights, I think about not goin' to work, but goin' to him, lyin' in his bed, walk in on his sleepin' ass and blow his brains out. I've got a double-barreled shotgun under my mattress. He don't know about that. Or he wouldn't have come up on me that Saturday. I'd been tastin' all day. I was in the wind. Standin' down on Cooper with some hard niggers. He came up and shook me down, down to the shorts. I had one of those twenty-twos taped to my leg. He stripped me. Right there. Arrested me. Just like I was a common criminal. And I was so high I couldn't move, or fight him off, or cuss, or even cry. He did his duty. Like Jesus, he judged me, and took me away. Don't I hate this man?

HATTIE: Why are you hidin' then?

(He laughs.)

BUBBA: Hidin'? Ho. I could ask you the same thing. Out here in your bare feet whistlin' up a heifer. Pretendin' to be thinkin' about daddy's good health. Could you be more confused?

(She puts the pie back in her bag.)

HATTIE: I've got work to do.

BUBBA: Hattie, let's not pretend. The man we call father is dead. Gone. Flown away. And the only thing *we* have to do is learn how to get up in the mornin', knowin' we are here, and are all that is left.

(She turns, runs toward the deeper marsh and stops.)

BUBBA: Go on.

(Pause.)

BUBBA: You want me to help you?

(She looks uncertainly at him.)

BUBBA: Then touch me. And recognize me.

HATTIE: I have to have my heifer now.

(The cow lows and thrashes in the distance.)

BUBBA: Touch me.

(She comes slowly to him with her hand out, slowly and tentatively touches him.)

BUBBA: That's better. I wouldn't want to go out in no swamp without the right charm.

(The cow lows again.)

BUBBA: You wait here.

(*He goes off in the direction of the sound. Pause. John Hicks slowly enters from the same direction the other two came. Though older, he looks like and is built like Bubba. He wears the policeman's outfit of gray short-sleeved shirt and blue pants. He has a gun, handcuffs and keys hanging from his belt. He also wears a brass bracelet. He carries a swagger stick. He stops and looks around, seeming almost not to notice Hattie. She turns toward him, but moves away from him. He speaks, looking away.*)

HICKS: I hear the boy's been botherin' you.

HATTIE: Boy?

(*He looks directly at her.*)

HICKS: You understand me.

HATTIE: Yes, I understand you. He's helping me. He's down there, fetching the heifer.

HICKS: I can't be everywhere. And I can't be lookin' out for those who take no care for themselves.

HATTIE: You can leave me alone.

HICKS: How I'm gon leave you alone? You've got everything turned around as it is. Is the heifer partial to this swamp? You got some ache in your knee that need this mud?

HATTIE: No need to tell you about my knees.

(*He snorts. Pause. He looks around, slaps the swagger stick in his hand.*)

HICKS: Where is he?

HATTIE: I told you. Down there. Fetching the heifer.

(*Hicks laughs.*)

HICKS: Fetchin' the heifer. Who gon fetch him? The boy needs somebody to prop him up all the time. A mama who got nothin' to do but follow him around.

HATTIE: Or a father who can see what a mother knows.

HICKS: Don't play with me now. You've got that thing in your voice again. I hear it, and I ain't gon suffer it. This ain't my day.

HATTIE: What is your day?

HICKS: You always stop short of callin' me by my name. Call me by my name.

(*He moves closer to her.*)

HICKS: I want to hear it.

HATTIE: I would gladly do that, if I knew your name.

HICKS: I see we gon go over the same ground.

HATTIE: Always.

(*He draws closer, takes his swagger stick to explore the hem of her dress and touch her right knee.*)

HICKS: No. 'Cause I'm not interested in what went down before. You may not believe me, but I'm not concerned with rumors, where you've been sleepin', the promises you made.

HATTIE: I've only promised one thing.

(He stops stroking her.)

HICKS: What's that?

HATTIE: That I will always be faithful.

(He snorts.)

HICKS: What does that mean? It don't take an owl's eye to see how far that goes.

(He gestures around him.)

HICKS: Here you are. You got this taste for swampy water and back roads now. Why?

(Pause.)

HICKS: Why is it so hard for you to say you love me?

HATTIE: When things are in order, I love you.

(He dismisses this.)

HICKS: That's what I mean. There's always a condition. Put up a house, take me to this village, put a cap on my boy, come back on Wednesday, don't speak my name so much, don't go away, don't come back, don't say a word, don't move.

(He shakes his wrist with the bracelet.)

HICKS: I still have the evidence that you belong to me.

HATTIE: No, that is the sign that you belong to me.

HICKS: Now how can that be? I make things happen around here. Why, some of these boys think *I'm* their mama.

HATTIE: All but one.

HICKS: I'm gon see to that. This little business between you and him is all I need. I'm the hawk gon catch the hawk, and shake him loose.

(Hattie now speaks as the first Hattie.)

HATTIE: That's goin' to be mighty difficult, Mr. Hawk.

(There's thrashing in the distance. He starts. She touches his arm.)

HATTIE: Take it easy. Why not just wait here with me 'til he comes back with the heifer?

(She takes out the bean pie.)

HATTIE: Take your mind off it.

(He takes the pie and starts to pop it into his mouth.)

HATTIE: I thought we'd share it.

(He stops and starts to break the pie.)

HATTIE: Don't you have a knife?

HICKS: No.

HATTIE: He does. Said he'd use it, too, when the time came.

HICKS: Oh?

HATTIE: Told me there'd be no more runnin' away, and no more embarrassment. Told me he was gon pull the heifer from the swamp and lay her at my feet as the first sign of his strength.

HICKS: Sounds like the boy refuses to learn from experience. I made him. Ain't gon be no cuttin' unless I'm the one doin' it.

HATTIE: We'll see.

HICKS: Yes, we will.

(*He straightens his armor, ringing it in the process.*)

HICKS: I don't know what you've promised him, but you've misled him.

(*Hattie speaks as the second Hattie.*)

HATTIE: It's just that he's become accustomed to my charms, and grown tired of defending you. I'm a new dawn. I promise him love and beauty and happiness.

(*Bubba enters energetically. He sees Hicks, hesitates, but then comes on forcefully. He addresses Hattie.*)

BUBBA: I've got her tied to a tree. Pick her up when we get ready to go.

(*He takes out his whiskey, opens it, offers the bottle to Hicks, who spits. Bubba shrugs and drinks. He sighs with pleasure.*)

HICKS: You finished, boy?

(*Bubba caps the bottle, puts it in his pocket.*)

BUBBA: Yeah. I'm finished. And I'm not your boy.

HICKS: Ho. I see. Spend a few minutes herdin' cow and you're equal to your old man.

BUBBA: I've done more than spend a few minutes herdin' cow. You may not have noticed, but then, where you've been you wouldn't have.

(*Hicks hands the pie to Hattie, who puts it in her bag.*)

HICKS: I'm not blind, and I've been close enough to you to see all I need to.

BUBBA: Good.

HICKS: Don't get sly.

BUBBA: Sorry, judge.

(*Pause.*)

BUBBA: Well, Sheriff, what's the charge?

HICKS: Only one. Bein' an offense to my name.

BUBBA: I thought you was gon say to your memory, since you dead anyhow.

(*Hicks reaches for his handcuffs. Bubba quickly draws his knife and snaps it open.*)

BUBBA: Don't do that.

(*Hicks releases the handcuffs and tosses away his swagger stick.*)

HICKS: We ought to settle this in the right way.

(*He starts to unbuckle his belt. Bubba snaps his knife shut and puts it away. Hicks pulls his gun and shoots Bubba. Hattie, stunned, raises her right arm. She stands statue-like with her mouth open in astonishment. Bubba falls at her feet.*)

HICKS: You thought you could redeem him, didn't you?

(*He holsters his gun.*)

HICKS: Well, that's all over, Hattie. Between you and me now there will never be any word but what is just.

HATTIE: So be it.

(*She takes off her hat and tosses it near Bubba's body.*)

HATTIE: No need to tell you what your love has cost me. Now that our son is gone, I will find it easy to be faithful. And to love the darkness.

(*She looks at Hicks. They stand still. The light fades and disappears. Black. The woman's voice singing wordlessly. Silence. The flutelike whistle. Silence.*)

Notes on Contributors

KATHY ELAINE ANDERSON is a published poet living in Washington, D.C.; she was cofounder and editor of the *Nethula Journal of Contemporary Art and Literature*. "Louisiana Shade" is her first published work of fiction.

HOUSTON A. BAKER, JR., is the Albert M. Greenfield Professor of Human Relations at the University of Pennsylvania. He has published three volumes of poetry, most recently, *Blues Journeys Home* in 1985. He is the author of *Blues, Ideology, and Afro-American Literature: A Vernacular Theory* (1984), and his *Modernism and the Harlem Renaissance* was published by the University of Chicago Press in 1987.

JOSEPHINE BAKER's career, which began at the age of eight when she started singing in Harlem nightclubs, included numerous appearances at Carnegie Hall and on Broadway. She gained her greatest fame as a dancer in Paris appearing in *La Revue Nègre, Folies Bergères*, and *Casino de Paris*, among other productions. Decorated with the croix de guerre and made a chevalier of the Legion of Honor, she was author of *Les Mémoires de Josephine Baker* (1927; expanded edition, 1949). But of all her accomplishments, she was most proud of her role as mother of twelve adopted children.

JAMES BALDWIN, essayist, playwright, and novelist, was born in Harlem, the eldest of nine children. He moved to Paris in 1948 and was residing in France at the time of his death in 1987. His works include *Go Tell It on the Mountain* (1953), *Notes of a Native Son* (1955), *Giovanni's Room* (1956), *Another Country* (1962), and *Just Above My Head* (1979).

AMIRI BARAKA's most recent publications are *Confirmation* (1983), edited with Amina Baraka, *A Unity of African Waivers* (1983), *The*

287

Autobiography of LeRoi Jones (1984), *Daggers and Javelins: Essays, 1974–1979* (1984), and *The Music: Reflections on Jazz and Blues* (1987).

ANTHONY BARTHELEMY is the author of *Black Face, Maligned Race: The Representation of Blacks in English Drama from Shakespeare to Southerne*, published in 1987 by Louisiana State University Press.

DAVID BRADLEY, winner of the 1982 Pen-Faulkner Award, teaches in the creative writing program of Temple University in Philadelphia.

CYRUS CASSELLS is the author of a highly acclaimed first book, *The Mud Actor*, one of the winners of the 1982 National Poetry Series and a nominee for the 1982 Bay Area Book Reviewers Award in poetry. In 1985 he completed a translation manuscript, "To the Cypress Again and Again," of the late Catalan poet Salvador Espriu, who was, until his death in 1985, Catalan Spain's leading contender for the Nobel Prize.

MELVIN DIXON is the author of *Change of Territory* (1983). He received a National Endowment for the Arts fellowship in poetry in 1984 and is the translator of Genevieve Fabre's study *Drumbeats, Masks and Metaphor: Contemporary Afro-American Theatre* (1983). His most recent work, published by the University of Illinois Press in 1987, is *Ride Out the Wilderness: Geography and Identity in Afro-American Literature*.

RITA DOVE, a recipient of both National Endowment for the Arts and Guggenheim fellowships, teaches creative writing at Arizona State University. In 1985 her third volume of poetry, *Thomas and Beulah*, for which she received the 1986 Pulitzer Prize, appeared, as well as a volume of stories entitled *Fifth Sunday.*

ROLAND L. FREEMAN is an internationally known documentary still photographer who is engaged in an ongoing project to record black life throughout the African diaspora. Since 1972 he has been a field research photographer for the Smithsonian Institute's Office of Folklife Programs. His latest book is *Southern Roads/City Pavements: Photographs of Black Americans* (1985).

HENRY LOUIS GATES, JR., W. E. B. Du Bois Professor of Literature at Cornell University, is the author of *The Signifying Monkey* (1988) and *Figures in Black* (1987).

MICHAEL S. HARPER's most recent volume of poetry is *Healing Song for the Inner Ear* (1985). He teaches at Brown University.

PINKIE GORDON LANE has written three volumes of poetry: *Wind Thoughts* (1972), *The Mystic Female* (1978), and *I Never Scream* (1985). She is a professor emeritus of English at Southern University in Baton Rouge.

JOHN McCLUSKEY, JR., is associate dean of the graduate school at Indiana University at Bloomington. He is also director of the CIC Minorities Fellowships Program, based at Indiana University. One of his recent projects has been editing *The City of Refuge: The Collected Stories of Rudolph Fisher* (1987).

ROBERT G. O'MEALLY is professor of English and Afro-American studies at Wesleyan University. The author of *The Craft of Ralph Ellison* (1980), he has also edited *Tales of the Congaree* (1987), and the forthcoming *New Essays on "The Invisible Man."*

BRENDA MARIE OSBEY, a native of New Orleans, is the author of three volumes of poetry: *Ceremony for Minneconjoux* (1983), *Desperate Circumstance, Dangerous Woman* (1987), and *In These Houses* (1988).

RICHARD PERRY teaches at Pratt Institute in Brooklyn, New York, and is a member of Teachers and Writers Collaborative. His novel *Montgomery's Children* (1984) won the Quality Paperback Book Club New Voice Award for 1985.

CHARLOTTE PIERCE-BAKER completed a doctoral dissertation on vernacular black English and now teaches at the Germantown Friends School in Philadelphia.

ARNOLD RAMPERSAD teaches American literature at Rutgers University. He is the author of *The Art and Imagination of W. E. B. DuBois* (1976), as well as an award-winning two-volume biography of Langston Hughes, the first volume of which appeared in 1986 and the second in 1988.

ISHMAEL REED is the author of *The Terrible Twos* (1982) and is currently at work on *The Terrible Threes* and *The Terrible Fours*. He also published *Reckless Eyeballing* in 1986.

CHARLES H. ROWELL, founder and editor of *Callaloo*, teaches English at the University of Virginia.

VALERIE SMITH teaches English and Afro-American literature at the University of California at Los Angeles. She is an executive committee member of the MLA Division of Black American Literature and Culture. Her most recent book is *Self-Discovery and Authority in Afro-American Narrative* (1987).

CLYDE TAYLOR teaches literature and film in the English department at Tufts University in Medford, Massachusetts. He received the 1982 Callaloo Creative Writing Award for Non-Fiction Prose and the Life-Achievement Award from the Association of Independent Video and Film Producers for criticism and advocacy. More recently, he received the Ford Foundation Fellowship for work at the Du Bois Institute, Harvard University, in 1987 and 1988.

MARGARET WALKER is best known for her novel *Jubilee* (1966). Her other books include *For My People* (1942), *October Journey* (1973), and *Prophets of A New Day* (1970).

MARILYN NELSON WANIEK is the author of *For the Body* (1978) and *Mama's Promises* (1985), both Louisiana State University Press publications. She teaches at the University of Connecticut at Storrs and is working on a translation of the poetry of Thorkild Bjornvig.

MEL WATKINS, a former editor for the *New York Times Book Review*, is the author of *On the Real Side: Black American Humor from Stepin Fetchit to Richard Pryor* (1988).

MICHAEL S. WEAVER, a recent graduate of the creative writing program at Brown University in poetry and playwriting, has published a collection of poetry entitled *Water Song* (1985).

JOHN E. WIDEMAN teaches English literature at the University of Massachusetts at Amherst. He is the author of three novels: *Sent for You Yesterday* (1983), which won him the 1984 Pen-Faulkner Award, *Brothers and Keepers* (1984), and *Reuben* (1987).

JAY WRIGHT is a bass player from Piermont, New Hampshire. Of *The Adoration of Fire* Mr. Wright says, "This play derives its impulse from, and is a synthesis of, some Egyptian and Yoruba myths."